The World Wars

An Enthralling Guide to the First and Second World War

Free limited time bonus

Stop for a moment. We have a free bonus set up for you. The problem is this: we forget 90% of everything that we read after 7 days. Crazy fact, right? Here's the solution: we've created a printable, 1-page pdf summary for this book that you're reading now. All you have to do to get your free pdf summary is to go to the following website:

https://livetolearn.lpages.co/enthrallinghistory/

Once you do, it will be intuitive. Enjoy, and thank you!

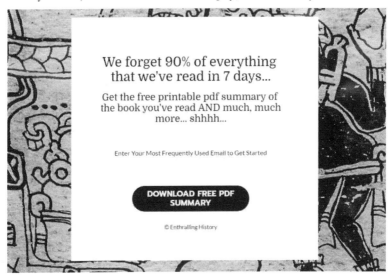

We forget 90% of everything that we've read in 7 days...

Get the free printable pdf summary of the book you've read AND much, much more... shhhh...

Enter Your Most Frequently Used Email to Get Started

DOWNLOAD FREE PDF SUMMARY

© Enthralling History

Table of Contents

Part 1: World War I

An Enthralling Guide from Beginning to End

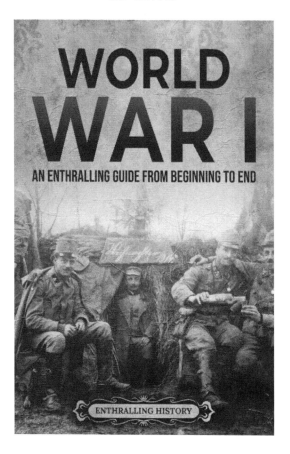

Introduction

The Great War, which lasted from 1914 to 1918, was referred to in Europe as the "war to end all wars." With a total number of casualties ranging anywhere from fourteen to twenty-five million people, history would remember the First World War as one of the deadliest and, at the same time, as one of the most influential wars ever. The four-year conflict was a long time coming for the world, which was rapidly undergoing fundamental transformations in all major areas of life. In fact, because the roots of the war went so deep, lying in historical rivalries and fueled by the desire for revenge, World War I had immense consequences for the international order. The struggle that started in June of 1914 in Serbia quickly spread through all parts of the world due to complex political and cultural ties. These ties were an underlying feature of an increasingly globalized 20th-century world, characterized by the increased importance of power politics and the selfish drive of the European superpowers to assume dominance over their counterparts.

It was this drive that caused the war to escalate to unseen levels, even though Europe had experienced warfare many times before. The war exceeded everyone's expectations; the tight but fragile international order was only one of the factors why the war was referred to as the "one to end all wars." In addition, the technological advancements of the time contributed to this iconic characterization of World War I. The great nations had achieved significant progress in regard to not only civic but also military technology, and the rapid militarization that followed the relatively peaceful period in the late 19ᵗʰ century reached its pinnacle when the war broke out. Thus, by 1914, the world had become increasingly militarized. The nations had grown wary of each other, caused by a multitude of complicated factors that will be explored throughout the course of this book.

Ironically, the First World War only became "the First" after the events of the 1940s, which saw the world descend into chaos yet again. The First World War did not "end all wars" like many, including the winners, had predicted it would. What emerged from the remnants of cities was an even more intricate global system, where the winners of the war enjoyed various privileges while the losers were purposefully isolated and made to feel guilt for the troubles they had caused. The victorious nations tried to implement changes that would ensure peace and stability, but as time would tell, their efforts were all in vain. The international order that was established immediately after World War I would barely last for thirty years. Their attempts failed miserably, and the quick disintegration into yet another world war in 1939 made everyone realize that the model adopted after 1918 was fundamentally flawed. It was based on the redistribution of power at the expense of millions of people who lived in the nations that lost the war. The hardships that were endured by the losers were effectively exploited by the winners, but no one thought that their actions would produce yet another conflict, one that would dwarf the First World War in almost every aspect.

This book seeks to explore the Great War from beginning to end by providing a chronological account of the relevant events that influenced the conflict. In the first part, we will take a look at what exactly caused the war to begin, diving deep into the heightened emotional and political tensions between countries. We will describe the history behind the distribution of power in Europe, as well as the arms race that preceded the Great War, which resulted in its rapid escalation.

Next, the book will cover the actual outbreak of armed warfare, providing a general overview of what the war looked like from the two opposing sides and what the stakes were. We will discuss and analyze the key events and the general characteristics of the first part of the war. Then, the book will focus more on the conflict's military developments by reviewing in-depth accounts of the most important battles that took place, reaching the bloody turning point of the war about two years after its beginning, and the pivotal occurrences that determined the final outcome. Finally, the book will take a look at the last year of the war and assess its conclusion and impact. The events that led to and followed the Paris Peace Conference are vital in truly grasping the long-lasting effects the Great War had on the world.

Section One: Underlying Tensions

Chapter 1 – Germany vs. France: Any Excuse for Revenge

This chapter will explore the power dynamics established in continental Europe in the later part of the "long nineteenth century," a period of immense importance stretching from the French Revolution until the start of the Great War. The events that occurred during this time are so intertwined that it is impossible to truly speak about them as separate entities, as they all influenced each other in different ways. From the end of the Napoleonic Wars through the unification of Italy and Germany, the developments that took place are pivotal in understanding the roots of the Great War. This chapter will touch upon those events and then focus on the rivalry that developed between France and Germany and the precarious position both sides saw themselves in before the start of the conflict.

The Long Nineteenth Century

The period from the French Revolution of 1789 to the start of World War I in 1914 has come to be known among historians as the "long nineteenth century." This is because the French Revolution is thought to have started a massive shift in the way Europeans looked at politics. The French Revolution saw the

French monarchy get overthrown by the people due to it increasingly ignoring the needs and rights of the majority of the population in favor of the nobility and the clergy. The movement that started in France quickly spread throughout Europe, eventually leading to the birth of nationalism, which became a driving factor in the formation of many European states during the 19th century. As a result, more and more European nations started forming their own defined identities and establishing strong nation-states.

Most importantly, following Napoleon Bonaparte's defeat in the 1810s, the Congress of Vienna determined what was next for the future of Europe. In 1815, the Congress of Vienna reorganized the power dynamics of Europe and drew new borders after Napoleon's military endeavors. The negotiations, led by representatives from the four "Great Powers," Russia, Britain, Austria, and Prussia, were perhaps Europe's first real effort at achieving long-term peace and stability in the continent. France was stripped of its recent territorial gains, going back to the borders before Napoleon, and multiple new states were officially recognized in its place. Mainly, the German Confederation was established, which was an entity that incorporated several German territories, including parts of Prussia and Austria. Italy was also divided, with Sicily, Piedmont, and the Papal States, among other Italian factions, emerging as the most important in the region.

Europe in 1815.

An underlying motive behind the Congress of Vienna was the suppression of the revolutionaries, who had become prevalent with the French Revolution and the rise of Napoleon, who had claimed that he wanted to liberate the Europeans from their tyrannical rulers. The Great Powers were all led by conservative monarchies that perceived the rising nationalist voices as a direct threat to their power. Thus, by manipulating the European order, they were able to successfully suppress them, at least for the time being.

The "Old Empires" of Russia and Austria-Hungary were the main advocates of the old regimes and arguably benefited the most from their strengthened position. Britain, on the other hand, was the most stable nation among the Great Powers. It had its house in order, as it enjoyed a balanced system between its parliament and monarchy. Overall, with the Congress of Vienna, the Great Powers managed to divide the continent as they pleased and agreed to pursue stable foreign policies in line with each of their national agendas. They each envisioned different European regions as their own spheres of influence and came to terms for the first time to not interfere with each other's matters.

The Rise of Nationalism and the Unification of Germany

German-speaking Central Europe had always been a strange and complicated political entity. The Holy Roman Empire incorporated the German-speaking peoples of Central Europe, but it was never a stable state because of a multitude of factors, including the sheer number of smaller political units that were under its rule and the unclear chain of command that was in place. As a result, the German provinces largely enjoyed their independence, acting in their own self-interests instead of coming together under a single united German state. Thus, the Holy Roman Empire's position weakened when a province grew more and more powerful because of its individual efforts, challenging the rest for dominance. Other major powers of Europe, like France and Austria, saw their own emergence during much of the late Renaissance. They further reduced Germany's already disjointed political power, as they recognized the threat a united German state could pose in an increasingly competitive Europe.

Thus, one can argue that the German unification process was long overdue and that the preceding events at the beginning of the 19th century were its precursor. Napoleon faced no real difficulties when he took over the disunified, small German states. After his defeat, however, nationalistic ideas became more prominent in all of his conquered territories, including the German Confederation. With the Congress of Vienna, the region saw a period of stability and tried to catch up with the rest of Europe. The Germans realized they were one people, speaking one language and sharing much of the same history, two of the most common factors for forming a nation.

International developments accelerated this process; the period from the 1820s to the 1860s saw massive socio-economic advancements. For instance, Prussia created a German customs union, where all participating states saw positive outcomes, reducing competition among them and paving the way for an even more interconnected road and railway system. The exchange of people and goods took place between the small German states, while Prussia in the north and Austria in the south became two powerhouses that oversaw the political activities in their spheres of influence.

The German dualism that emerged from the clashes of these two rivaling powers decided the course of German unification. One idea was a lesser German solution; in other words, a unification without Austria. The other was the greater Germany option, which included the Austrian-held Holy Roman territories as part of a unified German state. The main problem was that Austria was still largely an absolutist state, and the monarchy was not willing to give up its powerful position. This changed due to developments in Italy that further contributed to the revival of German nationalist sentiment.

In 1859, Piedmont, an Italian state, with the help of France, was able to defeat the Austrian resistance, which had wanted to maintain its influence in northern Italy. This meant Austria's supremacy was dwindling, something that was underlined by the emperor's decision to adopt a new constitution, shifting Austria to a less conservative state. These events demonstrated that a united effort would yield significant results. What was needed was a leader who would pave the way for consolidating the smaller German states into a larger political entity.

Otto von Bismarck.
https://commons.wikimedia.org/wiki/File:Otto_Von_Bismarck.jpg)

Otto von Bismarck would come to be known in history as the man who created a unified Germany. As the Prussian ambassador to Paris, he was appointed as prime minister by Prussia's Wilhelm (William) I in September of 1862, which was a surprising move to many. The liberal nationalists of the German community, who had advocated for more involvement of the people in governmental decisions, did not like Bismarck. Bismarck was known to have a relatively conservative approach to politics, so the nationalists were not hopeful that he would produce results in line with their views.

Interestingly, however, Bismarck's diplomatic and negotiating skills saw Prussia become increasingly involved in the process of German unification. Whereas the liberal nationalists relied mainly on rhetoric to promote a sense of German nationalism in the people, Bismarck adopted a Realpolitik method, using major developments in Europe to boost support for reunification. His smart, pragmatic approach to international events put Prussia in an increased position of power among its rivals.

With the victory in the Seven Weeks' War with Austria in the summer of 1866, Bismarck was able to significantly weaken Austria's position. He expanded the Prussian realm by annexing several major German territories and formed a new North German Confederation led by Prussia. He made it clear that the process of German unification was underway under the leadership of Berlin rather than Vienna.

German unification concluded some five years later with Bismarck's victory in the Franco-Prussian War (1870–1871). Austria's defeat had signaled grave news for France, which was the other major European power directly affected by the formation of the North German Confederation. A unified Germany meant that the power dynamic would completely shift and challenge French interests. Bismarck knew that Germany was not complete without the southern states joining the union and that the French would most likely oppose him. Thus, both sides were looking forward to an unavoidable conflict, which finally came, thanks to the complex nature of the succession of European monarchies. Prince Leopold of Prussia was considered a candidate for the Spanish throne in 1870, and if he became king, he could further threaten France, which was in danger of being surrounded by members of the Prussian royal family.

In a clever turn of events, Bismarck intercepted and altered the contents of an important diplomatic telegram, manipulating the French into declaring war in July. He motivated the Germans to stand up against the French threat since they were defending themselves. The North German Federation saw multiple victories, one after the other, against the French, eventually leading to the capitulation of Paris in January 1871.

By the time the peace negotiations came to an end in May, Bismarck had already used the patriotic momentum generated by the war to have the southern states agree to join the federation. France also ceded control over the territories of Alsace-Lorraine and was made to pay five billion francs in reparations. With the south German states joining the confederation to form a powerful, united German Empire, Kaiser Wilhelm I was officially proclaimed as the first German emperor in the Palace of Versailles, further adding insult to injury to France. The process of German unification was finally complete.

The Bismarckian Alliance System

THE GERMAN REICH
1871-1918

The German Reich after 1871.

*Deutsches_Reich1.png: kgbergerderivative work: Wiggy!, CC BY-SA 2.5
<https://creativecommons.org/licenses/by-sa/2.5>, via Wikimedia Commons. Accessed
from: https://commons.wikimedia.org/wiki/File:Deutsches_Reich_(1871-1918)-en.png*

Germany's triumph and France's humiliation did not end with Prussia's victory in 1871. The rivalry that always existed between these two was elevated to an even higher level now that Germany was fully united. In fact, one can argue that by the late 1870s, Germany was the second-most dominant European Great Power after Britain and was rapidly striving to advance in every aspect of life to catch up. The 1870s saw the balance of power that had been established in the Congress of Vienna shift dramatically with the formation of two strong states: Italy and Germany. Thus, the interests of other powers changed with the rise of these new nations.

Germany had immense economic potential and was industrializing more and more. Its military had become more professional and disciplined; it was on par with the rest of Europe. The opposite was true for Austria-Hungary and France. The Habsburgs started to struggle to keep unity among the many peoples in their vast empire. The different people groups of Austria-Hungary had different fundamental views regarding their political life. It was also becoming apparent that, with the exception of Napoleon's rule, France never really recovered from the revolutionary spirit of the late 18th century, as the sharp differences between the revolutionaries and the loyalists continued to drive a wedge from within.

Since Germany was a newly formed nation that had just been through a couple of wars, Chancellor Bismarck thought that it was logical for Germany to focus more on its internal development rather than divert its attention and resources to external matters. To ensure that the Reich would not be bothered by its neighbors, Bismarck implemented a foreign and security policy that would lay the foundations for the system of alliances that emerged in Europe shortly before the start of World War I. As we have already mentioned, both France and Austria-Hungary were troubled by an array of domestic problems, but the latter was seen as a dwindling empire on the verge of collapse. Although France had also lost a war with Germany, Austria was lacking in economic, social, and military developments.

The Austrian crown had always been hesitant to adopt progressive views when it came to state-building and policymaking since the several different nationalities that comprised the empire were never in tandem. The conservative Austrian Habsburg monarchy was outdated when compared to the ruling systems of other European powers. Plus, due to its lack of cohesion, Austria was not nearly as industrialized, with a major part of the economy being comprised of agriculture. However, despite the somewhat precarious position of Austria-Hungary in the 1870s, Bismarck saw a potential ally since he believed it to be a "European necessity."

Bismarck claimed that he needed Austria-Hungary to separate Germany from the Ottoman Empire and Russia, the latter of which was capable of handling the tension in the Balkans and preventing a war from breaking out in the region. In addition, Bismarck needed to dissuade the Austrians from potentially joining the French in an attempt to seek revenge on Germany. Thus, with all this in mind, he managed to form a *Dreikaiserbund*–the Three Emperors' League–with Austria-Hungary and Russia in 1873 to further isolate France. Struggling Austria was instantly on board, and Russia also accepted, happy to have its roles increased in European politics.

The Three Emperors' League did not continue its existence as a smoothly operating alliance, although it did partially serve its purpose as a balancing mechanism against France. Russia and Austria-Hungary confronted each other after a revolt in the Slavic territories of the Ottoman-controlled Balkans. Russia declared war on the Ottoman Empire, something that was met with fierce resistance from the Austrian crown, which was concerned about Russia's expansionist tendencies. Russia won the war and would have gained significant territorial gains as a result, but Bismarck managed to broker a new agreement at the Berlin Congress of 1878 between the Austrians and Russians to avoid further escalation of tensions. Thus, the renewed Three Emperors' League existed after 1881, despite Russia and Austria's poor relations. In 1879, Germany entered a mutual military alliance with Austria to demonstrate its firm support and dissuade Russia from potentially starting a war.

If having Austria on its side was not enough to isolate France, the joining of Italy and the formation of the Triple Alliance in 1882 really made it apparent. The Triple Alliance had subtle premises for all its members. Italy was promised help from Germany and Austria-Hungary in the likely event that France declared war— something that the Italians were increasingly wary of after the struggles between the two countries in North Africa. In exchange, Italy was to help Germany in case France attacked and pledged to remain neutral if a war between Austria and Russia broke out. The Austrian troops permanently guarding the Italian border (due to a somewhat hostile history between the two states) could then be freed up to face the Russians on other fronts.

Therefore, shortly after unification, Germany became one of the most active and effective players in European politics. Under Chancellor Otto von Bismarck's leadership, Germany assumed a commanding position in continental Europe with its clever foreign policy, which was aimed at keeping peace in the region so Germany could focus on developing domestically. By the 1880s, what became known as the Bismarckian Alliance System defined the power dynamics between the major European nations. Bismarck knew that Germany was potent enough to endure war with a single nation. Since the main threat was expected to come from the west in the form of revenge-hungry France, he spent a lot of time trying to isolate the French by allying with its rival factions.

Unfortunately, Bismarck's efforts are recognized as a factor in why World War I broke out. The system he organized did ensure peace among the allied nations, but it also promoted competition among those who were left out. As we will see, other European nations soon retaliated and tried to shift the balance of power in their favor.

Chapter 2 – The Age of Industrialization and New Imperialism

This chapter will focus on the international factors that are considered to be the precursors to the First World War. Understanding the power dynamics of the involved parties in World War I requires us to examine the states of these actors beyond the borders of the continent.

Pax Britannica

Several major developments took place in the "long nineteenth century" that influenced the political landscape of Europe before World War I broke out. Among them, of course, was the Industrial Revolution, which massively affected the socio-economic structures of European nations. The nation that led industrialization was Great Britain, which was where the Industrial Revolution first took place. Because of this, Britain was given a sort of head start compared to its rivals, causing it to undergo developments of immense magnitude much quicker than its European counterparts for most of the 19th century. Having already established a strong colonial foothold, Britain was able to import goods from its colonies in abundance for cheap and sell it, in turn, for a higher price in an increasingly competitive domestic market.

The profits that the British made from colonial trade were huge. And with the technology to process the raw materials into luxury and everyday goods available only to them, Britain quickly became one of the richest nations in the world by the 19th century.

Other factors contributed to Britain's success, such as its convenient geographic location. The British were kept safe from the wars of the tightly packed European nations due to their island locale. This did not limit Britain in asserting its influence in European relations, though. The rise of Napoleon is a clear example. The French emperor was never able to achieve meaningful success against the British, but Britain led the coalition that destroyed Napoleon's ambition to rule all of Europe.

Thus, after the Congress of Vienna, with Europe undergoing a period of stabilization from the Napoleonic Wars, Britain's power grew exponentially to the point that it was the undisputed hegemon of the world in the mid-19th century. This period of British dominance has come to be known as Pax Britannica—the British Peace—whose name was borrowed from the famous Pax Romana of the Roman Empire. Britain's achievements were felt by the whole world. It became an industrial and political powerhouse, fielding a professional army and a world-renown navy and instilling fear among other nations. With peace in Europe, Britain was able to divert its attention to growing and diversifying its domestic market while also extending its reach and becoming a dominant player in the emerging markets of the Middle East, Southeast Asia, Africa, and Latin America. For example, in the first part of the 19th century, Britain signed several agreements with the Arab rulers of the Gulf countries, pledging to protect them from external threats and piracy in return for economic benefits.

Perhaps the most iconic symbol of British dominance is the Royal Navy—something that has persisted as one of the most recognizable characteristics of the nation even today, and rightfully so. At the height of Britain's power, its possessions stretched from North America to Africa to Asia to Oceania. Guaranteeing peace and stability would never have been possible if it wasn't for the constant, effective presence of the British military. The British navy became so advanced and professional because it was the most experienced, having to conduct non-stop operations all around the world since the early colonial days. While other former major colonial powers, such as Spain and Portugal, for example, ceased much of their colonial activity with the turn of the 19th century and continued to lose their overseas possessions in the Americas, Britain largely maintained a firm grip.

The bases for the Royal Navy were scattered all throughout the British colonies, contributing to the formation of a cohesive, effective system and the increase of Britain's overall maritime power. The navy single-handedly controlled the world's trade routes and even provided services other than protection to merchants, such as transportation of expensive, luxury goods that needed to be defended. The unchallenged dominance of the Royal Navy paved the way for Britain's position as a global power and undermined its competitors' advancements for nearly a whole century. It ensured the nation's prosperity by providing protection to the most valuable part of the British economy—colonial and intercontinental trade—as well as to the British Isles in general by dissuading any potential invader from mounting a full-scale assault on British lands.

Resuming Imperialism

With the defeat of Napoleon in the 1810s and the stable period of Europe that followed the Congress of Vienna, what became increasingly clear was the fact that the European territories were not as much up for grabs as they had been before the 19th century. Although wars throughout the continent persevered, it seemed as if the balance of power was finally at a place that was largely acceptable to the European powers, which slowly ceased conducting long-term military campaigns against one another. With some exceptions like the Russo-Ottoman War, Europe in the second half of the 19th century saw no large-scale wars, with the nations instead focusing on internal issues that posed a threat to the political systems in place.

The nationalist movements in Germany and Italy advocated for the formation of a united state. But the conflicts that arose were never on a large, destructive scale, only lasting for short periods of time with low casualties since no side was prepared to contribute adequate resources. Besides, Austria-Hungary and the Ottoman Empires (the "Old Empires") had to deal with multiple rebellions within their borders. Thus, no one really had time to start a war just yet. The European powers became rivals of each other, but the situation never escalated to a large-scale conflict.

Instead, seeing that the options for expansion in continental Europe were limited, the Europeans indulged themselves by contesting each other in the rest of the world. Colonies were an efficient and reliable source of income, as is apparent from our earlier example of Britain. And now that Europe had been pacified, attention was diverted to challenging each other's interests in different regions of the world. As one could imagine, the technological advancements brought about by the age of industrialization helped the Europeans resume their imperialist intentions after an almost century-long halt. In addition to having access to more sophisticated weaponry, advancements in transportation and communication systems made it easier for the colonizers to better hold onto their colonial gains, which had been a problem in the past. For example, information and goods could be transferred quicker than ever thanks to new railway and telegraph systems, paving the way for a more cohesive approach when trying to increase their foothold in the colonies. Modern medicine also allowed the Europeans to better adapt to the climate and diseases of different geographic locations.

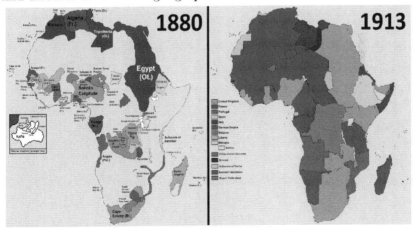

Scramble for Africa.

In the 1880s, after realizing the potential for economic exploitation of the colonies, the European imperialists simply partitioned foreign lands among themselves. During the Berlin Conference of 1884, the continent of Africa was divided by those European powers that had colonial interests. In the Scramble for Africa, as it would come to be known, France, Britain, Germany, Italy, Belgium, Portugal, and Spain drew up new borders of the African continent and came up with several regulations on trade.

As a result, only Ethiopia and Liberia remained sovereign African states, which was quite different from 1880 when only about 10 percent of the continent was effectively colonized. While Britain and France were very much present in the continent before the Berlin Conference, after 1884, the territories under their rule increased in size. Other European states claimed the rest of the continent for themselves. Belgium got the entire basin of the Congo and most of Central Africa; Italy established its colonies in Libya and Somalia; Germany took Namibia and Tanzania; Portugal chose Mozambique in the southeast and Angola in the southwest; France got hold of the island of Madagascar and nearly all of Northwest Africa, including much of the Sahara; and Great Britain's possessions followed the basin of the Nile (including all of Egypt with the recently opened Suez Canal) and included South Africa and parts of West Africa. In short, with the partition of Africa, a new age of imperialism took Europe by storm.

The Europeans vehemently justified their territorial gains in the Age of New Imperialism. They claimed that they brought spiritual and moral enlightenment and material development to the "savage" peoples of the colonies. This feeling of superiority was, in their minds, scientifically proven. In fact, Charles Darwin's newly published thesis, *On the Origin of Species*, perfectly coincided with the Age of New Imperialism. The colonizers used Darwin's scientific findings and manipulated them in a way that benefited their claims. The misinterpretation of complex concepts, like the theories of natural selection and evolution, was one of the reasons behind the Europeans' increased efforts to justify their actions in the colonial world.

Social Darwinism not only applied to the peoples of the world as a whole but also to the Europeans themselves, as different nations perceived one another as more or less culturally advanced.

Everyone agreed that Europe stood higher than all other civilizations and that being European was prestigious and beneficial, but the European nations challenged each other for cultural and moral superiority too. For example, the predominantly Orthodox Slavic Europe perceived Russia as their moral, spiritual, and political leader in the clash against Western Catholic Europe. The Germans believed that it was time for the Germanic peoples of Central Europe to reassert their dominance over the Franco-Latins, who had been in power since the days of the Roman Empire. Different statesmen and authors started romanticizing and idealizing this clash of civilizations, coming up with several justifications for why the Europeans should further pursue their efforts of colonization.

All in all, the colonies became a new frontier for the Europeans to challenge each other for regional supremacy. During the latter part of the 19th century, none of the big states were ready to risk war in continental Europe, knowing that a war would only bring destruction to their homes. However, the Europeans never stopped struggling for dominance; they simply moved it to other parts of the world. They were able to subdue much of the colonial world thanks to their technological superiority and the disjointed states of the African, Asian, and Oceanian people. Then, the Europeans justified their actions through pseudoscientific and cultural factors and enjoyed their position as the rulers of the world. The European imperialists significantly grew their power from their colonial gains, something that only contributed to increasing the competition between them. Thus, the renewed imperialist practices and the transformed world order that was established by the end of the 19th century are considered to be indirect but highly influential precursors of World War I.

European Militarism

As Europe became quieter in the 1880s and 1890s, the European powers started investing more in developing better military and weapons systems. The relative peace established after nationalism triumphed in Italy and Germany, in addition to the expansion of Europe's imperialist strength, resulted in the birth of militarism in major European nations. They spent a significant portion of their income on improving their capabilities during wartime. As a result, the final decades leading up to World War I are characterized by a European arms race.

The roots of 19th-century German militarism can be traced back to the years before its unification, right after Napoleon's defeat. When Napoleon defeated the Prussians, King Frederick William III agreed to reduce the Prussian military's size to a mere forty-two thousand active troops. However, the king implemented a smart tactic; he conscripted and trained new troops every year for a one-year period and then dismissed them from service. This meant that even though the Prussian military immediately after the Napoleonic Wars was comprised of 42,000 active men, ten years later, there were 420,000 Prussians who had undergone at least a year of military training and could have been called up if the situation proved dire.

The Prussian military's readiness during the events of the 1860s and 1870s helped the kingdom lead the process of German unification and defeat the Austrians and French without much difficulty. France's rapid defeat in 1871 further supported the fact that Prussia had a more professional force than its neighbors, and a unified Germany under Prussian leadership would expand the army's capabilities even more. Thus, to no one's surprise, the efforts to further modernize and improve the German military continued after the reunification, and the system became well organized, relying on a strict hierarchy with the Kaiser at the top followed by a military council comprised of generals and officers of landowning *Junker* nobility. The German parliament had no say in the military decisions; it could only advise the council and the chief of general on needed occasions and left the military in the hands of the professionals.

Overall, the spending on the German military after unification increased dramatically, almost by 70 percent, reaching about $460 million by 1913. France, Russia, and Italy soon followed, although the sheer industrial power held by the Germans made it difficult for the competition to catch up. It was correctly perceived by the European powers that if a conflict broke out in Europe, the direct clashes of armies on open fields would decide the outcome, thus justifying their decision to increase conscription to have as many men available as necessary.

Technological advancements also played a role. Military industrialists closely observed and studied the conflicts of the 19th century and introduced improvements to weapons systems. Again, the main focus was on improving heavy artillery by, for example, increasing the range of fire without sacrificing too much mobility. New types of explosive shells made their way into the arsenals of European nations, and small and large firearms were developed to be more portable and deadly. New regiments and battalions were created to field these improvements. All in all, the upgraded weapons systems slowly caused a shift in the way the European powers regarded warfare.

The abovementioned developments generally increased the competitiveness of European powers, but militarism managed to touch other parts of the world that would eventually become involved in World War I, namely Japan and the United States. Dominant actors in their own respect, these nations also built up their militaries and exercised similar practices in the decades leading up to 1914, in turn increasing their own positions of power in their respective regions.

From the second half of the 19th century to the start of the First World War, all of the major powers implemented significant reforms to boost the competence of their militaries. One underlying feature was the implementation of action plans in case a war broke out. Quick offensive strategies, which allowed the attacker to rapidly overwhelm the defenders to achieve decisive victories, became prominent. Nearly all of the powers had these plans ready before World War I.

In an interesting turn of events, Germany would find itself in a new rivalry with arguably the strongest power of the world at the time: Great Britain. As we have already mentioned above, the British Royal Navy proved crucial for Britain's international success and enabled it to reach a dominant position as a global hegemon. The navy was virtually unchallenged and the most experienced and advanced. It kept steadily growing in size since Britain's colonial activity never ceased, unlike other European powers in the 19th century.

In addition, after achieving victories in multiple naval battles, it became clear that having a powerful navy was the key to increasing a state's power. However, no state had invested as much as Britain in developing naval capabilities. They all, in a way, accepted Britain's supremacy on the high seas. The Spanish and the French had tried multiple times but suffered losses against the British on different occasions, most famously in the Battle of Trafalgar when a combined Franco-Spanish fleet was crushed by Admiral Horatio Nelson of the Royal Navy. The United States had practiced an isolationist policy for much of its existence and did not wish to challenge Britain on the seas. The disadvantageous geographic location of Russia and Austria-Hungary and their lack of access to the seas meant they had no interest in building up their fleets to compete with the British. Thus, with no competition, Britain continued to dominate.

The situation would change drastically in the 1890s when Germany prioritized building a strong navy. Several factors precipitated this development, the most important of which probably was the publishing of a very influential work about contemporary naval strategy titled *The Influence of Sea Power upon History* by an American naval officer named Alfred Thayer Mahan. Mahan asserted that there was a direct relationship between possessing a strong navy and global supremacy. He stressed that achieving world domination and emerging as powerful actors on the international scene was determined by sea power, and in the seas, whoever had the bigger fleet would usually reign supreme.

Influenced by Mahan's thorough analysis of the global balance of power and naval strategies, Germany diverted its efforts to building a naval force strong enough to pose a threat to the unquestionable British dominance on the seas. Kaiser Wilhelm II put Admiral Alfred von Tirpitz in charge of the navy since both had similar views on the matter. They increasingly lobbied the Reichstag for funding for their projects, leading to the five German Fleet Acts (1898–1912), which saw huge amounts invested in their cause and substantially increased Germany's naval power. Admiral Tirpitz envisioned Germany's fleet to be about two-thirds the size of Britain's so that, in case of war, it would not be possible for the latter to simply bully Germany on the seas.

However, Britain did not just sit back and watch as one of its main European rivals continued gaining power. The passing of the Second German Fleet Act in June 1900 served as a wake-up call for the British, who tried to answer the Germans by increasing their own naval capabilities. British Admiral Jacky Fisher proposed different measures to counter German efforts in 1902. He ordered a large part of the Royal Navy, which had been scattered around the world to patrol the seas, to return to the British homeland so they could mobilize quicker.

The **HMS Dreadnought,** 1906.
https://commons.wikimedia.org/wiki/File:HMS_Dreadnought_1906_H63596.jpg

In addition, a major development altered the approach of the two powers when it came to their navies. A new super battleship, the **HMS** *Dreadnought,* was launched. It was equipped with the newest weapons and dwarfed all other warships. Upon its launch in 1906, the **HMS** *Dreadnought* was the most powerful—wielding the strength of three normal battleships—and the most expensive, with the British having spent upward of about 1.7 million pounds on just the first model. The commissioning of the warship gave birth to a completely new line of warships conveniently nicknamed "dreadnoughts." They modernized sea warfare and were viewed by the world as a necessity to keep up with militarization efforts. By the start of the war, powers around the world had invested in their own dreadnoughts, but it became clear that Germany had put the most effort into catching up with Britain since its funding and number of personnel increased dramatically.

The naval arms race, as it would come to be known, would continue on different levels until 1912. Different international events, like the Russo-Japanese War, would further prove Mahan's points about naval strategy. Beginning in 1912, German Chancellor Theobald von Bethmann Hollweg would prioritize building the army since Germany had achieved its primary objective of becoming a viable power on the seas. The situation in continental Europe was becoming more worrying, so it was practical to focus on building up ground forces. However, Germany also began the development of military submarines, a completely new and revolutionary technology that was kept secret from the rest of the world. Britain, on the other hand, stopped investing in the Royal Navy since it thought that it was still substantially ahead of the competition.

A 1909 cartoon from Puck showcasing the European naval arms race.
https://commons.wikimedia.org/wiki/File:Naval-race-1909.jpg

All in all, competition increased among the European superpowers, despite the fact that their rivalries never escalated to war. Each state prioritized militarization as they grew wary of the quiet international order and expected war. With the influx of new technology as a result of industrialization, they continued their struggle for dominance in the Age of New Imperialism by competing with each other through their colonies. At the turn of the 20th century, it seemed as if the world was ripe for another major war.

Chapter 3 – Setting the Stage

There is no doubt that after the age of Napoleon, the world underwent a massive transformation in all areas of life. Nationalist and liberal movements breezed through Europe, leaving their mark on emerging new powers. New players emerged in the new and old worlds as the Europeans sought to partition the colonial lands among themselves. And rivals began rapid military mobilization, cautious of a potential conflict that could break out.

This chapter will explore a major factor behind the quick escalation of World War I: the European alliance system. Shortly before the start of the war, two main alliances emerged that sharply divided the superpowers. Although the initial intent of both alliances was to balance the levels of power and influence as a countermeasure to war, ironically, this complex relationship would drag European states into the First World War not long after it started.

New German Foreign Policy

Chancellor Otto von Bismarck saw France as the main and natural threat to Germany, so the measures discussed in the previous chapters were aimed at preventing France from forming strong connections with other powers and from regaining some of the might the French had lost since the days of Napoleon. The Three Emperors' League served that purpose, and by working with Austria and Russia, Bismarck significantly strengthened Germany's position of Germany while undermining France. The Triple Alliance with Italy and Austria was also conceived to provide an effective response to a potential French offensive on Italian and German positions. The security provided by these treaties put Germany in a comfortable position, allowing it to focus on its internal development and build up its industry and military.

However, German foreign policy significantly changed after Bismarck left office in 1890. Kaiser Wilhelm II saw a different course for Germany, one aimed at increasing its influence and power not only regionally but also globally. This was in fundamental opposition to Bismarck's earlier policies, which were mainly directed at keeping peace in Europe by dissuading nations from going to war with each other and relying on domestic production to gain more wealth. In fact, Wilhelm II's efforts to make Germany a player in the colonial game were arguably based on the country's domestic improvements. Had Germany not achieved immense economic growth in the 1880s, the Kaiser's ambitions of expanding the country's power would have been baseless and illogical. The naval arms race with Britain served the same purpose. Germany was able to continue investing millions in developing its navy because of its strong economy.

Thus, Kaiser Wilhelm II decided not to renew Bismarck's agreement with Russia. According to the Reinsurance Treaty, which had been signed in 1887, both sides would declare neutrality in case of an attack on either France or Austria. The Reinsurance Treaty was a guarantee for Germany that Russia—a European power that had immense military potential due to the sheer size of its army—was not a threat.

After the treaty was dropped in 1890 by Germany, Russia naturally felt betrayed and started seeing its former partner as a potential enemy. This opportunity was used by the French. France and Russia entered into a mutual military alliance, something that was extremely beneficial for both sides since they lacked friends. The new Franco-Russian alliance redistributed the balance of power in Europe, with Germany now sandwiched between two nations that were unfriendly toward it. The alliance was especially crucial for Russia, as it borrowed millions from Paris to finance development projects in industry and infrastructure. These funds were mainly invested in building a trans-Siberian railway, which would connect the European part of Russia with the east. In addition, Russia managed to negotiate with Austria on the Balkan matter, signing an agreement and putting their differences aside for the next ten years. This freed up more of Russia's resources to be used elsewhere, further boosting internal development and raising its capability on the international stage.

Britain in Search of Allies

Additional events transpired that further intertwined the fates of world superpowers. A major development was a new British foreign policy. British concerns arose predominantly in response to the increased industrialization and militarization of the European powers, something that Britain correctly believed would challenge its supremacy as a global hegemon. Despite the fact that the Royal Navy was still the ruler of the high seas, the naval arms race with Germany, as well as the naval reforms of countries like the United States, Japan, and France, meant that the British might not enjoy such a prestigious position for long. For a very long time, Britain's isolation had managed to keep it out of complex foreign affairs and provided the kingdom with the possibility to expand its reach. However, it was becoming apparent that Britain needed friends it could rely on, especially since other states were forming close relations with each other.

Thus, Britain's foreign and security policies in the final years of the 19th century were directed to forge ties with states with which Britain shared interests, especially when it came to colonial matters in Asia—a region that had become of the utmost importance. While Germany was emerging as Britain's direct rival, a series of talks took place between the two sides to reach a mutual understanding regarding several pressing matters. However, between 1898 and 1901, in three different instances, Anglo-German talks broke down, leading to deterioration between the two states.

Britain decided to implement a smarter strategy by increasingly working with nations that were considered German rivals, which served to undermine Germany's progress by preventing it from further extending its global reach. Britain signed the Hay-Pauncefote Treaty with the United States in 1901, reaching an agreement about the terms of building the Panama Canal, which was extremely beneficial for both sides. About a year later, in January 1902, Britain managed to form an alliance with Japan—a nation that had significantly grown its power after the Meiji Restoration and had established itself as perhaps the most influential actor in East Asia. The relations between the two states were already on somewhat good terms after the signing of a new trade agreement in the mid-1890s, and the alliance was perceived as beneficial for both sides. It undermined Russia's power in the region and allowed Britain to focus more of its resources on India.

Then, in 1904, as Japan and Russia were about to descend into war over Manchuria, Britain realized that its alliance with Japan would potentially drag it into conflict with France, which was an ally of Russia. Thus, to avoid an escalation both in Europe and in the colonies, Britain and France set aside their historical differences and decided to sit together at the negotiation table. In April, the two sides agreed to the Entente Cordiale. This agreement was not an official defensive or military alliance but served to improve the relations between the two nations. The Entente Cordiale was the first real step in forming deep Franco-British ties. It focused on clearing up the colonial disputes of the two sides in previously contested territories, mainly by giving up French claims on British Egypt and by Britain supporting the French occupation of Morocco. Several other points of contention were also cleared up in other parts of the world.

In the big picture, this agreement between France and Britain was, in a way, the end to the international isolation both nations had experienced for much of the 19th century. France regained some of its power through a new ally, while Britain now had amicable relations with the Reich's main rival. As we will see later on, the Entente Cordiale became the foundation for the cooperation between France and Britain, with both continuing their efforts of deepening diplomatic ties in case of future international crises. All in all, in the span of four years, Britain managed to gain several partners it could rely on, something that served to reassert its position as the biggest global superpower and subdue its challenger, Germany.

The First Moroccan Crisis

The Entente Cordiale did not go unnoticed by Germany, which became wary of the improved relations between its rivals. Despite the fact that Germany had become one of the most economically prosperous nations with a professional military, the developments from 1901 to 1904 only served to reduce its overall influence on the international stage. Germany had not seen any benefits from allying with Austria and Italy since the Triple Alliance's nature was strictly defensive and served to deter a potential French invasion. France and Britain were happy with their increasing presence in their colonies and did not demonstrate an interest in expanding in Europe. What followed the signing of the Entente Cordiale was a provocatory German reaction aimed at undermining the relationship between the French and the British.

It is important to understand that by the time the Entente Cordiale was signed, Morocco was one of the remaining African nations not under the direct rule of a European nation. The French and Spanish had both expressed interest in Morocco during the Berlin Conference, but their approach did not include direct occupation or the use of force. Over time, Morocco became a sphere of influence for both of these nations, with France and Spain seeking economic gains, something that was frowned upon by the Germans due to the increased presence of the French.

When Kaiser Wilhelm II arrived in the Moroccan city of Tangier on March 31ˢᵗ, 1905, he toured the whole city, which had gone into a parade for his presence, on a white horse and declared his support for the Moroccan sultan. The move was seen by Paris as an insult to France. After the Kaiser's speech, Sultan Abdelaziz felt compelled to invite the European powers to advise him on how to reform the country instead of going through with the reforms presented to him by the French prior to the Kaiser's visit. France naturally believed there was no need to hold such a conference, while German Chancellor Bernhard von Bülow threatened to sign an alliance treaty with the sultan if the French presence in Morocco was not discussed with the other nations.

Thus, France was forced to take part in the Algeciras Conference, which took place at the beginning of 1906. Despite this, only one other nation at the conference—Austria—supported

Germany. The overwhelming majority, including the US, Russia, and Italy, took France's side. Most importantly, Britain decided to firmly side with France, demonstrating that it was more than ready to pursue the Entente Cordiale. In fact, it is argued that Germany had acted to see how strong Franco-British relations were and undermined the treaty's importance by provoking both nations. France saw success in reorganizing Morocco by increasing its presence through several policies while leaving some power to the sultan. Additionally, France and Spain signed the Pact of Cartagena a year later, officially recognizing each other's spheres of influence and excluding Germany from matters in Morocco. All in all, the First Moroccan Crisis did not diminish the Franco-British relations as Germany had desired. Instead, it made it clear that both Britain and France were willing to challenge Germany.

The Russo-Japanese War

Along with the First Moroccan Crisis, the Russo-Japanese War was another major international development that contributed to the world alliance systems.

Japan was a rapidly modernizing nation that sought to catch up to the European powers and become an influential actor on the world scene. It had made quite an effort to increase its regional presence since the Meiji Restoration in the mid-19th century. In fact, Japan's imperial ambitions, as well as many of its ideas regarding modernism and development, were influenced by prior European endeavors. After defeating China in the Sino-Japanese War, it became clear that Japan was the strongest independent power in East Asia since the rest of the region was composed of European colonies. None of them were strong enough to challenge Japan except for Britain, but the two sides had agreed to an alliance in 1902 that permitted them to pursue mutual interests—economic gains and rich naval trade routes for Britain and the ability to expand for Japan.

Naturally, the main rival that emerged against Japan's imperialistic intentions was Russia, a nation that had expanded its possessions to include all of northern and northeastern Asia. The founding of the major Pacific port city of Vladivostok (which translates to "the ruler of the East") was the most apparent sign of Russia's ambition to secure its eastern flank and cement itself as a major actor in East Asian politics. The Russians wanted to establish a permanent presence in the Pacific to enable an influx of new trade routes to the country from the east. For that reason, Russia leased the naval base at Port Arthur from the Chinese in 1897. However, both ports were only operational during summertime and froze during winter. Thus, both the Russians and the Japanese eyed Manchuria and Korea.

Japan acted first. It realized that neither Korea nor Manchuria would be able to resist the two countries and offered to divide the territories with Russia. Korea would become part of Japan's sphere of influence, while Russia would be free to pursue its interests in Manchuria. As a counter-offer, Russia wanted to organize a buffer zone between the two sides along the 39th north parallel in Korea, which directly clashed with Japanese ambitions, prompting them to declare war. In a surprise attack, the Japanese engaged with the Russian fleet stationed at Port Arthur in February, striking a heavy blow. The Russian response was swift but not effective. The Russian army lacked discipline and heavily relied on numbers to overwhelm the opposition. But the majority of Russia's forces were not mobilized in the east, and transporting them from western Russia was a long and tenuous process. Even when they came into contact with the Japanese, they suffered multiple defeats since Japan had a more professional, battle-ready core with high morale. In addition to that, Russia's main fleet was also in Europe, and it only managed to get to the Sea of Japan in May 1905, by which time the Japanese had significantly reduced the Russian presence and achieved a decisive victory in the naval Battle of Tsushima.

The war ended with the Treaty of Portsmouth, which was negotiated by US President Theodore Roosevelt. After it became clear that the Japanese were on par with the Russians, anti-war sentiment swept the country. Combined with an array of social and economic problems, it resulted in the 1905 Russian Revolution. Tsar Nicholas II, who fully believed that Russia was capable of defeating Japan, and had hoped to achieve a quick victory to pacify his critics, was forced to agree to difficult terms. Japan got hold of Korea, which it eventually annexed in 1910, while Russia evacuated all of its forces from Manchuria, significantly reducing its strength in East Asia.

More importantly, the Russo-Japanese War proved that Japan was a true superpower and had the ability to challenge and even defeat the Europeans. The Japanese victory made it clear that Britain had made another successful foreign policy move by allying with Japan and had correctly predicted Russia's demise in East Asia. On the other hand, Tsar Nicholas II realized that his prospects of expanding in the Pacific had dwindled. The defeat made him reignite Russian interest in the Balkans.

The Triple Entente

The First Moroccan Crisis and the defeat of Russia in the Russo-Japanese War had repercussions on the European balance of power. In an interesting turn of events, the British alliance with Japan had proven to be a smart move, as Japan established itself as a force to be reckoned with in the Pacific.

Naturally, the nation that did not see any real benefits from the two international events was Germany. German efforts to undermine the Entente Cordiale between France and Britain were ineffective. In fact, its efforts in Morocco had the complete opposite effect, strengthening the ties between the two nations. Germany only found support from the Austrians during the Algeciras Conference. Even Italy, which supposedly had friendly relations with both Germany and Austria, backed French interests in Morocco in exchange for French support in Libya.

The Russo-Japanese War showed that the Russian army, despite its size and former glory, still needed to undergo massive changes to modernize, thus undermining the severity of the Russian threat to Germany. However, France was more than happy to provide funds to Russia to rebuild and play catch up. In short, after Bismarck left office in 1890, with the exception of the Berlin Conference, nothing had really played out in favor of the Reich. The arms race with Britain had prompted it to abandon isolation, causing Germany's main threats to come together to unite against the rising German nation.

The troubles for Germany did not end there, as Britain, France, and Russia continued to engage with each other in new diplomatic talks. Tsar Nicholas II was desperate to consolidate his internal power. Faced with instability and revolution back home, he was ready to give up much of Russia's imperial interests in exchange for much-needed economic support. Thus, in another shocking foreign policy move, Britain decided to backtrack from its not-so-positive relations with St. Petersburg and initiate the Anglo-Russian Convention of 1907. The two sides agreed to terms regarding their interests in Afghanistan and Persia. Britain was heavily dependent on imports from the Indian subcontinent. Since the territories in contention directly bordered India, it was happy to clear up the disputes it had with Russia, which considered Persia and Afghanistan as its own sphere of influence. As in the case of the Entente Cordiale with France, Britain was willing to put an end to its old rivalry for the sake of pursuing mutual interests that indirectly contributed to Germany's further deterioration.

It made sense that the bilateral agreements between Britain and France, France and Russia, and Britain and Russia finally led to the creation of the most important World War I alliance—the Triple Entente. Although the Triple Entente was not a mutually defensive alliance (meaning that in the case of an attack on one member, the other two did not have to necessarily interfere), it clearly underlined that cooperation existed between the three countries. It was more of a coalition, similar to what the European powers had done during Napoleon's reign. It served as a balancing mechanism against the German-Austrian axis and emerged as a direct rival to the Triple Alliance between Austria, Germany, and Italy.

France and Britain continued their efforts of clearing up colonial disputes while also sending economic aid to Russia to speed up its development and help St. Petersburg overcome the effects of the revolution. In addition, they mediated better relations between the Japanese and Russians to avoid another potential conflict in East Asia, which likely would have been more destructive. Paris concluded an agreement with Tokyo in 1907 that tied the two nations closer together and played a big part in stabilizing the relations between Japan and Russia. Putting the war behind, Japan willingly accepted France's proposal and no longer perceived Russia as a threat to its interests in East Asia, something that was also partly due to the close relations between Moscow and Paris.

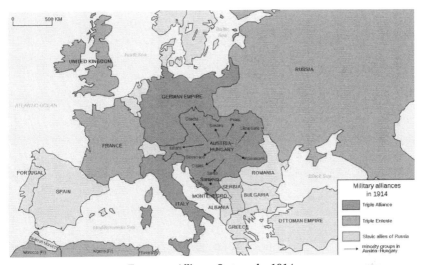

European Alliance Systems by 1914.

Historicair (French original) Fluteflute & User: Bibi Saint-Pol (English translation), CC BY-SA 2.5 <https://creativecommons.org/licenses/by-sa/2.5>, via Wikimedia Commons. Accessed from: https://commons.wikimedia.org/wiki/File:Map_Europe_alliances_1914-en.svg

Thus, in the first ten years of the 20th century, the international order saw yet another fundamental transformation. The German efforts to abandon Bismarck's foreign policy of keeping peace in Europe by isolating their direct rivals in favor of pursuing a more prominent *Weltpolitik* did not prove to be a smart decision. Challenging Britain for international dominance in the naval arms race was becoming more and more costly for Berlin, and the active role that the Reich assumed did not go unnoticed by Germany's rivals. Britain realized that it was impossible to keep its vast empire without international partners and started to slowly forge relations with different actors to obtain a firmer grip on its colonial possessions, which were the main source of its income and prestige. Britain's alliance with Japan, agreements with the United States, and ententes with Russia and France served the British government well.

The Triple Entente was an immensely beneficial agreement for France as well. It tried to retaliate against Germany, which had pursued a policy of isolating France since the early 1880s. By forming close relations with Britain, Russia, and Japan, France was given a much-needed way back into becoming one of the biggest players in world politics. In addition, the Triple Entente could be helpful against a potential German threat. Russia, unlike the other powers, just sought to buy time and solve an array of problems, such as the revolution and the war with Japan. It was becoming evident that the next major European conflict would have massive repercussions for the whole world.

Chapter 4 – On the Brink of War

The emerging alliance systems were a byproduct of new powerful international actors that had risen into prominence in the later part of the 19th century. Britain recognized that Germany's rise might challenge its global hegemony and decided to forge connections with nations to govern its vast colonial possessions and potentially deter the Germans from catching up. Germany, on the other hand, abandoned the Bismarckian alliance system that was primarily aimed at keeping peace in Europe. Instead, it shifted its focus to world domination, something that proved to be costly since its rivals soon realized the threat Germany posed and balanced it out with their own efforts.

This chapter will explore the final pieces of the puzzle of what led to World War I. We will take a look at the old-fashioned structures of the European empires, as well as one of the most politically complex regions—the Balkans—and how the developments that transpired in the early 20th century accelerated the start of the conflict.

The Question of Austria-Hungary

Up until this point, we have not paid much attention to the developments involving Austria-Hungary. In a way, this "prejudice" against the Habsburg Empire is for a good reason. In the "long nineteenth century," as other nations sought to modernize by promoting more liberal views and rapid industrialization, Austria-Hungary was perhaps the loudest advocator and best example of the older, more conservative regimes. The Habsburg royal family, unlike other European monarchies, was unwilling to give up much of the influence and power that they held. The Austrian rulers enacted ineffective measures to combat the empire's problems, which caused Austria to fall behind in development. It was unable to keep up with the standards of modern empires.

Austria-Hungary's structure is crucial to understand. Because of the geographical location of the Habsburg Empire—stretching from the provinces of Bohemia and Galicia of Central Europe to parts of northern Italy and the Adriatic coast of the Balkans—Austria-Hungary was a very complex political entity. Many different ethnicities and nationalities were almost equally prominent.

The ethnic groups of Austria-Hungary in 1910 according to *Distribution of Races in Austria-Hungary* by William R. Shepherd, 1911.

Different ethnic groups in Austria-Hungary.
https://commons.wikimedia.org/wiki/File:Austria_Hungary_ethnic.svg

By the early 20th century, Austria-Hungary had stopped many of its expansion efforts and had reached the maximum extent of its historical borders. It included many different peoples of Europe: the Germans made up a good part of the population, concentrated in the northwestern regions of the empire; Czechs were prominent in the north, while the Ukrainians and Poles lived predominantly in the northeast; Slovaks and Hungarians dominated the central part; Romanians were focused in the east; Croats and Serbs occupied the southern parts of the empire on the coast of the Adriatic; and finally, although they had a smaller presence than the other peoples, the Italians and Slovenes lived in the western and southwestern parts.

All in all, Austria-Hungary was a geopolitical mess of several European nationalities, which caused an array of problems for the empire time and time again. For example, when new monarchs ascended the throne, their policies could not address the issues of all these different peoples equally. Some parts of the empire felt left out, while others enjoyed more privileges. In addition, most of Europe's transformation since the French Revolution had happened due to the increase of nationalist sentiment that swept through the continent. In Italy and Germany, the majority of the population were ethnically the same. They shared similar cultures, traditions, sets of values, language, and other characteristics that contributed to their efforts of achieving statehood. Austria-Hungary, on the other hand, was not a nation-state, and the nationalist movements in different parts of the empire were crushed time and time again by the royalist forces. The suppression of these movements only caused more discord in Austria-Hungary, requiring stricter measures from the empire, thus sending it into a vicious cycle.

Thus, despite its vastness and past might, Austria-Hungary was plagued by the problems all ethnically diverse empires are eventually doomed to face. It had to concentrate on dealing with the rising nationalist sentiments within its borders, which undermined the centralization of the Habsburg rule and caused the collapse of the empire. Austria-Hungary did not have time or was willing to undertake fundamental transformations. Additionally, it still considered itself an influential player in European power politics, something that mainly derived from its role in the past, although the other European nations knew they were far more powerful and influential than the Austrians by the late 19th century.

The internal instability can be perceived, alongside Austria-Hungary's unfavorable geographical location, as the reason behind its noninvolvement in the colonial game, something that had come to be seen as vital for any empire desiring to be looked at as dominant on the international scene. Austria-Hungary could not even aspire to be a dominant global player if it could not deal with its internal problems first. In a way, the imperialist practices of the other colonial powers were being practiced by Austria-Hungary within its own borders, as the monarchy sought to balance the dynamics between the different struggling nations.

Since internal stabilization was the main factor behind industrialization and rapid development, Austria lagged behind in almost all aspects, unlike its German, British, French, and, to some extent, Russian counterparts. The Austro-Hungarian army was not as professional and disciplined, having been defeated multiple times over the course of the 19th century. Its military technology, strategy, and general outlook on war were not up to standard. Industry and infrastructure were less developed, and Austria-Hungary lacked a competent fleet to challenge even regional rivals. But perhaps most importantly, the monarchy was reluctant to grant more freedom to its subjects.

Chancellor Otto von Bismarck's decision to ally with Austria-Hungary can be justified since Germany was primarily focused on regional security at that time and needed Austria as an ally against France, which was perceived as more powerful and more competent. But as Vienna's only ally diverted its attention to pursue global imperialist endeavors and challenge the British for dominance, it became more difficult for the Habsburgs to keep a firm grip on their subjects. As time would tell, Austria-Hungary, despite its relative backwardness, was indirectly responsible for keeping Europe from bursting into an all-out war. Russia, which was the main regional rival of Austria, was willing to encourage internal conflicts and undermine the Habsburg rule for its own benefit, while France and Britain believed that Germany could not stand a chance against the Entente Cordiale without powerful allies. In the end, the Habsburgs' inability to resolve the tensions within their borders became one of the most prominent causes of World War I.

The Sick Man of Europe

Another formerly great power that played an important role in World War I was the Ottoman Empire. Just like Austria-Hungary, the power held by the Ottomans at the height of their existence was immense; the empire stretched from southeast Europe to Anatolia, the Middle East, and North Africa. But the Ottoman rulers also faced similar problems as Austria-Hungary, resulting in a backward empire on the brink of collapse. In fact, since the Ottoman lands stretched farther than the Habsburgs' domain, they experienced tougher times because they were not able to keep up with industrialization and modernization. Sometimes, the later Ottoman Empire is referred to as the "sick man of Europe," a name first used by Tsar Nicholas II of Russia.

One of the Ottoman Empire's main struggles was the fact it had a different religion from Europe and was perceived as a natural enemy to the Christian Europeans. Although Christianity saw divisions among itself, the Muslim Ottomans were never considered to have been a friend. The clashes between the Europeans and Ottomans were always, in some way or another, a manifestation of the underlying rivalry between Christian and Muslim ideologies.

This proved to be a disadvantage, as the Ottomans had to sometimes face multiple Christian nations at once in battle. For example, during the siege of Vienna in 1683, the Ottomans had made significant progress toward capturing the Austrian capital but were stopped in their tracks after the arrival of a Polish relief force, which forced the Ottomans to abandon the siege and retreat. The Polish had been motivated by the pope to aid Vienna and stop the Muslim invaders. Despite the general disunity of the European nations, they came together time and time again once they realized the Ottoman threat had arrived at their doorstep.

The Ottoman Empire's decline was gradual, starting mainly in the 17th century. When the Ottomans were at the height of their power, no European nation dared to challenge them. Before the Age of Exploration, the Ottomans became the masters of the Mediterranean and controlled much of the trade flow between Europe and Asia, immensely profiting from the trade routes that had to pass through their territories. It was their monopoly over

Eastern trade that forced the Europeans to find alternative routes to Asia. They were finally able to circumvent the Ottoman obstacle after they discovered the route around the African continent that led to Asia. Over time, this diminished the Ottoman Empire's economic strength since the European merchants did not have to go through the Turkish lands anymore to reach the rich Indian markets.

In addition to economic struggles, the Ottoman Empire experienced a similar industrialization problem as the Austrians and the Russians. Unlike Britain, France, and Germany, where rapid industrialization had taken off because of the countries' relative stability, the Ottomans did not have the same luxury. Stretched over three continents, the Ottoman Empire struggled to keep order in its distant provinces and was unable to suppress the rebellions that popped up. Out of the major actors of World War I, the Ottomans were the ones who never truly let go of the conservative monarchy. Even Austria-Hungary was less dependent on it. The lack of centralization and the emergence of nationalist sentiments, especially in the European part of the Ottoman Empire, caused many provinces to break off. They were supported by the Ottomans' regional rivals, which wished to see the collapse of a once-mighty empire.

The technological disparities that emerged after the industrialization period also impacted Turkish rule. For instance, European nations adopted new military technologies that gave them a huge advantage over the Ottomans. In fact, much of their strength lay in the size of their armies. The Ottomans were able to muster up armies composed of tens of thousands of men regularly, unlike their European counterparts for much of the late medieval times. Back then, the fate of a battle was largely decided by whichever side had a bigger force.

As time and technology progressed, it became clear that numbers alone did not guarantee success. The Ottoman soldiers were simply outclassed in wars, not only lacking modern equipment to competently conduct battles but also lacking the morale, professionalism, experience, and general discipline of European troops. Its loss in the war with Russia over Crimea demonstrated the disparity that existed between it and the Europeans even more clearly. Everything is relative when it comes to development. The Russian army was never considered to have been up to "true" European standards, but it managed to crush the Ottoman forces relatively easily.

The Balkan Powder Keg

Many underlying problems troubled the Ottoman Empire for a long time. When the European powers noticed their superior position, they actively got involved in the processes that led to the empire's collapse. The Ottoman rule was centralized in Istanbul and the ethnically Turkish Anatolia and Asia Minor, but it was very weak in the peripheral provinces, which seceded from the empire first. The independence movements in Egypt, for example, were quickly supported by the British, who also actively funded the construction of the Suez Canal. The British and French were also increasingly involved in ending the Ottomans' control in regions that were of interest to them due to their proximity to their colonial holdings. Thus, by the late 19th century, Istanbul had lost control of the entire North African coast with the exception of Libya, as well as many of its European possessions. The Ottomans only effectively controlled modern-day Turkey and most of the Middle East.

However, the biggest point of contention between the Ottomans and the Europeans was the Balkans—an ethnically diverse and strategically important region whose developments were influenced by the foreign policies of neighboring empires, namely Austria, the Ottoman Empire, and Russia. The Balkans constituted a natural buffer zone between the Ottomans and Europe, and because the Balkan nations did not enjoy independence, the Ottomans posed a big threat to Europe's security. Each actor saw the region as their own sphere of influence. The Ottomans had controlled most of the region since their early days as an empire, and their claim and ideological strive that they were "European" was heavily based on them being in control of the Balkans. Austria-Hungary was a conglomeration of many nations and included a large part of the Balkan peoples within its borders. The Habsburgs' foreign policy was always based on increasing the empire's reach to rejoin their brothers and sisters who had been left behind, trapped under the tyrannical Muslim rule of the Ottomans. Russia saw itself as a natural leader, a big brother of all ethnically Slavic and Orthodox peoples of Europe, and had tried to increase its presence in the Balkans on multiple occasions. All three sides had their own reasons to challenge each other for dominance in the Balkan Peninsula.

But achieving stability in the Balkans was extremely difficult because of the presence of so many nationalities and ethnicities, each with its own unique identity. Nationalist sentiment was very strong in the Balkan region, and such movements, especially when paired with a rapidly declining Ottoman Empire, saw major success throughout the 19th century. For example, Greece's struggle for independence in the 1820s and the 1830s was supported by Britain, France, and Russia, and the country succeeded in breaking free from the Ottomans in 1832. This weakened the Ottoman presence in Europe and also inspired bordering nations to fight for their own independence.

Serbia gained its autonomy from the Ottoman Empire in 1830. Since Serbia was Orthodox, its independence was guaranteed by Russia. The Russian protectorate proved extremely beneficial, as Serbia managed to achieve territorial gains after Russia's victory in the war against the Ottomans in 1878. Bulgaria was also granted autonomy in 1878. In addition, the autonomous region of Bosnia and Herzegovina was occupied by the Austrians, sandwiching the Ottoman Balkan possessions between independent states and autonomous provinces.

The Ottomans truly lost their grip over most of the Balkans by 1908, when a major change occurred in Istanbul. The Young Turk Revolution managed to gain a lot of traction since it advocated for the promotion of more liberal values and fundamental changes in the sociopolitical structure of Ottoman life, including granting its provinces more autonomy. In 1908, Sultan Abdul Hamid II was forced to accept the terms put forth by the revolutionaries and reinstitute a constitutional monarchy, giving up much of his privileges as the sultan and weakening Ottoman influence in the Balkan region.

This opportunity was quickly realized by Austria-Hungary, which already saw itself as the rightful ruler of Bosnia, annexing the territory by the end of 1908. The crisis within the Ottoman Empire did not end there, as the country saw itself go to war with Italy just three years later in 1911 over Italy's colonial ambitions in Ottoman-controlled Libya. The Italians wielded a more professional, disciplined, and overall superior army with higher morale. They were able to quickly assume a dominant position in the war and forced Istanbul to give up its control over Tripoli and the rest of the empire's North African possessions about a year later in October 1912.

The Ottomans just could not keep up. The empire's crises never seemed to end. The empire was torn between needing to implement major domestic reforms and spending more resources on keeping peace within its borders. Thus, even before the war with Italy was officially over, the Balkan nations declared war, now united under the banner of the Balkan League, in early October 1912. The Balkan League had been formed after a series of secret negotiations between Greece, Serbia, Bulgaria, and Montenegro. The four former Ottoman provinces signed multiple bilateral agreements that bound each other as defensive or military allies, aimed at keeping themselves safe from the bigger regional threats, namely the Ottomans and Austrians.

Seeing that the war with Italy was going terribly for Istanbul, the Balkan League realized that it was the perfect time to strike against the empire and drive the Turks out of Europe once and for all. The members of the Balkan League were inspired by the nationalist movements of the 19th century and firmly believed they could overcome Ottoman tyranny if they all came together. They devised a plan of action, acknowledging the fact that they lacked the numbers to go up against the Ottomans. However, the Ottoman Empire's main forces were either busy with the Italians or scattered in Asia. Thus, it would take a lot of time and effort for the Ottomans to transport the majority of their troops to the conflict zone, which was not only right at the border of the Balkan nations but also extremely close to Istanbul. The Balkan League decided to strike quickly and decisively.

In early October, the Balkan nations declared war on the Ottomans one after the other and launched a united offensive on multiple parts of Ottoman holdings in the region. Serbia, Montenegro, and Bulgaria led the assaults on land since they fielded the majority of the ground forces, while Greece's main role was to delay the Ottoman reinforcements in the sea since the

Greeks possessed a pretty capable navy that was experienced in maneuvering around the area.

The war effort was successful. The Balkan League caught the Turks off-guard and managed to achieve small victories in nearly all the land battles, while the Greeks held off the Turkish fleet in the Aegean and the Mediterranean. The victorious nations signed a peace treaty with the Turks in May 1913, ending the Ottoman presence in Europe after nearly five hundred years. With the Treaty of London, the great powers decided the territorial gains for each participating nation, eventually leading to the creation of the independent state of Albania, the Greek occupation of nearly all the formerly held Ottoman islands, and the clear definition of the borders of the rest of the Balkan states.

With the Ottoman Empire's defeat, the regional balance of power had dramatically shifted once again. But the victorious Balkan nations could not come to terms with the spoils of war, spiraling the region into yet another armed conflict known as the Second Balkan War. Bulgaria declared war on its former allies Greece and Serbia, challenging them for regional dominance. Bulgaria had initially been promised more gains according to the secret agreements prior to the First Balkan War but was left disappointed when the Serbs and Greeks refused to make more territorial concessions. Thus, the Bulgarians invaded, hoping to catch their former allies by surprise. However, they overestimated their own capabilities. Although Bulgaria achieved some progress, it was forced to surrender in thirty-three days, in the summer of 1913. As a result, it lost even more territories to Serbia and Greece and made some concessions to Romania, which had joined the conflict toward the end.

The events that transpired in the Balkans over the 19th and early 20th centuries earned the region an infamous name. By the start of the Great War, the Balkans had a reputation as being one of the most politically unstable locations in Europe. The multitude of ethnically diverse groups with distinct national identities had complicated the political landscape, and while the European superpowers tried to influence the developments in the Balkans time and time again, by the start of World War I, none of them had assumed a dominant position in the region.

Meanwhile, Russia, another interested player in the Balkans, was regarded as the big brother to all the Slavic peoples concentrated in the Orthodox Balkan nations. Russia promoted a Pan-Slavic ideology and supported the independence movements. Strategically, Russia knew that the independence of the Balkan countries would significantly weaken its rival, the Ottoman Empire, and potentially give Russia access to the warm ports of the Mediterranean. Russia also hoped that the instability would be detrimental to Austria-Hungary, another empire that had historically struggled with the Balkan peoples.

Austria-Hungary was put in a very precarious position after the Balkan Wars, as it included a large number of Balkan peoples within its vast borders and was worried that its subjects would also rise up, motivated by their brothers who had managed to achieve independence. The Habsburgs and the newly freed Balkan nations, especially Serbia, did not get along with each other for that reason, and it wouldn't be long until the Balkan subjects of Austria-Hungary started protesting the rule imposed over them by the Habsburgs.

The "Balkan powder keg," as it would be referred to by its contemporaries due to the political instability innate to the region, would eventually decide the fate of the world since World War I would begin shortly after the Balkan Wars. In 1914, the rest of the world truly felt the impact of the Balkan powder keg's explosion.

Section Two: The Outbreak of War

Chapter 5 – The Gunshot Heard around the World

It is now time to divert our attention to the events that directly led to the outbreak of World War I and the early stages of the Great War. We have already observed the complicated, competitive sociopolitical climate in Europe by the end of the 19th and the start of the 20th century. Rivals challenged each other at every opportunity, organizing themselves in complex, intricate alliance systems. It was becoming more and more apparent that war was imminent. All that was needed was a spark, something to ignite the tensions between the global superpowers and lead the world into chaos.

As the dwindling Austro-Hungarian Empire tried holding onto its influence over the Balkan nations, complicating the situation even more by trying to exert power, perhaps the most infamous assassination in history would lead to a chain of unfortunate events, eventually ending with the outbreak of World War I.

The Austrian Problem

The Ottoman Empire's decline did not directly translate into an increase in power for Vienna. The emergence of the Balkan nations as independent states posed a threat to the Habsburgs' unity. The Habsburg ruler was worried that the developments immediately on the empire's southern borders would spill over to

Austria-Hungary, which included a lot of ethnically diverse groups—peoples whose brothers and sisters had achieved independence and were urging others to join them. The Habsburgs had tried time and time again to deal with the nationality problem, but the measures they implemented were never truly effective, serving mostly as temporary rather than long-term solutions. Austria-Hungary's ruling elite were split between advocating for a federalist system, which would grant a large degree of autonomy for the empire's provinces in return for relative stability, and more imperative measures, such as directly intervening in the political life of their diverse ethnic groups to discourage and punish any nationalist movements.

The developments preceding the Balkan Wars also influenced the dynamics between Austria-Hungary and the newly independent nations. Most importantly, in 1903, the royal Obrenović family of Serbia, which generally had somewhat stable relations with the Habsburgs, was ousted by the Serbian army during the May Coup. The king and queen of Serbia were brutally assassinated, and the Karageorgević family was put in charge. The Karageorgević family's rule was characterized by increased nationalist sentiment, something that led to worsening relations with Vienna and Serbia taking a more pro-Russian course.

For the next few years, Serbia became more and more involved in the events that unfolded in the Balkans. It tried to increase its borders and muster up a professional army to challenge regional rivals. At the same time, the Austrian annexation of Bosnia and the events of the Bosnian Crisis of 1908 to 1909 left Serbia disappointed and angered because many of the annexed territories were predominantly inhabited by Serbs. Serbian nationalism took off, with the Serbs in Austria-Hungary organizing several secret societies with the aim of promoting nationalist values to achieve liberation while disrupting and undermining Vienna's regime. The *Narodna Odbrana*, which was formed in 1908, is an example of one of these societies. It sought to show that the Serbs did not belong as subjects of the Habsburg Empire.

However, their efforts proved somewhat ineffective, leading to the formation of more radical nationalist groups. These organizations operated largely like terrorist groups, as they planned the assassinations of many Austrian officials. The Black Hand rose to prominence, regarding itself as the next logical evolution of the *Narodna Odbrana*. Its members mainly advocated for the formation of a Greater Serbia—an entity that would include many of the predominantly Serb territories and would be a precursor for an eventual Pan-Slavic state, one led by Serbia.

The Serbian nationalist movements became a significant problem for Vienna. They created instability and encouraged conflict between the subjects and rulers of the empire. If the problem was not addressed quickly, it had the potential, at least in the eyes of the Austrian elite, to cause the complete dissolution of Austria-Hungary. Thus, Austrian statesmen increasingly started lobbying to solve the problem. Among them was Archduke Franz Ferdinand, son of Archduke Charles Louis and the nephew of Emperor Francis Joseph of Austria. In 1889, due to the untimely death of the heir apparent, Prince Rudolf, and then Archduke Charles, Franz Ferdinand became the next in line for the throne of Austria-Hungary.

Archduke Franz Ferdinand.
https://commons.wikimedia.org/wiki/File:Franz_ferdinand.jpg

Despite having unfavorable relations with the throne because of the issues that had arisen with his marriage, Franz Ferdinand was a prominent figure in the empire and enjoyed a relatively comfortable position of power. This was mainly due to his influence on the imperial military, as he had become the inspector general of the army in 1913. His political views, however, were very different from most of his contemporaries, as he did not really support one side over the other. For example, Franz Ferdinand believed the best way to stabilize the empire was to listen to the ethnic groups and grant them relative autonomy.

He demonstrated more tolerance and sympathy toward some groups, like the Czechs, while frowning upon others, like the Serbs and Hungarians. This assertion mainly came from the fact that he criticized the Hungarian branch of the dual monarchy for its inability to significantly contribute to the empire's joint rule. Archduke Ferdinand also wanted to increase Austria-Hungary's role on the international stage. He believed the empire should be more actively involved in world matters as a European superpower and saw the modernization of the military and the creation of a competent navy as precursors for a more powerful Austria-Hungary.

Archduke Franz Ferdinand was one of the most vocal people when it came to the Serbia problem. His peculiar approach of encouraging a version of federalism without necessarily undermining the monarchy's position was hopeful, as it aimed to achieve the best of both worlds and balance the crisis. However, it was unknown how he would be able to put it into practice. Still, because of the prestigious position Ferdinand was in, he was adamant about adopting a careful approach to Serbia, recognizing that an all-out war would be devastating for both sides.

But despite undoubtedly being one of the most powerful men in the empire, the archduke was highly unpopular. The conservative Hungarians despised him for his federalist views, and many different ethnic groups, including the Serbs, did not support him because they believed his efforts would lead to a pacified nationalist sentiment and stand in their way of reunifying with their brothers and sisters over the border.

The Assassination

So, when Emperor Francis Joseph sent Archduke Franz Ferdinand to the Bosnian capital of Sarajevo to conduct inspections of the imperial army stationed in Bosnia, he arrived at a location where the aggravated public's opinion was largely not favorable toward him. As we already mentioned, due to the significant presence of Serbs in Bosnia, anti-Austrian sentiment had grown, something further instigated by the rise of Serbian nationalist organizations. These groups knew the archduke would visit the capital in June of 1914 and wanted to exploit his visit, planning an assassination to send a clear message to the empire that they were not messing around. In a way, in hindsight, Franz Ferdinand's visit to a place that was so hostile toward him was not exactly the smartest decision.

Several extremist organizations would get involved in planning and carrying out the assassination. Young Bosnia, which was largely comprised of Bosnian-born ethnic Serbs, took the lead. Strongly motivated by popular accounts of heroism from local folklore and legendary historical stories of Serbian heroes, the members of Young Bosnia were eager to put everything on the line to achieve their goal for the greater good, believing that Franz Ferdinand's eventual accession to the throne would end their dreams and hopes for unification. Supplied with arms from the Serbian Black Hand, the assassination plan was put in place.

The day of the archduke's visit to Sarajevo fell on Vidovdan, a Serbian national holiday that memorialized the 1389 Battle of Kosovo between the Ottoman Empire and Serbia. For the conspirators, it was, in a way, symbolic, as a Serb assassin had managed to assassinate the Ottoman sultan back then. They hoped they could repeat the events. Franz Ferdinand was supposed to ride through the streets of Sarajevo with his wife in an open car as part of a motorcade with a police escort. Six assassins knew the predetermined route and armed themselves with hand grenades. They assumed their positions and patiently waited for Franz Ferdinand to pass by.

However, despite the readiness of the assassins, the first attempt to murder the archduke was unsuccessful. The first assassins— Muhamed Mehmedbašić, a veteran Black Hand member, and Vaso Čubrilović—failed to act. Both of them were armed with hand grenades and pistols, but neither of them decided to strike when the motorcade passed them. The next assassin, Nedeljko Čabrinović, was stationed on the opposite side of the road, farther down the route. Čabrinović threw a bomb but missed. The grenade bounced off the archduke's car and fell back onto the streets. It detonated when the next car of the motorcade was on top of it, causing a massive explosion that injured up to twenty people.

Čabrinović saw that his effort was unsuccessful. He popped a cyanide pill and jumped in the Miljacka River, but he survived and was dragged out by the crowd before eventually being arrested by the police. The motorcade realized that the archduke's life was in danger and sped up, breezing past the other assassins without giving them a chance to react. Franz Ferdinand survived the attempted assassination, fleeing to the town hall.

There, the archduke discussed the situation with officers and the governor, expressing his anger over the fact that somebody had just tried to kill him. The parties agreed that the disaster had been avoided, and Archduke Ferdinand, motivated by his wife, decided not to stay in the town hall and pay a visit to those who had been wounded in the attack. The archduke went back to the car with his wife and the mayor, and the motorcade drove off to the nearby hospital. What transpired next is probably the most ironic development that changed the course of the world forever.

In an unfortunate turn of events, the new route that was proposed by Governor Oskar Potiorek was not effectively communicated to the drivers of the motorcade. This meant that instead of altering their route according to the new plan, the drivers proceeded to follow the old route, taking a wrong turn at Latin Bridge. This would prove to be a fatal mistake. After the first failed assassination, one of the assassins, a nineteen-year-old Bosnian Serb student by the name of Gavrilo Princip, decided to abandon his position and move to a local food shop at Latin Bridge, where Archduke Franz Ferdinand was accidentally led to by a mistaken motorcade.

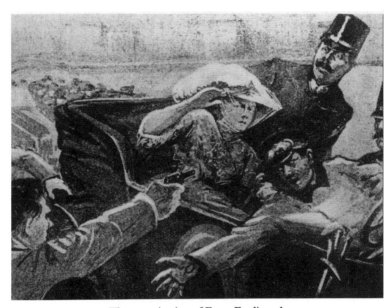
The assassination of Franz Ferdinand.
https://commons.wikimedia.org/wiki/File:Assassination_of_Archduke_Ferdinand.jpg

Once the motorcade took a wrong turn, Governor Potiorek shouted to the driver of the first car from the third car, where he was sitting with the archduke and Duchess Sophia, to stop and back up to the main road. When the motorcade stopped, Princip realized that the archduke was stuck on a bridge just in front of him at point-blank range. He proceeded to fire two shots from his FN Model 1910 pistol, fatally wounding the archduke and his pregnant wife before being immediately seized by the crowd.

Thus, Archduke Franz Ferdinand of Austria had successfully been assassinated by the radical Serb extremists, an event that would have massive implications for the rest of the world.

July Crisis

The assassination of Archduke Franz Ferdinand would eventually cause a chain reaction that would see all the rival European powers go to war with each other, falling like dominoes in a line, with one side dragging the other into the conflict with them. As the next heir of Austria-Hungary, Franz Ferdinand was a very important political figure in Europe, and it was logical that the empire would be aggravated, even though the archduke did not enjoy much popularity. Because of the tense relations between the Habsburgs and the Serbs, the assassination had an even stronger underlying political meaning.

As we have already observed, Austria-Hungary was aiming to spread its influence to the smaller, weaker states of the region. Austria needed an event to justify a potential war, and the assassination of its heir apparent was more than enough. The events that followed Archduke Franz Ferdinand's assassination have come to be known as the July Crisis. Throughout July, different actors tried to justify or prevent war. It would become clear that the balance of power that had been carefully established over the past decades was about to come crashing down.

Although the people of Austria-Hungary were appalled by the archduke's murder, the immediate reaction in Vienna was not what one might expect. Emperor Francis Joseph knew about the region's complex political climate and preferred to conduct investigations about the assassination to determine whether or not Serbia's government had anything to do with it. The interrogations of the arrested assassins determined their Serbian origin, as well as their membership in radical extremist organizations. However, Serbian envoys immediately claimed they had warned Austria-Hungary of the potential dangers associated with Archduke Franz Ferdinand's visit prior to his arrival and also denied that Belgrade had anything to do with the assassination.

By early July, it had become clear that the archduke's assassination was yet another crisis Austria-Hungary had to face. It pointed at the empire's long-standing inability to effectively deal with the upset peoples who dwelled within its borders and posed a legitimate challenge to the Habsburgs' competence. The Austrian government started debating whether or not war with Serbia was a real possibility, discussing the European powers' potential reactions to the conflict.

Serbia was Russia's ally, but would the Russians be willing to support such a small nation and risk fighting an all-out war with the Austrians? If Vienna could successfully expose Serbian involvement in the events that had transpired in Sarajevo, it would have the perfect justification to go to war, and it would be much quicker to conduct a successful offensive. Russia would simply have no time to respond to Austria's actions in Serbia because it was so far away. Plus, Russia's army would need rapid mobilization, something that Moscow was not really capable of doing.

For Austria, localizing the conflict and quickly defeating the Serbs would be the best outcome. It would not only prevent the war from escalating with Russia but also be perceived as a decisive action by Vienna in dealing with the assassination crisis. Still, the emperor chose to wait before making such a major decision, preferring to consult with his military staff and allies.

By the first week of July, Austria-Hungary had gotten the backing of Germany, which pledged to support any Austrian military action against the Serbs. Germany believed that Russia would not pose a threat to the German military. This confidence was justified, as Germany had invested much more in modernizing its forces since the 1870s compared to Russia. The German high command unanimously supported the idea of Austria-Hungary going to war with Serbia and eliminating the newly established nation-state since it would further increase the Habsburgs' presence in the region and weaken Russia. In fact, German officials openly stated that the situation was an opportunity for Austria and declared their firm support for any Austrian action with the infamous "blank cheque," which essentially means that Germany gave Vienna unlimited freedom to solve the crisis.

Still, the evidence of Serbian involvement in the assassination was lacking. Austria-Hungary's cabinet of ministers assembled to properly discuss a joint plan of action. War was certainly popular among the majority, but ultimately, the officials decided to present an ultimatum to Serbia so Austria-Hungary could have a proper, legal justification for war. The main supporter of this decision was Prime Minister István Tisza of Hungary.

The council wanted to present Serbia with a list of demands that would be impossible to meet, a provocative action that would definitely result in war. However, Tisza managed to persuade the ministers to draft another set of ultimatums, a list that would still be harsh on Serbia but still somewhat acceptable to the Serbians. Tisza believed that Austria-Hungary would be in a win-win situation. If Belgrade accepted the terms, it would be seen as a diplomatic feat for Vienna. If the terms were denied, Austria would be compelled to go to war and would most likely emerge victorious. Several versions of the ultimatum were drafted and presented to the emperor. By July 19th, the final draft was ready to be sent to Belgrade.

However, the Austrians decided to wait a few more days. At the time, the French delegation, including President Raymond Poincaré and Prime Minister René Viviani, was visiting Tsar Nicholas II in St. Petersburg. The date of the visit merely coincided with the crisis; it had not been planned as a response to the assassination. Still, the two sides discussed the assassination and the potential of a war breaking out. The Franco-Russian alliance had proven to be beneficial for both sides. France was happy to have friendly relations with Russia because of its reduced international position and saw it as a deterrent against Germany. Russia benefited from the funding provided by Paris to modernize its army, support infrastructure projects, and keep up with the rest of the developing world. President Poincaré assured Tsar Nicholas II that France would commit to the alliance with Russia, even if the situation escalated to more severe levels. The visit proved to be a crucial one, as Russia now had France backing it.

On July 23rd, as the French delegation left St. Petersburg for Paris, Austria-Hungary presented its finalized version of the ultimatum to Serbia. It contained ten points that had to be met by Belgrade within forty-eight hours. If Serbia refused any of the terms in the given timeframe, the Austrian ambassador was to leave immediately and suspend all diplomatic activities. The ultimatum, in hindsight, was unrealistically demanding. It was very unlikely for Serbia or any other sovereign nation to unanimously accept all ten terms. They heavily undermined the Serbian government's power but increased Austria-Hungary's power dramatically.

Serbia needed to suppress all anti-Austrian movements, publications, and teachings and disband nationalist organizations, such as the *Narodna Odbrana*. Austria claimed that the situation in Serbia threatened the empire's security, something that was made clear with the archduke's assassination. The Austrian side also wanted to become increasingly involved in Serbia's sociopolitical processes, demanding that Serbia allow the arrival of Austrian officials to monitor the actions of its government and military and to ensure the elimination of anti-Austrian sentiment. It also demanded the immediate arrest of all suspects involved in the assassination and the start of a new Austrian-led investigation. All in all, the ultimatum was a condescending, humiliating document, the main purpose of which was to assert Austro-Hungarian dominance over the small nation of Serbia and provoke Belgrade into starting a war.

The week after July 23rd saw the whole of Europe in a never-before-seen uproar. Serbia was compelled to respond quickly but knew that accepting the ultimatum would infringe on its sovereignty and set the nation back after successfully regaining independence. Serbia consulted with its ally, Russia, but the tsar was not ready to fully back Belgrade and would only respond if Austria-Hungary acted first. Russia suggested to Serbia that it should accept the terms of the ultimatum or at least partially accept some of the demands and seek an extension of the deadline. Russian foreign minister Sergey Sazonov also tried to persuade the European powers to urge Austria to extend the deadline and requested that Vienna prove official Serbian involvement in the assassination. This request was, of course, denied by the Austrians since they did not have sufficient evidence.

Britain acted as a mediator between Austria and Serbia. Britain's foreign minister was wary of the consequences and recognized that Europe was bound to descend into all-out war if the crisis was not properly addressed. An assembly was convened in London to discuss the matter and determined that the ultimatum would be unacceptable for any sovereign nation. Europe became increasingly worried about the situation's potential escalation.

On the next day, July 24th, Serbia had come to realize that war with Austria was imminent and started to mobilize its army. At the same time, Russia ordered a partial mobilization, influenced by Foreign Minister Sazonov, who had been in talks with the French ambassador to St. Petersburg, Maurice-Georges Paléologue. By that time, the French delegation had not yet returned to Paris, and Ambassador Paléologue urged Sazonov to truly grasp the state of the crisis. Sazonov was convinced that Russian inaction would result in unchallenged Austrian dominance in the Balkans. He persuaded the tsar to order a partial mobilization, despite the fact that most of the Russian ministers believed that Russia was not ready for a full-scale war with both Austria-Hungary and Germany.

Still, perhaps afraid that a potential Austrian takeover of Serbia would be yet another defeat of Russia on the international scene, Tsar Nicholas II was compelled to act, putting the army on high alert. The tsar knew that he had backing from France, having just met the French president, and decided to take a more proactive stance in the Austro-Serbian crisis, even though Russia's military reforms had not been completed yet. The tsar also hoped that the partial mobilization would dissuade Austria-Hungary from immediately declaring war and instead think about solving the matter diplomatically. Instead, it produced a more aggravated response from Vienna, as the Austro-Hungarians, motivated by Germany, realized that Russia was serious.

On July 25th, Serbia officially responded to Austria-Hungary's ultimatum. Although the exact response is not known, Serbia is thought to have accepted all but one or two demands, which were believed to have been a direct infringement on Serbia's independence and sovereignty. The international community received this as good news. Britain believed that Serbia's response was understandable. France and Russia also believed that the Serbian response was more than satisfactory and that Austria-Hungary should not proceed with declaring war. Even Kaiser Wilhelm of Germany, who had been absent all this time on his annual North Sea cruise, stated that Austria should have reconsidered an all-out war and only occupied Belgrade to punish the Serbs and force them to carry out the terms of the ultimatum.

However, Austria-Hungary did not listen to any of these remarks, nor did it really need to. It had the German "blank cheque" and believed that it had a legitimate reason to justify war against Serbia. In addition, Vienna thought that it would act quickly and decisively, eliminating Serbia's army before the bulk of the Russian forces would be able to intervene. And even if St. Petersburg did decide to act, Germany would help in dealing with the Russian forces. Thus, on July 27th, Austria-Hungary finalized its war preparations by mobilizing the army. Germany assured Austria-Hungary of its unshakable position.

By that point, it was clear that war was imminent, but each actor perceived the scale of the coming conflict differently. The July Crisis was still not over, as the next three days would also see critical developments, but after a month of political maneuvering, war could not be prevented.

On July 28th, 1914, Austria-Hungary declared war on Serbia, starting World War I.

Chapter 6 – Europe at War

The assassination of Archduke Franz Ferdinand spiraled the European continent into a month of uncertainty. Austria-Hungary, seeking an opportunity to increase its presence in the Balkans, perceived the assassination of its heir as a justification for war with Serbia, despite the fact that the Serbian government had nothing to do with the murder. Throughout July, the blame game Vienna played with Belgrade peaked with Serbia's refusal to accept all of the ultimatum's demands, giving what Austria-Hungary perceived to be a legitimate reason to declare war. However, Austria's perception that the war would be quick and decisive proved to be wrong. Following the declaration of war on July 28th, the rest of Europe would get involved in the conflict, starting World War I.

Europe Enters the War

Despite the remarks of the international community to resolve the disputes with Serbia diplomatically, Austria-Hungary proceeded to declare war and invaded Serbia on July 28th, 1914. After hearing the news, Tsar Nicholas II of Russia ordered his troops to assemble in the four provinces that directly bordered Austria's territories. This was Russia's final effort to dissuade Austria from pursuing an all-out war with Serbia, but it was not successful. The next day, Austrian artillery bombarded Belgrade, causing Russia to fully mobilize its army. Germany ordered partial mobilization. It has to be noted that Tsar Nicholas II and Kaiser Wilhelm II both tried to keep the war from escalating, supporting a peaceful resolution of the conflict. However, their opinions were undermined by the war-hungry military personnel of Austria-Hungary. The German and Russian leaders exchanged a series of letters with each other, exchanging their concerns, but it was too late. The war was already underway.

As Germany and Russia stared one another down and Austria bombarded Belgrade, French President Poincaré finally arrived in Paris from his journey to St. Petersburg. Although he had been somewhat aware of the transpiring situation, he was met with patriotic and anti-German sentiment in Paris. The French urged their president to act decisively. Parallel to Poincaré's arrival, Kaiser Wilhelm II decided to finally mobilize all of Germany's forces, preparing the nation for war on two fronts. The French also responded, demanding that Germany back down, threatening war.

On July 31st, Germany sent out two ultimatums: one to Russia and one to France. Berlin demanded that Russia stop its mobilization and that France declare neutrality in the next twenty-four hours. However, as one would imagine, this was in vain. Russia and France decided to ignore Berlin's demands.

Thus, on August 1st and August 3rd, Germany declared war on Russia and France, respectively. To proceed with their pre-planned offensive, the Germans approached Belgium to let their army pass through neutral Belgian territory to France but were denied. Germany then declared war on Belgium.

Italy, seeing the events unfold and its allies descend into warfare with other major European powers, decided to declare neutrality. The Italians were not required to join the war because the war was not defensive. By the terms of the secret Triple Alliance between Germany, Austria, and Italy, the three powers only had to participate in each other's wars if the war had been declared on them by the enemy. So, because Austria had been the one to declare war on Serbia and because Germany declared war on both France and Russia, Italy did not have to act. Realizing the potential destruction an all-out war could bring, the Italians decided to pursue neutrality.

By August 4th, another major power would enter the war: Great Britain. The British position on the conflict had been made clear; London had urged Austria to resolve the crisis with Serbia through diplomatic means and was generally opposed to war since it was dealing with the Irish independence movement, which had gained prominence in the years leading up to the war. The British Parliament debated Britain's entry into the war for the first few days but was compelled to declare war against Germany after the latter invaded Belgium, whose independence had been guaranteed by Britain. The British demanded the Germans retreat from Belgium on August 3rd, and when they were denied, they officially entered the war on August 4th.

Different powers then proceeded to declare war on each other's respective allies. Austria-Hungary on Russia on August 5th, Serbia on Germany on August 6th, and Great Britain and France on Austria-Hungary on August 10th and August 12th. This latter declaration of war followed Japan's declaration of war on Germany on August 23rd and the subsequent answer of Austria-Hungary on Japan on August 25th. Austria-Hungary also formally declared war on Belgium on August 28th.

This domino effect seems logical and inevitable in hindsight. Bound by intricate alliance agreements rooted in mutual hatred and national interests, nearly all of the great powers of the world, save the United States and Italy, had joined the war by the end of August 1914. Thus, within two months of Archduke Franz Ferdinand's assassination, the world was divided in two: the German-Austrian axis known as the Central Powers and the Triple Entente of Russia, France, and Great Britain and their respective allies, referred to as simply the Allies. This quick and sharp polarization was a long time coming. The two sides had indirectly challenged each other for decades, avoiding military confrontation in multiple tense instances. Perhaps they were aware of the fact that a potential conflict could reach a previously unseen level.

It is worth taking one last look at the positions of both the Allies and the Central Powers and discussing what exactly was at stake for each nation that had entered the war.

The Central Powers

We have already covered the motivations behind Austria-Hungary's actions. The dual monarchy had experienced tough times after the defeat of Napoleon and the reorganization of the international world order. Austria-Hungary's main problems lay in the fact that the ruling Habsburg family had refused, time and time again, to reduce their own power and allow the implementation of more liberal, democratic practices. By the time World War I broke out, Austria-Hungary was still a conservative monarchy with old standards and beliefs.

The recent regional and global developments affected the effectiveness of the Habsburg rule. Austria-Hungary could not keep up with its European counterparts when it came to modernization. The rise of nationalism directly contributed to the weakening of Austria-Hungary as a political entity—a result that was logical, given the fact that the empire was comprised of multiple nations. These nations, although always having known and practiced their own customs and traditions and spoken their own languages, became increasingly aware of their distinct identities after Napoleon's conquests, igniting nationalist sentiments. In a region as diverse as the Balkans, this proved to be very problematic, as there were many groups yearning for independence.

Austria-Hungary was wary of these developments, recognizing that if it loosened its grip on one nation, letting it break away and achieve independence, it would start a chain reaction that would eventually lead to the dissolution of the whole empire. The Balkan Wars had demonstrated a similar consequence to the Ottoman Empire, another troubled entity that suffered from the same nationality problem as the Austro-Hungarians. The assassination of Franz Ferdinand was an opportunity for the Habsburgs to reassert their dominance and make it clear that they were still strong enough. In a way, one could argue that Austria-Hungary cared little about the international consequences that followed its war on Serbia, focusing only on what the victory in the war would mean for it.

Austria-Hungary's ally, Germany, was in a drastically different position than its southern ally. The German Reich was a direct consequence of nationalism, as this strong sense of German identity had motivated the nation to emerge as a regional and global powerhouse. Having been formed as an independent nation-state way later than its European counterparts, Germany realized early on that to catch up with the rapidly modernizing world, it needed to divert all of its attention to increasing domestic development. Unlike Austria-Hungary, which suffered from having many people groups within its borders, Germany did not have an underlying problem that hindered its rise to dominance. On the contrary, it was a nation-state, meaning that the majority of the population was German and, for the most part, had similar concerns and goals in mind. Germany had great material resources that had not yet been exploited to their fullest extent because of the former disunity of smaller German states. It had an organized civil society and political structure, with a perfectly balanced relationship between the monarchy, the government, and the people. And last but not least, Germany possessed a large, experienced, and disciplined army, one of the best in the world.

Through unification, Germany had all of a sudden been put in a powerful position to challenge its rivals and play a more active role in international politics. By the 20th century, Germany had achieved such substantial progress that it challenged Great Britain as the world's undisputed hegemon. Germany wished to evolve from being the most dominant in Europe to being the most dominant in the world, which contradicted the earlier efforts of Bismarck. The diversion from the Bismarckian course only meant that Germany was left with Austria-Hungary as its ally. Having this dwindling, old monarchy on its side was certainly useful as a deterrent against France, but it was useless for Germany's larger ambitions. On top of this, the rest of the world acknowledged the potential threat of Germany and, led by the efforts of Britain, had come together to undermine it.

By 1914, Germany was aware that it needed to break away from this precarious position and prove its might internationally. Thus, it searched for an opportunity to justify war on its regional rivals. Bound by its old alliance with Austria, Germany realized it could use the assassination to achieve this goal. The Germans were perhaps too confident in their ability to pursue a war on two fronts. They relied on the quick defeat of Serbia by Austria-Hungary's forces and believed they were in a good position to challenge the Triple Entente. Unlike Austria-Hungary, the Germans knew exactly what war on Serbia meant for the rest of the world but thought they had had enough time to prepare for it. Time could only tell if their feeling of superiority over the other nations would be justified or would be yet another instance of overconfidence.

The Allies

The Allied Powers had drastically different motivations. Russia's position was perhaps the closest to that of Austria-Hungary, as St. Petersburg had failed to keep up with the changing times, much like Vienna. With an older political structure and limited channels of political participation, Russia was perhaps the most conservative Great Power at the beginning of World War I. Russia also experienced an ideological struggle. As different monarchs came and left, Russia's perception of itself changed time and time again, with some advocating for Russia to assume a modern European position and increased liberalization, while others wanted Russia to embrace its unique status that incorporated the empire's European and Asian characteristics.

Overall, by the end of the 19th century and in the first decade of the 20th century, St. Petersburg started to perceive itself as the protector of all Orthodox Christian nations in Eastern Europe and the big brother to the Slavic nations that were under Austria-Hungary's and the Ottoman Empire's control. Moscow was seen as the "Third Rome." Enforcing and preserving this attitude of a divine Russian responsibility to exert influence over the Orthodox Slavic nations of Eastern Europe had direct consequences on Russian foreign policy in the early 20th century.

The main point of contention for Russia was the Balkans, a region where many Orthodox Slavic nations were concentrated, giving Russia justification to be involved in their politics and influence major decisions. In addition, Russia was the largest and most populous nation, which gave it constant leverage against its rivals. At times, they were so intimidated by the sheer size and potential of the country that they refused to make any moves against it. However, the size of the empire made cohesiveness difficult, with St. Petersburg stretching its capabilities over two continents. Russia also fell behind in industrialization, as it was still mostly dependent on agriculture and the export of raw materials, both of which were becoming outdated. The other Great Powers had switched to promoting their industry.

Russia was thus a superpower that had not truly unlocked its potential—a factor that served as an advantage and as a disadvantage to its friends and enemies. After having achieved favorable relations with Britain and France and having resolved past disputes with Japan, Russia was more than happy to focus on challenging Austria-Hungary in the Balkans to reassert its dominant position as the protector of the Slavic nations. Protecting Serbia was a symbolic move. In hindsight, if Russia had chosen to let Serbia fight the Austro-Hungarians alone, maybe the whole war could have been avoided. However, to cement itself as a European superpower, Russia firmly believed that it had to be decisive when it came to its sphere of influence.

As we have already mentioned, Tsar Nicholas II of Russia was somewhat hesitant to fully back Serbia against Austria-Hungary and did not believe that risking an all-out war was worth it. However, one of the main reasons behind Russia's decisive position in July of 1914 was France's full support. Despite the fact that the two nations had been allies since their agreement in 1891, the alliance had never truly been tested until Russia decided to directly confront Austria-Hungary. Their alliance dragged France into the conflict in 1914.

The French position is perhaps the most interesting to analyze since the nation had nothing to directly gain from the Balkans. Instead, what France hoped for was to reassert its position in Europe and the world. German efforts to isolate France proved to be pretty successful, as the latter was deprived of any allies for a long time. Everyone was aware of France's might. Napoleon had shown how strong France could be with a competent enough leader with strong backing. In fact, during Napoleon's time, France had the military and economic capabilities to challenge the whole continent by itself.

However, Napoleon's defeat and the redistribution of power were followed by a gradual decline in influence. This became especially clear in the humiliating defeat during the German unification process. The Germans were able to crush the French resistance, reaching Paris. Once there, the Germans signed a declaration for the official formation of the German state, crowning Kaiser Wilhelm as the emperor. In addition to taking away France's prestigious position as the strongest power in continental Europe, Germany also annexed the French provinces of Alsace and Lorraine.

France was then forced to divert its efforts to increase its colonial power. France was still strong in its colonies, arguably the second strongest after Britain, and continued to search for partners on the international stage. Perhaps as a desperate measure, France decided to ally with struggling Russia. At that time, it was clear that France was gambling with its newly gained partner; as we talked about above, Russia was not exactly reliable, lagging behind in development. But if Russia's potential was realized, it could be of help against Germany, which had humiliated and overtaken France as the strongest in Europe.

Thus, in the 1890s and the 1900s, France helped its ally finance many important projects relating to the military, industry, and infrastructure. By 1914, France had made a significant investment in Russia, an investment that had not yet been paid back. Paris believed that the best way for St. Petersburg to pay this investment back would be by taking France's side in a war against Germany. France contributed massively to funding Russian military reforms, which sought to fully modernize all of Russia's army by 1917. France was hoping to get a lot of help in return to undermine Germany's position.

During the Moroccan crises, the situation between France and Germany had deescalated, as neither side was brave enough to risk war over their interests in the colonies. But the opportunity that had arisen with Franz Ferdinand's assassination was too good to let pass. It did not matter for France if Serbia survived or fell. What mattered was a justifiable cause to crush the Germans, and the French did not hesitate.

We have also already addressed the last great European power: Great Britain. Much like France and unlike Russia, Britain had nothing to directly gain by getting involved in the conflict. The smart thing would have been to get away from the imminent explosion of the Balkan "powder keg" and not be consumed by the underlying political tensions that were rooted in the region. In fact, many British officials adamantly opposed intervention in Serbia for that reason, proposing that London should play a passive role and act solely as an intermediary to resolve the conflict between Belgrade and Vienna. In addition, Britain was experiencing a domestic crisis of its own; nationalist sentiment in Ireland had grown, with the Irish demanding more and more autonomy from the British. The tension between those in Ireland advocating for independence and the British government reached alarming levels, providing yet another reason the nation should not have been involved with matters in Eastern Europe.

However, the motivations behind British actions were largely similar to the decisions made by France. Britain had been challenged by the German powerhouse for the position of global hegemon, and it felt that it needed to remind its challenger of its might. Britain could not effectively limit Germany's economic and military advances, but it could rally other great powers under an anti-German umbrella. In the changing times, Britain felt compelled to cling to its position as the strongest in the world, and it would not be able to do so if it let the German machine run rampant over the continent.

This is why the British did not back down from the challenge once Austria-Hungary declared war on Serbia. Britain knew that Germany was strong enough to engage in a war on two fronts and was worried about the consequences a German victory might bring. As Britain saw it, Russia was not ready to withstand a German offensive, and France would eventually fall against a unified German-Austrian effort, even if it could put up a decent fight in the beginning stages of the war. Thus, Britain, much like France, needed a reason to put an end to German domination.

This justification came when Germany declared war on Belgium, a nation whose independence and neutrality had been guaranteed by the Great Powers in 1839 when they all signed the Treaty of London. The treaty bound Belgium to remain neutral in all conflicts but promised that it would never have to worry about a potential war with another Great Power. Germany was very much aware of the treaty when it demanded Belgium grant its forces the right to pass through to French territories. When the request was rejected, Germany declared war, perhaps hoping that Britain would not come to Belgium's defense.

So, by September of 1914, all of Europe's greater powers, save Italy, were at war with each other. The two alliance systems that had emerged in the years prior to World War I to keep each other from escalating conflicts were now involved in armed hostilities against one another. On one side stood the Central Powers:

Austria-Hungary, which was desperately trying to keep the empire from crumbling, and Germany, which hoped to finally demonstrate its might as the most developed and strongest nation in Europe. The Central Powers were opposed by the Allies: Russia, which believed it had a moral and strategic obligation not to give up its influence in the Balkans; France, which had decided to honor its alliance with St. Petersburg and stop Germany; and Great Britain, which had come out of its "splendid isolation," recognizing the German threat.

The Great War was underway.

Chapter 7 – The Start of the Hostilities

The Central Powers and the Allies were at war. Both sides were adamant about seeing how the new methods of warfare could influence the outcomes of battles. Military strategists, generals, and soldiers all had their own views and expectations and were eager to test out new equipment on the front lines. Before World War I, the Russo-Japanese War was a clear indication of how things had changed when it came to warfare, and the new opportunities were exciting. However, as the opening stages of World War I would show, much of the military's expectations would be subverted, and the two sides would be shocked, if not disappointed, by the results.

The Cult of the Offensive

In the years prior to World War I, historians have observed a tendency within the Great Powers that has been deemed the "cult of the offensive." Characterized by the glorification of rapid offensive maneuvers rather than defensive warfare, the cult of the offensive can be identified in all the actors of World War I. In fact, some have argued that this cult was one of the principal causes of the conflict's escalation.

The underlying factor of the cult of the offensive is the misconception that was present in Europe with the development of military technology and newly invented armaments, such as the machine gun, different types of rifles and small arms, modernized heavy artillery, and so on. Europeans were correct to recognize that these new weapons were much more powerful than their predecessors, but they wrongly assumed that the advantage would be held by the attacking side rather than the defenders. This misconception was based on the fact that no large-scale conflict had broken out in Europe that was "worthy" of attention. Yes, there was the Russo-Japanese War, which demonstrated the real effects of the new weapons' implementation in battles, but these results pointed to the defender's might; for some reason, this was overlooked. Instead, military personnel believed that in the new age of weapons, the best way to conduct battles would be to try and quickly seize the advantage over the defenders.

The infamous phrase "attack is the best defense" was perceived during this period as a result of the German military's efforts to glorify offensive attacks. In Germany, a nation with arguably the strongest army in Europe by the early 20th century, this view was very much present, with different high-ranking members of the military advocating for a cohesive, rapid offensive with new weaponry.

France and Britain, two nations whose histories had been forged in constant warfare, became obsessed with the narrative of the attacker being more virtuous. British and French officials stated time and time again that their soldiers were suited to conduct decisive offensive operations rather than proceed slowly and wait for the opposing side to attack. They claimed that the justification for this partially derived from the "superior" nature of their soldiers over the enemy, a point deeply rooted in nationalist sentiment. Similar views were even present in Russia and Belgium. Together, these countries assumed that a greater advantage would go to the attackers, who would have higher morale due to their eagerness and perseverance to bravely charge the enemies first. For some reason, offense was synonymized with strength, virtue, and glory, while defense meant cowardness and fear.

It is strange, to say the least, the extent of the Europeans' efforts to glorify offense and discredit defense. If nothing else, throughout most of history, the course of a battle was not solely decided by one side being the first to attack. Many other factors played a significant role in determining the outcome. For example, whichever side had more numbers was usually favored to win, regardless of whether it was attacking or defending. An advantage would often be gained based on the army's position on the battlefield, as terrain and general conditions were important. Not only that, but in siege battles, even after the development of gunpowder and the modernization of artillery, the attacking side was cautious when it came to mounting a full-on assault, as it would result in a lot more casualties because the defenders would shell the approaching troops from fortifications. Instead, waiting out the enemy and depriving them of food and resources was the optimal decision and was pursued in the vast majority of cases.

When taking all of these factors into consideration, it is interesting to see why the Europeans decided to glorify the cult of the offensive and completely disregard defense as a viable battle strategy. As we will discuss later on, the Europeans' keenness to favor the offense would manifest itself in the tactics adopted by the war participants and shape the course of the war, especially during its opening phase. In practice, the cult of the offensive would be proven wrong, as the two sides would be forced to respect the destructive potential of each other's weaponry and adopt a completely new approach to warfare.

The Schlieffen Plan

The European powers had long been developing military strategies in case a war broke out. One such strategy was Germany's Schlieffen Plan, named after the mastermind behind its conception, General Alfred Graf von Schlieffen. In development for nearly fifteen years, from 1891 to 1904, the Schlieffen Plan is one of the most famous tactics of European militarism in the late 19th and early 20th centuries.

The plan itself is relatively easy to understand. Borrowing from the cult of the offensive, Schlieffen's main idea was to find a way to defeat Germany's potential enemies quickly and decisively on two fronts: France and Russia. According to the plan, conducting military activities on both the Eastern and the Western Fronts would be exhausting for Germany, even though the German military was one of the best in the world. If a war broke out on two fronts, the plan suggested to first deal with the French in the West by directing the vast majority of Germany's resources to an all-out offensive on Paris through the Low Countries. Once France fell, Germany would then divert its attention to the Eastern Front, where a large and underdeveloped Russia would not be able to mobilize in time.

The Schlieffen Plan believed that if most of the effort was concentrated on defeating France first, dealing with the Russians would be an easy task since the German military could outclass anything Russia could field in battle. British involvement was also taken into consideration, although not sufficiently enough. When devising the strategy, Schlieffen believed that British intervention, which would come about due to the involvement of the Low Countries, would be too slow and too late. By the time the Brits were able to cross the English Channel with a competent enough force to stop the German advance, Germany would have achieved its goal and defeated the French.

The Schlieffen Plan was very ambitious. Still, the German high command fully believed in the plan's high-risk, high-reward style. Germany thought the plan had taken all of the potential factors into consideration and that its army was capable of executing it flawlessly. Germany believed that it would be able to carry out the Schlieffen Plan without any hindrances. But, of course, it would not be that easy.

Fiasco in Serbia

One other thing the Schlieffen Plan did not take into consideration was the actions of Germany's ally. Austria-Hungary had its own interests that it prioritized over those of Germany, meaning that in order to smoothly carry out the developments outlined by the German offensive, Austria needed to be fully on board. However, as it turned out, this was not the case. The cohesiveness of the Central Powers was crucial if they wanted to see their efforts yield the results they hoped for.

The main problem showed itself at the beginning stages of the war. What were they going to do about Russia? Germany had already proceeded to carry out the Schlieffen Plan and declared war on Belgium to get to France, focusing most of its strength on the Western Front. This left Austria-Hungary in a weird situation, as Russia was unattended by the Germans on the Eastern Front and threatened the Austro-Hungarians. The Germans had hoped that while they were busy fighting the French in the West, Austria would hold off the Russians in the East. But Austria-Hungary did not move its armies across the border until August 12th, delaying the start of the hostilities and angering Germany. The delay gave Russia just enough time to mobilize whatever it could. The 2nd Austrian Army had to move northeast to support the war against the Russians instead of focusing on taking out Serbia. The situation was very complex, and the efforts of the Central Powers were disjointed.

As a result, three European theaters emerged simultaneously in the first weeks of the war. The Germans fought the combined forces of the French, Belgians, and British on the Western Front. The Austro-Hungarians were trying to break through against the Serbians on the Serbian Front. And the Russians were hoping to undermine the lack of German presence by trying to advance on the Eastern Front.

The main indicator of the Central Powers' incohesive offensive is the disappointing Serbian campaign in 1914. Austria-Hungary had a part of its army depart to aid the Germans in stopping Russia on the Eastern Front, so its efforts to defeat the Serbians proved unsuccessful time and time again in the beginning stages of the war. The Serbs were able to stand their ground against the invaders, proving those who doubted their ability to defend wrong. Serbian commander Radomir Putnik correctly recognized that the Austrians, having split up their forces, were lacking numbers and fully believed that he would be able to keep them at arm's length while aid arrived.

The first battle between the two sides unfolded on August 15th, three days after the Austro-Hungarian armies crossed the border from the north. General Oskar Potiorek of Austria, who was in charge of conducting military operations in Serbia (and the governor who had been with Franz Ferdinand when he was assassinated), overestimated the capabilities of the forces under his command. Perhaps he was eager to win a major battle before Emperor Francis Joseph's birthday and be the bearer of some good news back home. In the Battle of Cer, the first encounter between the Austrians and the Serbs that lasted until August 24th, his forces were not able to break through the Serbian defenses and suffered heavy losses. The Serbians acknowledged that defending the whole border would be in vain and fell back to assume a more advantageous position. After fierce fighting, the Austrians were forced to retreat, marking the first Allied victory in World War I.

The next battles that ensued also saw disappointing results for the Austrian military. In the Battle of the Drina, the Austrians were unsuccessful in trying to cross the Drina River and were forced to retreat, suffering over ten thousand casualties. They had to dig in the trenches and be satisfied with shelling the Serbian positions on the other side. When Austria-Hungary realized that it had weakened the Serbian position through constant bombardment from the trenches, it launched another offensive in early November, forcing the Serbs to retreat at the Kolubara River, where the two sides engaged once again in fierce fighting. By that time, Belgrade was under Austria-Hungary's control. However, as the Austrians achieved progress, the Serbs retreated farther into their territory, which caused the attackers to feel confident. The Austro-Hungarians chased the Serbians, splitting up their army. The Serbian forces, having just received new weapons from Greece, were able to capitalize on the fact that the bulk of the Austrian army was lagging behind and crushed the Austrian vanguard, something that changed the course of the battle and helped the Serbs achieve victory in several consecutive encounters. General Potiorek was forced to order yet another retreat, giving up Belgrade.

The first Serbian campaign produced disastrous results for the Central Powers. To the surprise of everyone, including the Allies, the Serbians managed to hold off an Austrian offensive on three separate occasions, defending every inch of their lands to the best of their ability. This was even more impressive considering the fact the Serbians did it all alone, without any real help from their allies who were busy fighting on other fronts. Austria-Hungary was disappointed but had not lost all hope. The imperial forces knew the importance of this war and were determined to take out Serbia.

Thus, despite the failure of the 1914 Serbian campaign, it was clear that Vienna was not done. However, this failure was even more catastrophic for the Germans, who were relying on the Austrians to quickly defeat Serbia and then divert the bulk of their forces to fighting Russia on the Eastern Front. The Schlieffen Plan had clearly outlined the objectives of the German offensive and the circumstances in which it would be successful, but one of the most important parts of the strategy—Russia's participation in the war—was becoming more of a problem for Germany. With the Austro-Hungarians' inability to quickly win against Serbia, Germany was forced to keep a part of its forces in the East, therefore harming its own campaign in the West.

The 1914 Serbian campaign showed that the overly optimistic and glorified cult of the offensive was not rooted in reality and resulted in a drawn-out conflict on multiple fronts for the Central Powers, something that Germany had hoped to avoid.

Chapter 8 – The Theaters of War

As the Serbians were putting up a valiant fight against the Austro-Hungarian offensive, the Germans were trying to break through on the Western Front against the French, Belgian, and British resistance. At the same time, Russia was in the process of mobilizing its scattered forces and preparing to launch a full-scale assault on German and Austro-Hungarian positions. In addition, new theaters of war emerged throughout the world as new actors joined the two sides, seeing the war as an opportunity to achieve their personal interests. This chapter will focus on the major developments in the different theaters of war by the end of 1914 and look at the consequences that followed.

German Offensive in the West

The military activity on the Western Front started as early as August 2nd, when Germany crossed the border of Luxembourg and occupied the tiny nation without meeting any resistance. Luxembourg was just one piece of the puzzle according to the Schlieffen Plan. In fact, the plan had been slightly modified when it came to the details of the German offensive in the West. Although the underlying principle of focusing the vast majority of German forces on taking out France still defined the strategy, the plan had been changed to exclude the invasion of the Netherlands as a means of getting the German army to France.

The Netherlands was one of the three Low Countries, along with Belgium and Luxembourg, and the original Schlieffen Plan envisioned the German army passing through the Netherlands. However, the German general chief of staff at the time of the war, Helmuth von Moltke, modified the plan since the Netherlands was a valuable trading partner. The number of soldiers that would take part in the Western offensive was also lowered, with Moltke firmly believing that more troops would be needed to pursue the war on the Eastern Front due to the Austro-Hungarians' inability to provide support quickly.

After entering Luxembourg, the German soldiers stormed through the Belgian positions, bombarding and capturing a pivotal Belgian stronghold at Liège by August 12th. The German 1st Army took the rest of the Belgian forts relatively quickly, while the 2nd Army followed close behind, reinforcing the German vanguard and securing most of Belgium, including Brussels, by August 20th. By then, only a small part of the remaining Belgian forces had managed to escape and entrenched near Antwerp, while the rest fled to the French border, seeking help from their allies.

The initial stage of the Schlieffen Plan had been carried out. The next stage included quickly overwhelming the French forces from the north and encircling their troops, which were supposed to be defending Paris and conducting their own offensive at the Franco-German border.

France had its own offensive ready to carry out against the Germans. Named Plan XVII, the French offensive envisioned a quick and decisive strike, something that was very much in fashion during World War I, on the provinces of Alsace and Lorraine, which Germany had annexed during the War in 1871. With similar ambitions as the Schlieffen Plan, Plan XVII dictated the French efforts of armament and mobilization in the two-year period leading up to the war. With everything in place, the plan was set into motion parallel with the German invasion of Belgium on August 14th. Nineteen French divisions crossed the border into Lorraine to mount a rapid attack on the German positions.

However, the French efforts were disastrous, especially when compared to the Germans' success. The German 6th and 7th Armies had anticipated a potential French assault and were lying in wait with their positions heavily fortified when the French attacked, crushing them in the battle of Morhange-Sarrebourg a week after the French troops crossed the border.

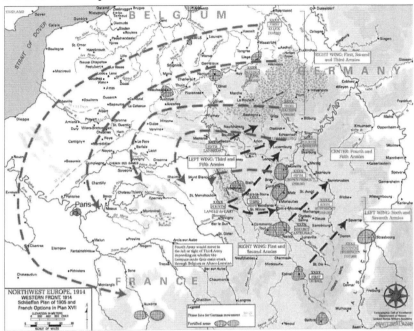

The Schlieffen Plan and Plan XVII.
https://commons.wikimedia.org/wiki/File:Schlieffen_Plan.jpg

In an interesting turn of events, the French advances in German territories managed to tempt General Moltke to alter the Schlieffen Plan. Germany was aware that France would have likely tried to break through to Alsace and Lorraine, so to counter this, the Germans decided they would not engage in an all-out battle with the French to fully drive them out. Instead, the Germans would retreat after dealing significant blows to the French forces. Then, according to the Schlieffen Plan, once Germany emerged victorious in Belgium, it would send its forces to wrap around the French positions from the north to encircle the bulk of the French forces.

However, Moltke did not expect the French to accept the German bait so naively. Seeing that the French troops had thrust deep into the German positions but had not achieved any significant victories and suffered a lot of casualties, Moltke diverted six German divisions from the Belgian wing to attack the French at

Lorraine. This move directly clashed with the intended outcomes of the Schlieffen Plan. The Germans dealt heavy losses to the attacking French and forced them to retreat from Lorraine, but they achieved it by sacrificing the cohesiveness of the Schlieffen Plan, weakening their own wing in the north that was supposed to deal the decisive blow to Paris.

The fighting that ensued in the first month of World War I on the Western Front is collectively referred to as the Battle of the Frontiers. Germany successfully surmounted the Belgian resistance and entered France from the northeast, while the French tried to break through to its long-lost provinces of Alsace and Lorraine on the Franco-German border. Over two million soldiers participated in this group of engagements. The Allies suffered over 300,000 casualties, while Germany lost about half of its troops. By late August, the French advance in Lorraine had been halted, and the German armies had secured a safe passage to northeastern France through Belgium.

The international community was shocked, not because of Germany's success but of the wicked ways in which the Germans treated the defeated Belgians. The Germans set fire to several towns and executed hundreds of civilians. They were accused of committing war crimes and atrocities that did not serve the purpose of emerging victorious in war. "The Rape of Belgium," as the German actions would come to be known, significantly damaged Germany's image, with anti-German sentiment rising across the nations that declared neutrality. This sentiment was further propagated by the Allies.

All Quiet on the Western Front

To salvage the relatively unsuccessful French offensive, French General and Commander-in-Chief Joseph Joffre decided to launch a counteroffensive on the German positions in the northeast with his troops in the south. General Joffre was hoping for aid from the British, who had sent an expeditionary force to get involved in the war. Supported by the BEF (British Expeditionary Force), the 3rd, 4th, and 5th French Armies led an attack on the Germans south of Liège but suffered a crushing defeat. Underestimating the German numbers, the French and British were trapped between the enemy forces, forcing General Joffre to order a retreat to save as many troops as he could. This defeat was followed by a retreat of all Allied forces, even the ones that had made headway in Lorraine.

Plan XVII was completely abandoned in favor of a new strategy. Joffre tried to reorganize the Western Front, giving up a significant part of northeastern France to the Germans, who had already established their presence in the region, and setting up a new united front. Joffre concentrated the majority of the Allied forces tens of kilometers northeast of Paris in the area around the Marne River, where they assumed a defensive position.

Still, the German advance would not have been fully overcome by the Allies if it wasn't for miscommunication between the German officers. As the Allies reorganized their forces under General Joffre's orders, Germany was slowly closing in on Paris, trying to gather up the remainder of the troops from the northern wing to join together for a united offensive and the final stage of the Schlieffen Plan. Following their mass retreat from the frontier, the military governor of Paris, Joseph Gallieni, was charged with creating a plan to defend the French capital and its outskirts. At the same time, Commander Moltke ordered the German 1st and 2nd Armies to join up under the command of General Alexander von Kluck. However, due to a communication error, Kluck proceeded to change the direction of his forces, marching them northeast of Paris in the valley of Marne instead of southwest, abandoning the original plan that sought to fully encircle the French capital. This meant the German army under Kluck had exposed its right flank, providing an opportunity for the Allies to strike.

The Allies sought to be the first to encircle the enemy, and their counteroffensive started on September 4th when Governor Gallieni convinced Joffre to try and exploit the German position. The First Battle of the Marne, as it would come to be known, would last from September 6th to September 12th and would catch the German forces off-guard. The opportunity was successfully seized by the united French and British armies, as they managed to split apart different German divisions and quickly overwhelm them. The Allies risked exposing new flanks of the German forces, so the Germans decided to retreat and abandon their initial plan of encircling Paris.

In addition to the risk of getting flanked, which would mean fighting with a constant disadvantage due to disrupted supply lines, the German forces were also exhausted from their continued advance through Belgium. They were pretty deep in Allied territory, and suffering a heavy defeat would detrimentally affect German morale. Thus, the Germans retreated, digging in at the Lower Aisne and successfully withstanding the following Allied offensives. The Battle of the Aisne demonstrated that the power dynamics in trench warfare were swayed in favor of the defenders. They enjoyed a much safer position when compared to the attackers, whose only move to break through was to charge head-first at the entrenched soldiers while being subjected to heavy machine gun and artillery fire.

Thus, the repelled German offensive on Paris was followed by a failed Allied counteroffensive. Both sides had exhausted their resources, and neither had the capability to break through. So, instead of trying to engage in full-on frontal combat, which would not have been beneficial for either side, the Germans and the Allies instead tried to outflank each other. This produced what is now known as the "Race to the Sea," as both sides maneuvered their forces from northeastern France all the way to the North Sea in the hopes of catching the other off-guard and exploiting a potential gap by flanking the enemy. In the span of a month, the two sides dug a complex network of trenches that ran parallel to one another from the North Sea all the way through northeastern France to the Franco-German-Swiss border.

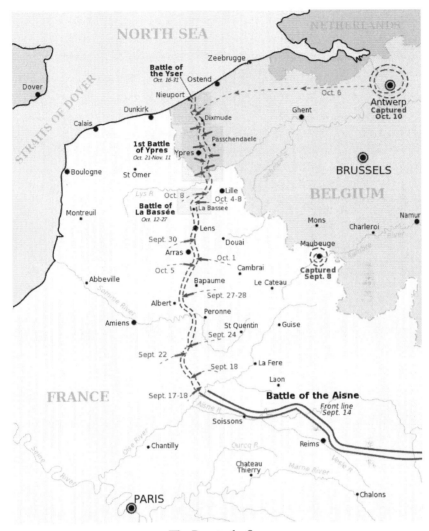

The Race to the Sea.
https://commons.wikimedia.org/wiki/File:Race_to_the_Sea_1914.png)

By December 1914, the military confrontations between Germany and the Allies had largely died out. The two sides had established two opposing trench systems, and neither wished to make the first move to try and break through, knowing that any efforts to overwhelm the other side's position would only end in disaster. While the Schlieffen Plan had seen partial success, the French were unable to mount a significant counteroffensive in line with their original Plan XVII. Still, the Allies had managed to prevent the fall of Paris and driven the Germans out of the immediate vicinity of the French capital with the Battle of the Marne. This meant the Allies' morale was still somewhat high on the Western Front.

On the other hand, Germany had seen success against the Belgians. Only Antwerp was effectively under Belgian control, with the Belgians surrounding the city with trenches. The Germans had also taken control of a large portion of northeastern France—a piece of land that produced much of France's coal and steel, affecting the French war effort.

In the opening months of World War I, the Allies in the West suffered up to a million casualties, with over 300,000 dead soldiers and 600,000 wounded, while the Germans had suffered about 200,000 less in total. What followed the chaotic and bloody developments of the first months on the Western Front was years of stalemate, with the other theaters of war being of more interest. The Western Front, with the entrenched Germans on one side and the British and French on the other, saw no real action for the remainder of World War I. The iconic novel by German writer Erich Maria Remark, who served on the Western Front during the war, perhaps best describes the situation that ensued after the two sides entered a long stalemate: it was all quiet on the Western Front.

The Bear in the East

The war on the Eastern Front developed quite differently. Russia was supposed to launch an offensive on the Central Powers to help relieve some of the pressure on the Allies in the West. However, as we already mentioned, the Russian military reforms that were funded by France had not yet been fully completed, meaning that much of Russia's vast army was not quite ready to fight. The Russian troops were scattered all around the country, and their hasty mobilization was not nearly as cohesive as the Germans, who, according to the Schlieffen Plan, had adopted a defensive approach toward the Russian threat during the opening stages of the war. Germany believed that with the help of Austria-Hungary, Russia would not be able to achieve meaningful success on the Eastern Front. The Germans were fully confident that they would have enough time to transfer a large part of their forces from the Western Front to the East.

But to Germany's dismay, things did not go according to plan. Despite seeing initial success, the Germans could not finish off the Allied resistance in the West, instead forcing a stalemate, with the two sides staring each other down from the trenches. Germany had to constantly keep a significant part of its force on the Western Front since there was a realistic chance of an Allied counteroffensive, which would have been enough to overwhelm the German positions and nullify their progress. In addition, Austria-Hungary faced resistance in Serbia. Since it had not taken out the Serbian forces, it could not contribute an adequate number of troops to battle Russia. By the end of 1914, Austria-Hungary had not made any real progress against Serbia. It split off its army to help Germany defend against Russia and, in turn, requested Germany's help with invading the Serbs.

However, this disadvantage was leveraged by the fact that Germany's army proved to be superior to Russia's army. It was better equipped, demonstrated more bravery, and had higher morale compared to the Russian forces. In nearly every encounter, the Russians had to rely on superior numbers or the element of surprise to achieve any success. And even then, they would still lose tens of thousands of soldiers every time they approached the Germans because of the latter's more advanced artillery. Unlike the Western Front, where entrenchment resulted in a deadlock, giving the defenders a massive advantage, the German army was so superior to the defending Russian forces that the trenches did not slow them down as much. The Russians were also plagued with problems of overextension and disrupted supply lines. The Russian army was probably a better match for Austria-Hungary. When these two nations clashed in the southern parts of the Eastern Front, Russia did see some success.

The Fight for East Prussia

The war in the East between Russia and the Central Powers unfolded separately in two different locations. One part of the Russian army launched an offensive on East Prussia and fought off the Germans, while the other half of the mobilized Russian forces held up the combined Austro-Hungarian and German forces in Russian Poland. The Russians did see initial success against the Germans, who suffered defeat in the Battle of Gumbinnen on

August 20th, 1914. Three days earlier, a quick strike by the German vanguard at the Battle of Stallupönen yielded no significant results for Germany, although it did provide some intel on the intended route the Russians planned to take. Paul von Rennenkampf and Alexander Samsonov led the Russian 1st and 2nd Armies, respectively, in a combined effort to overwhelm the German defenses in East Prussia. Instead of solely acting defensively, Maximilian von Prittwitz, who was in charge of the German forces, hastily decided to attack the Russian armies while they were recovering from the initial blow of the Germans, but his attack was repulsed. Seeing that Samsonov's troops could converge on his position, Prittwitz ordered the Germans to retreat.

Two days later, Chief of Staff Moltke decided to replace Prittwitz on the Eastern Front, believing that the latter had been consumed by panic after suffering defeat and having to retreat. He placed Paul von Hindenburg and Erich Ludendorff in charge of the German 8th Army in East Prussia, confident that the experience of these two commanders would turn the tides in their favor. This decision proved to be extremely successful. After having achieved victory, the Russian 1st and 2nd Armies threatened the capital city of Prussia, Konigsberg, and Moltke knew that letting the enemy take the city would shatter the soldiers' morale. Konigsberg was a historical military hub and held symbolic value to the German troops, most of whom were from East Prussia.

So, instead of falling back and allowing the two Russian armies to join up, Hindenburg and Ludendorff decided to launch a counteroffensive and converge on the 2nd Russian Army under Samsonov. Having intercepted Russian communications and utilizing the local railway systems for quick maneuvering between positions, the Germans devised a plan to overwhelm Samsonov's left flank, relying on the element of surprise to crush the Russian advance.

Paul von Hindenburg.
https://commons.wikimedia.org/wiki/File:Paul_von_Hindenburg-2.png

In a five-day battle that began on August 26th, the Germans perfectly carried out their plans. The rapid attacks on Samsonov's massive army, which in total counted about 230,000 troops, could not be answered by the Russians. By splitting off a part of the German forces to delay the 1st Russian Army, Hindenburg and Ludendorff managed to shatter the morale of Samsonov's soldiers, who started retreating despite having numerical superiority. The Germans were able to effectively exploit every opportunity that presented itself in their favor and achieved a decisive victory.

By August 30th, the Russians had lost a majority of their initial forces, with more than eighty thousand killed or wounded. Even more were taken by the Germans as prisoners of war. On the other hand, the Germans only suffered thirty thousand casualties at most. This piece of military brilliance has come to be known as the Battle of Tannenberg and had immense implications for the war on the Eastern Front. Samsonov, who had managed to escape the slaughter, committed suicide, ashamed of his defeat. Devastated by the defeat, the Russian high command tried to hide the news of the battle from the public, afraid that an already strong anti-war sentiment could grow to new limits and cause an array of internal problems.

The Germans were able to convert the victory at Tannenberg into another successful offensive against the Russian 1st Army under Rennenkampf in the northern part of East Prussia. Being in better shape and in a better mood from defeating the 2nd Army under Samsonov, Field Marshal Hindenburg and General Ludendorff ordered their troops to prepare for another attack. The Germans wanted to force a general Russian retreat from their territories. Their goal was achieved with the Battle of the Masurian Lakes, which lasted from September 4th to September 13th. The German army managed to successfully catch the Russian 1st Army off-guard and completely surround it. The Germans' main advantage was the region's railway network, which enabled the rapid transportation of troops and supplies. The Russians' numerical advantage did not amount to anything in this case either, as they were forced to retreat back to the border and leave the German territories.

In the fight for East Prussia, Russia suffered more than 230,000 casualties, with about 100,000 men taken as prisoners. The German losses were probably a third of that number. In the end, despite seeing some initial success, the Germans were able to successfully repulse the Russian advances with competent leadership and buy time for their armies in the West.

Galicia

East Prussia was not the only region on the Eastern Front where fighting unfolded in the beginning months of World War I. Clashes between the Central Powers and Russia also took place in the province of Galicia. A province historically populated by ethnic Slavs, Galicia was right on the border of Russia, making it an easy and logical target for the Russian forces. The Austro-Hungarian efforts to defend the province seemed disjointed and incoherent, as the imperial army was also busy fighting in Serbia, a fight that cost them much time and resources in the war's opening stages.

Realizing the importance of Galicia as a gateway that connected Russian Poland with the heart of Austria-Hungary, both sides thrust into the province with whatever strength they could. Of the mobilized Russian forces, nearly half of them were sent to fight in Galicia, with the Russian 3rd, 4th, 5th, and 8th Armies counting about a million soldiers combined. They heavily outnumbered the Central Powers when fighting began in late August, as Germany had sent most of its troops to the West and only had its 8th Army in East Prussia. The Austro-Hungarian forces were mobilized mostly against Serbia. Still, in true fashion of the over-glorified cult of the offensive, Austrian Chief of Staff Franz Conrad von Hötzendorf believed the best way to stop the Russian advance was to confront them directly and be the first ones to strike instead of trying to delay before help arrived. Thus, the Austrian 1st, 3rd, and 4th Armies waited for the Russians to approach Galicia, spreading out to cover a front over 240 kilometers (149 miles) long.

In late August, the two sides clashed relentlessly on several different occasions. Unlike East Prussia, where the Germans had a more advanced army than Russia, the latter's strength was almost evenly matched with the Austro-Hungarians. In fact, because of numerical superiority, the Russians were able to swing the battles in their favor multiple times. Initially, however, the Austrians were successful, as they managed to defeat the Russian northern flank in the battles of Kraśnik and Komarów, inflicting heavy casualties and taking more than twenty-five thousand men as prisoners.

But these efforts were undermined when the Russians achieved victory at the Battle of Gnila Lipa, where the Russian 3rd and 8th Armies crushed the attacking Austrians. By August 30th, after two days of fighting, the Russians were able to drive the Austrians back, forcing Commander Hötzendorf to recall his northern force to reinforce the Austrian center and south. However, this was not enough, as the Russian forces that had retreated in the north rejoined with the 3rd and 8th Armies and launched a massive counteroffensive that lasted a week, from September 3rd to September 10th. They were able to exploit the fact that the Austrian army was not united, picking it apart in the Battle of Rawa and forcing an all-out Austrian retreat from Galicia. The Russians captured more than seventy thousand prisoners.

In the Battle for Galicia, the Russians managed to advance in Austro-Hungarian territory by about 160 kilometers (99 miles). Crucially, they managed to take the important city of Lemberg, which reassured the Russian public, which had grown increasingly upset over the Russian losses in East Prussia. By mid-September, the Russians had managed to inflict an estimated 370,000 casualties to the Austrians, including more than 100,000 soldiers captured as prisoners of war, while suffering about 250,000 themselves. It was an important psychological victory for the Russians too. They hoped to continue their successful advance against the Austro-Hungarians to recoup their losses against Germany in the north.

Russia's success was certainly concerning for the Central Powers, to say the least. For Germany, it was vital that the Austro-Hungarians hold up the Russians as the Germans dealt with France in the West, but the Austrians' inability to stop the Russian advance required extra German attention. The Russian army, on the other hand, had successfully pushed the Austrian resistance to the Carpathian Mountains and continued their efforts to take more of Galicia. Immediately after taking Lemberg, the Russian armies converged on Przemyśl. With over 300,000 troops, the Russians laid siege to the town, which was garrisoned by about 130,000 Austro-Hungarians. The siege would last for more than six months.

Losing Przemyśl would be a disaster for the Central Powers, as Russia would have weakened their positions and threatened the German province of Silesia, which was an industrial hub and necessary to continue the war effort. After Russian General Radko Dimitriev's initial attempts to storm the fortress ended with about forty thousand casualties, the Russians decided to take a slower approach and wait out the surrounded city, which, in addition to the army, housed up to twenty thousand civilians.

After seeing that the Austrians could not hold out against the Russians for much longer, Germany decided to transport a significant number of its forces to Galicia to help its ally. Having achieved a decisive victory at Tannenberg and having driven out the Russians from East Prussia, Field Marshal Hindenburg felt confident that, with German aid, the Central Powers would be able to surmount the Russian resistance and prevent them from advancing. The Germans and Austrians decided to strike together, but the Russians were still able to defeat them at the Battle of the Vistula River, near Warsaw, a battle that lasted for most of October.

Eastern Front, 1914.
https://commons.wikimedia.org/wiki/File:Eastern_Front,_1914.jpg

Despite their inability to break the Russians, the Central Powers inflicted 150,000 casualties to the enemy while suffering about 70,000 of their own. This engagement was another example of the two allies' inability to properly coordinate, as they both blamed each other for the defeat, saying that their retreat was only a strategic move to assume better defensive positions and await the Russian advance. The victory at the Vistula River filled Russia's army with confidence. The soldiers and officers naively believed they were capable of beating Germany despite the obvious disparities between the two sides. In the long term, the Russians' overconfidence would have detrimental effects on their campaign of Prussian Silesia.

Section Three – 1915–1916

Chapter 9 – New Players, New Developments

The opening months of the war saw many interesting developments that challenged the preconceived notions held by the participants. Although the cult of the offensive had been disproven wrong, with the first battles of the war strongly suggesting that head-first strikes only meant thousands of casualties for the attacking side, the warring nations were still confident in their abilities and tried to follow their war plans to the fullest extent with rare exceptions.

In Europe, the war had unfolded in unexpected ways, with Germany unable to achieve the intended outcomes of the Schlieffen Plan, Austria-Hungary foiled in Serbia, and Russia making partial progress on the Eastern Front. However, as the months passed, new actors began to enter the war on both sides, something that truly gave the conflict the fitting title of a "world war."

The Ottoman Entry

The Ottoman Empire, as we previously discussed, was in a tough situation before World War I broke out in 1914. In fact, the Balkan Wars, which heavily affected the "sick man of Europe," were an indirect cause of World War I. The Ottomans had not only lost a lot of territories and resources with the events of the

First Balkan War, but the defeat had also taken away Turkish pride. The world now knew that the Ottoman Empire was weaker than ever, so weak, in fact, that several small nations were able to easily achieve victory against it. The empire was also undergoing a massive political and cultural revolution, which contributed to the development of a new Turkish identity, one based largely on irredentism. The Young Turk government, which had been in power since 1909, advocated for modernization and the spread of more democratic values. But by the start of the war, the Ottomans were still in a deep political crisis. The country was also viewed unfavorably by almost all of the European powers, with Germany, France, and Britain all turning down the Ottoman Empire's offers for an alliance by 1911. Bulgaria was the only nation that accepted an alliance with Constantinople, doing so in August 1914.

However, when the war broke out, the Great Powers' perception of the Ottomans started to change. The empire still had a large military, and it bordered the war's participants in different regions. It was very close to the Serbian and Eastern Fronts, directly bordered Russia with the Caucasus, and shared borders with Britain in the Middle East and India. Even though Constantinople had officially declared neutrality in the first few days of the war, it became clear to the nations that having a favorable relationship with the Ottomans could potentially swing the tides. Thus, Britain and Germany increasingly started lobbying the Ottoman government. In the end, Germany gained the upper hand by "selling" two German warships, the *Goeben* and the *Breslau,* with German crews to the Ottomans. The Turkish government also adopted an increasingly anti-British stance, provoking Britain on multiple occasions and rejecting British requests regarding naval activity in the Mediterranean. In September, it became clear that Constantinople was a German ally, as it closed the Turkish straits that linked the Black Sea with the Mediterranean, inflicting a massive blow to the Russian economy and further infuriating the Allies.

The Turkish government debated on whether or not to enter the war. The German warships signaled that Germany wanted the Ottomans on its side. The pro-British and the pro-German debate in the Ottoman parliament ended in favor of the latter, and by October, the Ottoman government had made up its mind to join the Central Powers. This meant the Ottomans would most likely be confronted by resistance on different fronts, especially in Egypt and on the Turko-Indian border.

The leader of the Young Turks, Enver Pasha, hoped that by the time Britain would be able to respond, the Turkish and Austro-German forces would have diverted all of their strength to defeating Russia, giving them time and resources to deal with the Brits. In late October, led by the German *Goeben,* the Turkish fleet sailed up the Black Sea and started bombarding the Russian port cities, including Odesa. Russia swiftly declared war on November 1ˢᵗ, and the rest of the Allies followed suit in the next three days.

Europe and the two alliance systems by the end of 1915.
https://commons.wikimedia.org/wiki/File:Map_1914_WWI_Alliances.jpg

In a shocking move that showcased Germany's diplomatic brilliance, the Central Powers now had manpower from Turkey to hold up the Allied forces on different fronts and leverage their advantage by creating more problems for Britain. As for the Ottoman Empire, the sick man of Europe, the war promised payback from the disasters of the Balkan Wars, with Constantinople hoping to receive a significant portion of Russian-

and British-held lands in the Caucasus and Asia.

Gallipoli

The Ottoman entry into World War I resulted in interesting developments all around the world, the most famous of which was the Allied campaign at Gallipoli. In January 1915, Russia urged Britain to do something about the Ottomans, as the latter had increasingly pressured Russia with its blockade of the straits and constant bombardment of Russian ports. The British had been debating the right course of action to further weaken Germany's position since the Western Front had come to a stalemate. Forced to act to relieve pressure on Russia, which had been fighting alone for almost six months against the Central Powers, the British high command devised a plan—a naval expedition into the very heart of the Ottoman Empire. According to the plan, the British would sail to the Gallipoli Peninsula, a small area on the western bank of the Dardanelles, and try to take it. If they were successful, they could establish a secure spot for future operations and put British troops dangerously close to Constantinople.

In February 1915, the British Royal Navy set out on one of the most ambitious landing operations in its history. The naval bombardment began on February 19th when a combined Franco-British navy opened fire on the defenders' positions. But this resulted in no real progress, as the Turkish defenses still stood strong after a week. The Allies were dissatisfied with the results, and Winston Churchill, First Lord of the Admiralty, urged the fleet's commander to increase his efforts and pressure the Ottomans.

The main problem was the area's awkward geography. The Dardanelles Strait was pretty narrow, and it was hard for large ships to effectively maneuver through it. In addition, the banks of the sea were hilly, giving the defenders a massive advantage since they could set up their forts and trenches along the high ground and answer the Allied navy with machine gun fire.

Thus, no progress had been made by March. In mid-March, the Allies sent eighteen warships to the Dardanelles. This also yielded no results, as the increased number of warships only made it harder for them to move around and dodge the mines. The Allies had managed to exhaust the defenders' resources by the end of the month but were reluctant to continue their efforts and recalled the naval forces by April.

This did not stop the Allies from devising a new strategy for Gallipoli. They envisioned landing on the peninsula instead of utilizing constant naval bombardment. Britain, demonstrating its true colonial power, transported trained troops from Australia and New Zealand to Egypt, organizing them into the combined ANZAC (Australian and New Zealand Army Corps) to use in the campaign. In total, the ANZAC counted about sixty thousand men. The bulk of the landing force was comprised of 345,000 soldiers from the British Mediterranean Expeditionary Force and 70,000 soldiers from the French Oriental Expeditionary Corps. Together, the Allies decided to land at every possible point on the Gallipoli, hoping to disorient the defenders and overwhelm them with their superior numbers.

French troops landing at Gallipoli.

Thus began the biggest amphibious landing operation in history, with the ANZAC forces successfully breaking through and landing at a small cove on the Aegean side of the Gallipoli Peninsula, fittingly nicknamed "ANZAC Cove." The Turkish machine gun fire made it hell for the colonial forces to achieve their intended objectives, but by nightfall on April 25th, the ANZAC had managed to set up a small beachhead and awaited further orders. At the same time, the main Allied army tried to land at five different points around Cape Helles, of which three attempts were successful. The advantage that the defenders held proved to be too much for the Allies to overcome, though. They made no significant advances on the Turkish positions in the first few days.

The Allies asked for reinforcements, but the beachheads they had established were too small for more troops to arrive. So, the soldiers that had landed on the peninsula were forced to dig in to avoid Turkish fire to the best of their ability. The British high command was indecisive when it came to the next stage of the operation. Every time the Allies tried to break through, they suffered thousands of casualties. Back in London, after fierce debates, it was reluctantly agreed that the operation would continue. New troops were sent to reinforce the landing in the summer of 1915. The reinforcements also managed to establish a beachhead in the northern part of the peninsula in August at Suvla Bay. Still, the combined offensive yielded no significant results for the Allies, who had not seen any real progress anywhere else by mid-1915 either. So, after further discussion, the Allied high command decided to fully call off the operation and evacuate all the soldiers who had landed on the beaches by January 1916.

It was a painful decision and a disastrous development for the Allies, who lost more than 250,000 men in the whole campaign, with about 60,000 dead and the rest injured or sick. As time would show, the whole operation was poorly planned, and the cult of the offensive once again proved ineffective. The Ottomans managed to hold out thanks to the defenses they had set up around the hills on Gallipoli. They suffered about the same number of casualties themselves, but at least they managed to dissuade the Allies from continuing their efforts and kept the heart of the empire—Constantinople—safe from the enemy.

Interestingly, not all historians regard the Gallipoli campaign as a total fiasco, with some believing that the Allied efforts to land on the peninsula distracted a significant number of Ottoman troops from being involved in other theaters.

New Frontiers

With the Ottoman Empire's entry into the war, several new frontiers emerged. In some cases, the Turks tried to weaken the Allied positions with surprise attacks, while in others, the Allies sought to achieve quick victories to dissuade the Ottomans from continuing the war. While the conflicts involving the Ottomans in the Caucasus, Egypt, and Mesopotamia are not nearly as iconic as the Gallipoli campaign, it is worth taking a look at them to understand the state of the war in the years following its escalation.

When the Ottoman Empire entered the war on the side of the Central Powers, it was hoping to deal blows to the peripheral regions of Russia and the colonial holdings of Britain and France. The Ottomans hoped the Allies would divert a lot of their resources away from the European theaters, where much of the war effort was concentrated. The fight for the Caucasus served that purpose, with the Ottomans wanting to take Baku, a city that would give them better access to the heart of Britain's possessions in Asia. However, to do that, the Ottomans needed to overcome Russian resistance and fight through Russian-controlled Armenia, which had been heavily fortified since 1878.

The Russians would be the first to engage in November 1914, right as they declared war, advancing toward the Turkish city of Erzurum. The Turkish counteroffensive was launched soon after, with Enver Pasha in command. The Ottoman 3rd Army, counting about 300,000 men in total, was divided into three and ordered to attack the Russian positions separately, something that proved to be a fatal mistake. Initially, the Ottomans took the city of Ardahan but suffered heavy casualties and could not hold onto it for long. They also were decisively defeated in the Battle of Sarikamish, losing more than half of their forces and giving the Russians a much-needed boost in morale.

The Turkish forces suffered from exhaustion and overextension, losing more men to disease and desertion than in battle. By the spring of 1915, it was clear that the Turkish efforts to take Baku would be in vain, and the Ottomans decided to retreat after the Russian offensive in March in Azerbaijan forced them back. What followed were several Russian victories: Erzurum and Trabzon were taken by the end of April, followed by Erzincan in the summer. By that time, the Caucasus was the only region where the Russians had seen massive success, with Tsar Nicholas himself arriving in Armenia in 1915 to show that he would not abandon his Orthodox subjects.

The Armenians preferred living under the rule of Russia instead of Muslim Turkey, and they often sabotaged the Ottoman forces during the campaign, something that led to the rise of anti-Armenian views in Constantinople. Beginning in early 1915, the Ottomans deported millions of Armenians from their Turkish homes, committing atrocities in the process and killing more than one million innocent civilians. The Armenian genocide would be one of the most horrifying war crimes of World War I. As for the war in the Caucasus, the situation would largely be under Russian control, and no real progress would be made on the front by the Ottomans.

In addition to the Caucasus, fighting also unfolded in Mesopotamia and Egypt, where the British tried to retaliate after the humiliating events of Gallipoli. Before the fight reached Mesopotamia, Britain managed to successfully take the Turkish port city of Basra on the Persian Gulf in November of 1914. Soldiers from the British Raj were organized into an expeditionary force to carry out this operation. With the capture of Basra, Britain assumed a more favorable position and awaited Turkish action.

The activity resumed in December of 1915 when the British tried to force their way to the Turkish city of Kut but abandoned the siege after suffering heavy casualties from the Ottoman defenders for four months. Much of the fighting stopped in Mesopotamia for almost another full year, with only minor skirmishes being carried out in the meantime. For the rest of 1916, the British regrouped and planned an offensive on Baghdad, capturing the city in 1917 with the help of local Arabs who were promised liberation from Ottoman rule. After taking Baghdad, the British in Mesopotamia adopted a more defensive role, instead focusing most of their attention on other fronts in the Middle East.

The situation in Egypt also escalated after the Ottoman Empire's entry into the war. Controlling the Suez Canal and the Red Sea was pivotal to the economic stability of not only Britain but also most of Europe, as every nation relied on trade from Asia, which mostly ran through the canal. The Ottomans directly threatened the safety of the Suez. However, the Ottomans were not aware that the troops who survived Gallipoli would be transported to Egypt to support the Egyptian Expeditionary Force (EEF) in defending the canal. So, the Ottoman efforts to seize the Suez in 1915 and at the beginning of 1916 were largely unsuccessful.

The EEF was more accustomed to fighting in harsh conditions, so they led the Allied forces, who benefited from a newly developed railway system that they used to repel Ottoman attacks. Fighting escalated in August 1916. The British forces of the ANZAC and the EEF were able to defeat a combined Germano-Turkish offensive at the Battle of Romani. Motivated by their success, the British launched a successful counteroffensive to capture the Sinai Peninsula in Palestine, driving out the Ottomans from the area by early 1917.

All of these developments unfolded parallel to each other. Out of the campaigns in which the Ottomans participated, they were only able to find relative success in Gallipoli, but even there, they lost almost 250,000 soldiers. Everywhere else, the superior British and Russian forces were able to easily overcome much of the Ottoman resistance. The Ottoman Empire was plagued with political instability and multiple coups instigated by British intelligence. The Central Powers were left disappointed with the Ottoman Empire's involvement in the war.

Italy Joins the Allies

Italy was perhaps in the most awkward position when the Great War broke out in August 1914. Being a member of the Triple Alliance with Germany and Austria-Hungary, it was bound by the treaty to support its allies in the event of war. However, the treaty stipulated that war had to be declared on them, not the other way around. As you now know, Germany and Austria-Hungary declared war on the Entente, which meant that Italy did not have to side with the Central Powers. The Italians had long been reconsidering their relations with European powers and had never really supported the Triple Alliance in times of crises on the international stage, something that was clearly demonstrated when Italy took the side of France during the First Moroccan Crisis instead of Germany.

Italy had the smallest and the least experienced army out of all the major war participants, so it had to be careful when it came to choosing its role in the conflict. In fact, Italy pursued neutrality for all of 1914. However, as it became clear that neither side had an advantage after the first few months and the countries realized that the war was going to drag on, both sides considered asking the Italians for help. Finally, in April 1915, Italy signed the secret Treaty of London with France, Britain, and Russia, in which the Allies offered Rome the Austro-Hungarian-held provinces that were mainly populated by ethnic Italians, including Trentino, Trieste, South Tirol, Istria, Gorizia, and northern Dalmatia.

This was an offer Rome could not refuse, especially considering the fact that Italy, much like every other nation in 1914, was swept by nationalist sentiment. The people wanted to see a strong and prosperous nation, and the best way to demonstrate Italian might was to "reclaim" the lost territories. Thus, in late May 1915, Italy joined the Allies by declaring war on Austria-Hungary and then on Germany fifteen months later.

The Italian military's inferiority showed when they launched an offensive on the Austrian positions at the Isonzo River in northeastern Italy. Italian commander General Luigi Cadorna wanted to break through modern-day Slovenia but was met with fierce Austrian resistance. Cadorna was also urged to act by the Allies, whose main strategy envisioned the creation of new frontiers since the Western Front had come to a complete standstill.

The Allies were hoping to achieve new breakthroughs against the Central Powers, and the Isonzo and the Gallipoli campaigns held that objective. However, the Austro-Hungarians, perhaps due to the fact that the Italian front was closer to the heart of the empire, did not give the attackers an inch for most of 1915. In what has come to be known as the Battles of the Isonzo, the Italians under Cadorna tried to seize the Austrian positions on twelve different occasions.

Italian troops at the Isonzo River.

Much like Gallipoli, the region was surrounded by hills, and the troops could only maneuver through the narrow valleys of the Isonzo. This naturally gave the defenders a huge advantage, as they would have more time to set up defenses. The imperial forces would often willingly retreat to the hills to reposition and gain a better defensive foothold. Of the initial five Italian assaults, all of them were repelled successfully by the Austrians by December 1915, with Cadorna losing more than 250,000 men in the process.

The Austrians then launched their own counteroffensive in May of 1916, motivated by the Italians' failure to make progress. They attacked from the Trentino region, which bordered the Alps, and threatened to cut off the rest of the Italian forces at Isonzo if they gained headway. Realizing the danger, General Cadorna recalled the Isonzo offensive and diverted the forces to drive out the Austrians in the north. By late July, the Italians had managed to recover some territory that had been lost to the imperial forces but had still not seen significant results.

New Developments in the Balkan Theater

As we already mentioned, the Ottoman Empire and Bulgaria signed a mutual defensive alliance when the war broke out. And while the Ottomans were being lobbied by the Germans to join World War I on the side of the Central Powers, so were the Bulgarians. Bulgaria, which had been somewhat isolated since its defeat in the Second Balkan War, was in a pretty precarious position and wanted to get revenge on Serbia. The obvious threat that existed with Bulgaria's entry into the war was a potential Russian invasion, which would have been almost impossible to handle. There was also a threat of a united counteroffensive by Serbia and Montenegro. Still, the Bulgarians were easily persuaded to join the Central Powers, which promised to reclaim some of Bulgaria's lost territories. Despite being the smallest Central Power, Bulgaria played a pivotal role due to its active involvement in the Balkan theater. It greatly contributed to Serbia's defeat and provided the Central Powers with a crucial overland route that connected the Ottoman Empire to the rest of Central Europe.

Bulgaria's entry into the war followed a catastrophic Austro-Hungarian invasion of Serbia. By the end of 1914, the imperial army had not gained much progress against the Serbians, who were being supplied by the Allies to hold up the Austrian forces. In early 1915, soon after Serbia reclaimed Belgrade and drove out the enemy forces, the Austrian war effort would mostly be concentrated on the Eastern Front against Russia and at the Isonzo against the Italians. Austria-Hungary requested help from the Germans, who were becoming increasingly annoyed and frustrated by the constant failures of the Austrian army and its inability to perform. Germany sent reinforcements in September of 1915 to renew the invasion of Serbia and make sure that it went smoothly. And to make matters worse for the Serbians, Bulgaria formally declared war in October. By mid-October, Serbia was sandwiched from the north by the Austrians and Germans and in the east and southeast by the Bulgarians.

Bulgaria provided an additional 600,000 troops to the war effort, and it was clear that Serbia did not stand a chance. Thus, in late 1915, the Serbians organized an all-out retreat, hoping to receive at least some assistance from the Allies. After reaching the

Adriatic, the Serbs suffered several defeats against the combined forces of the Central Powers, and their Montenegrin allies fell to the invasion. The Serbs were forced to flee to Greece by sea.

The Allies had not expected the war to escalate so quickly in the Balkans. Having just devoted a lot of men to the campaign at Gallipoli, they decided to send a relief force from the amphibious operation to help the Serbs retaliate. The Allied forces, under the command of French General Maurice Sarrail, arrived at the Greek city of Salonica (modern Thessalonica) in early October with the intention of getting to the Serbian border. However, the reinforcements were delayed since King Constantine I had pro-German sentiments. He dismissed the pro-Allied government and did not allow the expeditionary forces to advance any farther.

The situation escalated to the point where the Allied forces effectively took part in the Greek political revolution to install a favorable ruler. They were held up in Salonica until the spring of 1916. Eventually, the Allies managed to defeat the royalist resistance and force King Constantine I to abdicate. By that time, the Serbian positions had been completely overrun by the German-led invasion from the north and the Bulgarian armies from the east, complicating the situation even more.

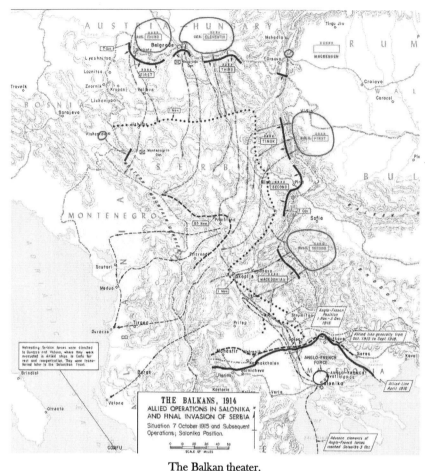

The Balkan theater.

The Balkan theater would not see any more significant actions for more than a year. By 1916, the Central Powers had managed to defeat Serbia, destroying much of its army and driving them out past their border. Bulgaria occupied the territories that it had wished to regain in the war, but this, paired with the fact that Romania joined the war in mid-1916 on the side of the Allies, complicated matters for the Bulgarian public and the high command. The Bulgarians had achieved their initial goals, but since they had been dragged into an all-out war where the interests of multiple nations had to be taken into consideration, they could not simply abandon the war effort. Forced by the Germans and Austrians to keep up the pressure against their enemies, Bulgaria stayed in the war for longer than it should have, suffering about

300,000 casualties in total—the most losses per capita out of any participating nation.

As for the Allies, after the successful Greek coup, they decided to launch a counteroffensive into Serbia and Macedonia while reinforcing their armies that were stationed in Greece. However, despite seeing some success against the Bulgarians with the Monastir Offensive, the Allies suffered many casualties without being able to achieve meaningful progress. The war effort had been thwarted in the Balkans. And since Serbia had been taken out, the war there favored the Central Powers. By 1917, when Greece formally joined World War I on the side of the Allies, almost 500,000 French, British, Serbian, and Russian troops were being held up in Greece, unable to break through the resistance.

Chapter 10 – The Years of Stalemate

By 1915, both sides had seen an increase in their allies, with the Central Powers being joined by the Ottoman Empire and Bulgaria and the Allies getting Italy. As these new actors became involved in the conflict, it became clear that they provided new opportunities for exploitation. Each side tried to shift the conflict from the heart of Europe to other regions to weaken the enemy.

Since the war developed differently in the new theaters and did not really amount to a decisive swing in the overall balance of power, it is a good time to take a look at what was happening on the Western and Eastern Fronts from early 1915 to 1916. This chapter will focus on the Allied efforts of breaking the stalemate on the Western Front, as well as more exciting developments on the Eastern Front, where Russia was confronted by a new challenger.

Allies Fail on the Western Front

The 740-kilometer (460-mile) front, which was established after the defeat of Germany in the Battle of the Marne, resulted in a complete deadlock for both sides. After entrenching in late summer/early autumn of 1914, no advance whatsoever was made by either the Allies or the Germans, nor was it really possible to break through. The Germans were the first to realize that trench warfare meant a stalemate on the Western Front. As time went by, they started to shift more and more troops to the Eastern Front to help the Austrians against Russia. It was as if Germany was acting according to the intended tactics of the Schlieffen Plan. The nature of trench warfare made it clear that not a lot of soldiers were actually needed to defend a potential Allied advance. Instead, the German high command decided to play the long game by developing its trench systems and making sure that resources were allocated properly to other regions at war.

Chief of staff Moltke was replaced in September of 1914 by Erich von Falkenhayn, who pushed for a defensive strategy in the West and is partially responsible for the almost two-year stalemate in the trenches. By constantly sending supplies to soldiers in the trenches to ensure they would never be overwhelmed by an Allied offensive and even building a whole new "vertical" railway network to better connect the entrenched troops, Germany was in a good position to divert its efforts to the East.

The Allies had a completely different approach. They were eager to break through the German defenses and achieve at least some progress against the Central Powers. The Allied efforts to open up new frontiers served that purpose, as they hoped to pressure their enemies in different regions around the world to indirectly weaken the German defenses in the Western trenches. A coordinated offensive on the weakened Western Front would be the shortest way to the German heartland and, thus, to a victory.

For most of 1915, the Allies tried time and time again to rout the Germans on the Western Front, but the defensive capabilities of the trenches proved too difficult to overcome. The French were especially eager to keep trying to force the breakthrough but met with no success. The Allied high command even considered landing on the German Baltic coast to force the battle to shift away from the trenches, but the strategy was scrapped in favor of renewed efforts on the Western Front.

The constant Allied efforts to storm the German positions on the Western Front proved extremely ineffective, resulting in the loss of about fifty thousand Allied soldiers by early 1915. The high command incorrectly believed that the best way to deal with the enemy's defenses was to continually bombard them with artillery, but the shelling would never happen with a time window that would allow the Allied troops to approach within fighting distance. The German machine guns, which were unstartled by the artillery fire, relentlessly mowed down anyone who tried to cross "no man's land."

Desperate times called for desperate measures. In the late spring of 1915, the Allies launched a major offensive that became known as the Battle of Aubers. The objective was to capture the important Aubers Ridge from the Germans, and the French 10th Army and the BEF (British Expeditionary Forces) tried to break through the front line at three different points. However, their efforts were all in vain. The British forces were completely wiped out, and the French continued their assault until they were forced to retreat back to the trenches in June.

In late September, another combined Allied effort occurred, which also yielded no results and ended in terrible losses, despite unrelenting shelling of German positions. These bombardments, which were intended to weaken and disorient the enemy before the troops were ordered to cross no man's land, actually signaled to the Germans that an assault was imminent, giving them time to call up their reserves and reinforce the bombarded areas. This was the only tactic the Allies used to try and break through the trenches in 1915, and in the end, it resulted in the loss of more than 250,000 French and British lives. The Germans, on the other hand, only lost about half of that amount by the end of the year.

These unsuccessful Allied attempts also had an impact on the British and French economies, with both countries effectively running out of artillery ammunition by the end of 1915. It was clear to the Allies that a continued assault on the trenches would be very costly, and it prompted them to come up with new strategies to circumvent the deadlock. During this time, the war effort against the Ottoman Empire took its real shape, with the Allies sending more troops against the Turks to achieve at least some success in the war. As it stood, they had only suffered losses, and the public back home was growing increasingly weary.

The Great Russian Retreat

Unlike the deadlock on the Western Front, the engagements in the East proved to be much more consequential. After finally taking Przemyśl after months of siege warfare, the Russian troops made significant advances in Galicia, especially when compared to their efforts in East Prussia. The defeat of the Russian armies in the north by the Germans prompted the Russians to devise a plan that strengthened their northern flank while also pushing for the German region of Silesia farther in the west.

The situation was even more complicated for the Central Powers since Austria-Hungary was getting picked on from different sides by different enemies. As a consequence, by mid-1915, the empire had to split its forces to fight off the Serbians and Italians on two fronts while diverting a significant part of its armies to hold off the Russian advance. Although Germany had hoped that Austria-Hungary would be able to stall the Russians for as long as possible, the Austrian army never managed to achieve significant success on its own. Fortunately for Vienna, the stalemate on the Western Front allowed the Germans to shift their focus back to the East more quickly. Throughout 1915, more and more German troops arrived in Galicia to push back the Russians.

Thus, the Central Powers slowly started to consolidate their efforts. In one of the first encounters of 1915, the Germans were able to defeat the Russians in the Second Battle of the Masurian Lakes, dissuading Russian efforts from reinforcing the northern flank. This success prompted the Central Powers to devise a plan that envisioned a concentrated thrust through the Russian center, grouping up the available Austrian and German divisions to overwhelm the opposition. The Gorlice-Tarnów Offensive proved to be extremely successful, with the Central Powers achieving every major objective and pushing the Russians back about eighty miles by June. They even managed to take back control of the lost city of Lemberg and the newly captured Przemyśl.

However, the offensive was perhaps too successful, as the high command of Austria and Germany had not foreseen such progress before the launch of the attack. As a result, they delayed further orders to the troops and gave Russia an opportunity to fully withdraw from the center without suffering more casualties.

The Great Russian Retreat, 1915.
https://commons.wikimedia.org/w/index.php?curid=726155

As a result of the offensive, the Central Powers had effectively advanced through the very center of the Russian front lines, and Chief of Staff Falkenhayn realized that he needed to seize the opportunity to fully surround the Russian forces on the northern flank, which the Germans and the Austrians had bypassed. The new plan was carried out in July of 1915 and envisioned cutting off the Russian troops that had been stationed in the Warsaw area. However, despite capturing thousands of enemies in the northward offensive from Galicia to southern East Prussia, the Central Powers were not fully able to capitalize. To shorten the time it would take to get to Warsaw, they chose a shorter path rather than enveloping and circling the Russians more from the east. This, in theory, would have made it possible for them to surround even more Russian forces.

The Russians realized the danger they were in and ordered an all-out retreat from the area, giving up whatever progress they had made in the opening months of the war. The Great Retreat saved the lives of many Allied soldiers and allowed Russia to continue the war effort. Still, in total, the tsar's armies lost an estimated 750,000 troops in the span of five months, more than any other European power.

Verdun and the Somme

Parallel to the events on the Eastern Front in 1915, the Allies on the Western Front had largely been recovering from their failed assaults on the German trenches. As we already discussed, these attacks produced a shell shortage in Britain, in addition to costing hundreds of thousands of lives. Thus, for the remainder of 1915, the Allies came up with new plans to achieve success on the Western Front. After the failures of early 1915, Britain and France started conscripting more men, quickly replenishing their losses and preparing for a renewed offensive.

The German high command believed that the war had so far gone very favorably for them. With German reinforcements arriving in Serbia and Russian Poland, as well as the Austro-Hungarians managing to hold off the Italians, Chief of Staff Falkenhayn was confident that a slow approach would be best on the Western Front. Falkenhayn devised a plan that mainly envisioned dealing a significant blow to the Allied positions in the West through an assault on the town of Verdun, which lay in the salient (a narrow breakthrough in the enemy's front lines), favoring a German convergence. Falkenhayn believed that concentrated limited advances onto Verdun would prompt the French to send reserves to defend their positions, drawing out large numbers of enemy soldiers and exposing them to heavy German artillery fire. The French would be compelled to defend Verdun because of its strategic importance and, in the process, suffer a lot of casualties. In fact, Falkenhayn intended to make the French bleed as much as possible to hinder the Allies from launching yet another offensive that would hold up more Germans in the West.

The German troops went on the offensive on February 21st, 1916, bombarding the French positions and setting up for a full-frontal assault. The Meuse River, which ran through the town of Verdun, was crucial, and one of the Germans' initial goals was to successfully take hold of both banks of the river. The first German push was successful, capturing nearby Fort Douaumont after just three days of fighting. The French, realizing that losing Verdun would mean a significant German breakthrough on the Western

Front, turned to their allies, urging them to act.

In fact, prior to the German offensive of Verdun, the Allies had all met up in the French town of Chantilly to discuss a united, multi-pronged offensive on the Central Powers. As the fighting at Verdun had escalated, they felt compelled to attack at different points to try and relieve some of the pressure on France. The Italians resumed their offensive at the Isonzo, the Russians tried to break through in the East, and the British replaced the French at Arras on the Western Front, freeing up French troops to be used in Verdun's defense.

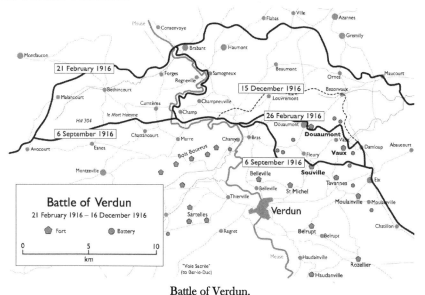

Battle of Verdun.

Drawn by Gdr, CC BY-SA 3.0 <http://creativecommons.org/licenses/by-sa/3.0/>, via Wikimedia Commons. Accessed from: https://commons.wikimedia.org/wiki/File:Battle_of_Verdun_map.png

Still, it was not enough to stop the Germans from advancing. Crucially, French General Phillipe Pétain refused to give up the defensive positions assumed by his forces, ordering fierce counterattacks on the advancing Germans, halting them. The counterattacks bought enough time for the French artillery to mobilize and significantly fire back by mid-March. The outnumbered French were slowly being pushed back, giving up forts along the way for the Germans to occupy and use as defenses. A month later, after the Germans had transferred even more men to reinforce the offensive at Verdun, they began to push even harder, switching from relying on artillery to relying on sheer numbers to break through and force the town to surrender. Eventually, by early June, after about four months of relentless fighting, the Germans came close to capturing the town of Verdun and defeating the French forces. But new developments on the Western Front forced them to delay their advance.

Having agreed to launch a counteroffensive against the Germans and relieve the French defenders at Verdun, the British and French came up with a plan for a concentrated assault in northern France at the Somme River. The Allies finally proceeded with a frontal attack on July 1st, 1916, after a week of heavy bombardment. The Allied offensive at the Somme dissuaded the Germans from sending more reinforcements to the Battle of Verdun, buying much-needed time for the French to retaliate.

Led by British Commander in Chief Douglas Haig, the first efforts to break through the German defenses at the Somme ended disastrously for the BEF 4th Army. The British were ordered to cross a couple of miles of no man's land. Burdened with heavy equipment and confronted with heavy German machine gun fire, the British lost about sixty thousand soldiers in the assault, the most suffered by the Royal Army in a single day. Despite this, General Haig firmly believed that the breakthrough at the Somme was the only way to save the French from being fully defeated at Verdun. After the failure of the first assault, he ordered another attack on the southern part of the German defenses.

Adopting a slower method proved to be more effective, as the Brits managed to achieve some success by July 14th by breaking the Germans at Ovillers. Even though Haig was optimistic about further advances, he decided to continue partial assaults on German positions for the next two months. No significant ground was gained, but the British were able to keep a large portion of the German army on the Western Front occupied. In September, the first tanks were used at the Somme, but it amounted to no real success for the British. In the end, the Allies decided to dig in, accepting the fact that further advancement seemed impossible. The British suffered an estimated 400,000 casualties at the Somme. The Battle of the Somme also saw 150,000 French causalities and about 550,000 Germans. By late September, the offensive had been abandoned, having gained no real victory, although it was justified by the fact that it was able to act as a diversion for the German forces at Verdun.

The British offensive at the Somme.

The Allied counteroffensive at the Somme dramatically influenced the course of the Battle of Verdun, where the French were able to transfer reinforcements and reorganize after the Germans' inactivity throughout the course of the summer. Starting in September, the French, now under the command of General Charles Mangin, retaliated, recapturing the important Douaumont and Vaux forts by December. The French advanced slowly and firmly, while the Germans, who had fewer resources, were forced to give up their gains at Verdun. The fighting largely ceased in mid-December, after which the French troops were able to stabilize the situation and reestablish defensive positions.

All in all, the Battle of Verdun lasted for 302 days, with about 350,000 casualties on each side. It has become one of the most famous battles of World War I, synonymous with bloodshed and French resilience.

The Brusilov Offensive

As two of the most famous battles of WWI unfolded on the Western Front, there was also significant activity on the Eastern Front, where the Russians tried to mount another offensive to weaken Germany and help relieve the pressure on the West. With many Germans occupied by fighting France and Britain and the Austro-Hungarians sending more forces to deal with Italy, the Russian high command believed that it was the right time to strike and recover from the Great Retreat.

Under the leadership of General Alexander Brusilov, Russia devised a plan to attack the Austro-Hungarians in Galicia and reclaim Russian Poland. By the start of the operation on June 4th, 1916, the front line between Russia and the Central Powers had been pushed to the east, stretching southward from the Baltic coast and the city of Riga to the Romanian border. However, in about two months, the Russians had managed to make significant progress and pushed the Austrian and German troops west of Warsaw, marking one of the most impressive offensives on the Eastern Front.

The success of the Brusilov Offensive is attributed to the careful planning that took place months before its launch, with the Russian high command correctly realizing that their forces would face limited Austrian resistance during the assault because of the latter's war with Italy. The four armies under General Brusilov coordinated remarkably well, easily crushing the ill-prepared Austro-Hungarian troops and forcing them to retreat after a series of rapid assaults on their positions. The Austro-Hungarians surrendered in large numbers, with the Russians capturing an estimated 200,000 soldiers at Czernowitz, a number that increased up to 400,000 by the end of the offensive in September. The total number of casualties for the Central Powers amounted to more than a million, with about 90 percent of the losses coming from the Austro-Hungarians. The Brusilov offensive was a remarkable victory that demonstrated the true military strength of Russia.

However, despite forcing the Austro-Hungarians all the way back to the Carpathian Mountains, the Brusilov Offensive did not end in the way the Russian high command had hoped for. The constant shortage of supplies and lack of proper communications were a massive problem for the Russians, who, after the arrival of the Germans, were forced to retreat, afraid that the salient they had established could be flanked by the German forces. In addition, Brusilov's advances came at a massive cost. There were an estimated one million Russian casualties, most of them being captured or deserted. General Brusilov was disappointed by the lack of discipline, which undermined his efforts to continue pressuring the Central Powers. The Brusilov Offensive was perhaps the final positive thing that would happen to Russia for the rest of the war.

A direct consequence of Russia's success in the offensive was Romania's entry into the war on the side of the Allies in August 1916. The Allies promised Romania the Austrian province of Transylvania, which had historically been a part of Romania and was largely inhabited by Romanians. However, Romania's entry into the war did not produce the results the Allies had hoped for. After a relatively slow offensive in Transylvania by the Romanian military, the Central Powers were quick to respond by organizing a counteroffensive from Bulgaria that easily thrust into southern Romania. The Bulgarians, with German reinforcements and under German command, quickly pushed their way through the Romanian defenses, achieving victory after victory until eventually reaching Bucharest in December. The Romanian capital fell on December 6th, 1917, and the army was forced to retreat north into Moldova and seek shelter under Russian protection.

Chapter 11 - The War at Sea

Having covered the most significant military developments since the start of the war up until late 1916, it is time to look at a crucial part of World War I—the war at sea. We briefly touched upon the naval side of the conflict when we discussed the Ottoman Empire's "purchase" of two German warships, the *Goeben* and the *Breslau*, something that was one of the precursors to the Ottomans' entry into the war on the side of the Central Powers. However, this was only a small part of the naval developments that took place during the Great War. This chapter will focus on the crucial events that shaped the naval war between the two sides, focusing on the rivalry between Britain and Germany that escalated to an all-out conflict at sea and revolutionized warfare.

The Early Encounters

Before the beginning of the war, Germany made significant efforts to try and catch up with Britain in terms of naval strength. By the end of the 19th century, it was increasingly believed that possessing a strong navy was the key to global domination. Britain had enjoyed naval supremacy for centuries, possessing the largest fleet out of all the major powers and having experienced and disciplined personnel. Still, Germany managed to make up the disparity that existed with Britain by the start of the war. Despite not outnumbering the Royal Navy, the Germans were confident they could hold their own against the British.

The dreadnoughts dominated the naval arsenals of both nations. The ships were armed with several large and small guns and reinforced with steel to give them durability. Throughout the course of the war, naval technology developed drastically, with the creation and increased use of battlecruisers, torpedo boats, and submarines. Battlecruisers were basically modified versions of the dreadnoughts, with some lacking armor for greater speed and others housing more artillery for power. Torpedo boats, also known as destroyers, were smaller ships that were very quick and effective in rapid encounters. The submarines, which became very prominent with the German U-boats, were not as good at fighting warships but were extremely effective at pressuring naval blockades and carrying out surprise attacks.

German U-boat with its crew.

The first major battle between the Germans and Brits on the high seas was the Battle of the Helgoland Bight in late August of 1914. A part of the British fleet managed to destroy several German light cruisers and kill about one thousand men while only suffering thirty-five casualties in return. The Germans retaliated, thanks to their submarines, which were still a fresh invention at the beginning of the war. Throughout October, the German U-boats proved to be problematic, as they were scattered in the North Sea, dealing significant blows to several British warships. Still, in the encounters on the ocean, the Brits were able to defeat parts of the German High Seas Fleet. In January of 1915, at the Battle of Dogger Bank, the German cruiser *Blücher* was sunk by the Royal Navy without suffering any casualties.

Where the Germans saw more success at sea were in other parts of the world, especially in East Asia, where the German High Seas Fleet held a squadron of four battlecruisers under Admiral Graf Maximilian von Spee. Through quick and concentrated bombardments, the squadron created a lot of problems for the British, who had to keep an eye on their vast possessions in Asia and Oceania, stretching their navy thin to defend different locations. In addition to damaging Allied trade, the Germans also sailed to the shores of British and French possessions, where they shelled the ports that were used to transport Allied colonial troops to the front lines in Europe. The German cruiser *Emden*, for example, was able to destroy up to fifteen Allied transport ships on its own by November of 1914 until finally being sunk off the Cocos Islands by the Royal Navy.

The rest of the squadron was reinforced by Germany by the end of the month, and it achieved an impressive victory against the British ships in the Battle of Coronel, where it sunk two British cruisers without losing any of theirs. To deal with the German East Asian squadron, Britain sent more ships to the Pacific and Indian Oceans. The Royal Navy was able to finally catch the Germans near the Pacific South American coast. Under Admiral Sir Doveton Sturdee, eight British cruisers chased down the German squadron and sank all of the enemy ships. Through this victory, they put a much-needed end to the disturbance of trade that had been caused by Germany.

Blockades

Since both sides realized they could significantly damage each other's economies by interfering with international trade and the colonies, Germany and Britain viciously engaged to dominate the transporting corridors and cut off each other's supply lines. Right at the beginning of the war, Britain organized a huge naval blockade of Germany by covering the two points at sea the Germans used to access international trade: the English Channel and the entry to the North Sea off the coast of Scotland. Covering the narrower Strait of

Dover with sea mines was enough to dissuade the German ships from taking that route. In the north, the Royal Navy deployed a squadron of heavy and light cruisers to patrol a large area and make sure that no material that could be used for the war reached the German coast.

To answer the blockade, Germany began relying on its submarines, which proved to be extremely effective at taking out merchant ships. In fact, partly due to the fact that the German East Asian surface squadron had been destroyed by the Royal Navy, the Germans upped their production and usage of U-boats. By early 1915, submarine attacks were carried out on non-military ships only after the Germans issued warnings to the target ships to ensure the safe evacuation of innocent crews. However, as time went by, the Allies adapted and began dealing with the U-boats by implementing new defense measures like underwater nets, new types of mines, special depth bombs to target the submarines, and new radars that were capable of detecting sound waves generated from the rustling German engines underwater. The Allies also started arming and reinforcing their merchant ships to avoid too much damage. France also helped out significantly, as it fielded a decent navy to support Britain. Together, the Allies managed to overcome the submarine problem.

The situation did not get better for Germany throughout 1915, as the Germans declared the waters near the British Isles were hostile, claiming that they were entitled to attack any ship, Allied or not, as they deemed necessary. The neutral countries did not welcome this decision, correctly believing that Germany had no right to open fire on ships that had nothing to do with the war and were just conducting regular activities. The public's discontent toward Germany reached its peak in May 1915 when the German submarines sunk the British liner *Lusitania*, which was one of the biggest transport ships in the world. It was on its way to Liverpool from New York. Over a thousand innocent civilians died, including 128 US citizens.

The international community, especially the United States, adopted an increasingly anti-German stance after this event, but the US government, staying in line with its neutrality policy, calmed public sentiment, which was clamoring for war with Germany. The Germans would provoke the US on several more occasions by sinking other non-military ships. The United States' protests would eventually lead to Germany ceasing all of its submarine activity west of the British Isles in late 1915.

RMS Lusitania in 1907.
https://commons.wikimedia.org/wiki/File:Lusitania_1907.jpg

Jutland

The most important and most famous development of the naval war would unfold in May 1916. The newly appointed commander in chief of the German High Seas Fleet, Admiral Reinhard Scheer, carefully observed the British Royal Navy's movements in early 1916, believing the Germans had an opportunity to exploit a temporary numerical superiority and deal a massive blow to the British. With the main part of the Royal Navy patrolling near the Orkney Islands, Admiral Scheer devised a plan that envisioned engaging with the British fleet on the English east coast. Scheer believed the Germans would be able to effectively overcome the British Royal Navy's strength and achieve a decisive victory.

Fortunately for the Allies, British intelligence was able to intercept and decode a part of the transmission from the German high command and immediately alerted Admiral John Jellicoe, who was in charge of the Grand Fleet, to reinforce Admiral David Beatty and his men. The Germans were still quick to attack Beatty's ships, overwhelming them with firepower and sinking one cruiser. After most of Beatty's ships were mobilized and returning fire, the Germans sent out their destroyers with a torpedo attack, sinking another battleship, the *Queen Mary*.

Admiral Beatty realized he could not hold the German fleet any longer and decided to retreat northward to stall for time until Admiral Jellicoe arrived. For the next hour, the Germans pursued Beatty's ships, which led them to Jellicoe's squadron that had set up a battle line, ready for the enemy to arrive. For the next half an hour, the Germans maneuvered through a barrage from the British Royal Navy, only managing to reorganize thanks to the durability of their ships and the discipline of the crew. They were able to return fire quickly.

Then, in an extraordinary turn of events, Admiral Scheer, realizing that his ships were still facing an organized battle line, ordered the Germans to carry out a 180-degree turn to avoid a full confrontation with the British. This was an extremely risky and difficult maneuver for one ship, let alone a whole array of massive cruisers and battleships, but it was executed perfectly by the experienced and well-trained German crew.

Scheer directed his ships south, and Admiral Jellicoe ordered his fleet to chase down the Germans in a parallel line from the east, leading the two sides to fire heavily on each other's positions. By 7 p.m., both sides had suffered significant casualties, and it became clear to Admiral Scheer that the Royal Navy's position blocked the German ships from the German coast, meaning the British had cut off their potential escape path.

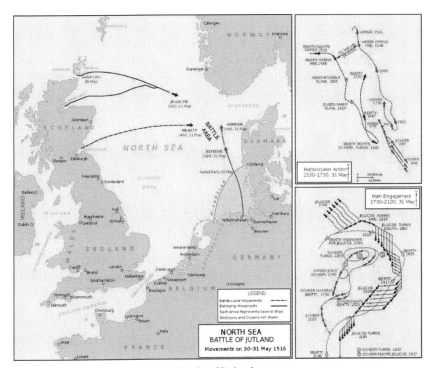

Battle of Jutland.

Grandiose, CC BY-SA 3.0 <https://creativecommons.org/licenses/by-sa/3.0>, via Wikimedia Commons. Accessed from: https://commons.wikimedia.org/wiki/File:Map_of_the_Battle_of_Jutland,_1916.svg

In a last desperate move to break the British, Scheer ordered a full-frontal charge with his cruisers, a move that was unheard of because it gave a massive advantage to the British, who could calmly fire on the approaching Germans. However, since Admiral Jellicoe had also seen a lot of damage, he was afraid the Germans might overwhelm his fleet. He ordered the Royal Navy to turn back and sail away from the charge. If Jellicoe had correctly weighed the danger posed to his positions by the German forces, he would have stood his ground and completely destroyed the Germans. But after hours of fighting and in total darkness, it was difficult to assume what the Germans were capable of, and Admiral Jellicoe acted accordingly, saving what was left of his forces.

The Battle of Jutland was the biggest naval battle in history up until that point. At the end of the battle, both sides claimed victory, while, in reality, the results were indecisive. The Germans had managed to inflict more losses on the British but could not capitalize and effectively carry out their intended objectives. In the end, despite the losses suffered by the British, the Germans were not able to undermine the Royal Navy's strength in the North Sea, as the British ships continued the blockade and still outnumbered the German High Seas Fleet for the rest of the war.

Chapter 12 – Russia Out, United States In

This chapter will focus on arguably two of the most important non-military developments in World War I: the Russian Revolution and Russia's subsequent exit of the war and the events that caused the United States to enter the war on the side of the Allies. These events significantly turned the tide of the war and affected its final outcome. Although they happened parallel to each other, we will first examine how the mass discontent in Russia resulted in a socialist revolution and then turn our attention to the fatal telegram from Germany that caused the United States to break its neutrality.

The February Revolution

The year 1917 turned out to be a momentous one for Russia. The events of 1917 did not only change the course of the country forever but also had long-lasting consequences that affected the rest of the world for decades to come. Of course, we cannot fully cover the political and social extent of the Russian Revolution; instead, we will be focusing on how Russia's participation in the Great War influenced the events of 1917.

When World War I broke out in 1914, Russia was swept up, much like every other nation, in nationalist fervor. People of all classes demonstrated their firm support for the war effort and were ready to prove their patriotism. Due to this, many overlooked the economic and social hardships the country had been struggling with for the past decades, giving the tsar and his regime hope that the Russian public would adopt a more royalist stance if they achieved success in the war. And they could see some favorable results in this regard when the Russian army achieved victories in Galicia and the Caucasus.

However, by the end of 1916, things were not going well for Russia. After two years, with an estimated five million casualties, the Russian army was losing more and more men after the partially successful Brusilov Offensive. The prolonged war had detrimental effects not only on the morale of the soldiers, who mutinied time and time again and deserted on multiple occasions, but also on the Russian economy, which still had not achieved similar levels of industrialization as other major powers in the war. This meant that Russia could not keep up the war effort on a similar scale and quality as its enemies. And when paired with the government's incompetence in finding solutions during wartime, the people were greatly discontented.

The crisis finally amounted to a series of protests in late February 1917 in St. Petersburg. The public took to the streets, protesting the inadequacy of the tsar's regime, as well as new food rationing laws that had been put in place a couple of days prior. During the next week, the protesters grew in numbers. The government became concerned that the demonstrations could turn into something bigger. At that time, Tsar Nicholas II was not present in St. Petersburg, having arrived at the Caucasian front to personally lead the Russian forces against the Ottomans. This infuriated the protesters even more, who viewed the tsar as a traitor, leaving the struggling people behind in search of some glory in the war.

From February 21st to February 28th, the protests slowly turned into armed confrontations with the city's police, but by the end of the week, even the city's garrison had joined the demonstrators, refusing to execute orders from the high command. Tsar Nicholas was forced to return to the capital after learning of the events that had transpired, but it was all in vain. Nicholas II failed to find enough support and was forced to abdicate three days later on March 3rd, nominating his brother, Grand Duke Michael Alexandrovich, to take his place. His brother declined the offer.

This marked the end of the Romanov dynasty. As a result, a provisional government was set up to lead the country during the crisis.

Peace, Land, and Bread

However, this was not the end to Russia's problems, nor to the revolution. The provisional government had no time to address the Russian people's immediate problems, as there was an empty treasury and limited resources. In addition, Russian troops, which had been suffering defeat after defeat and had been ill-supplied for months, lost practically all motivation to fight after having learned of the situation back home. Because of the change in leadership in St. Petersburg, the army's chain of command had been distorted, and the soldiers were confused about what to do. Thousands deserted every week. Still, the provisional government insisted on continuing the war effort and could not implement any substantial changes for the unhappy population. This caused yet another series of mass protests over the course of the summer. The protestors were dealt with violently.

In the wake of all of this, some political organizations recognized the opportunity to influence developments. Among them was the Bolshevik Party, which managed to gain a lot of traction. The Bolshevik Party was a far-left party led by Vladimir Lenin and stressed the necessity of a social revolution and the triumph of the lower-class proletariat over the corrupt bourgeoisie. Motivating the local soviets (civil society groups where people of the lower classes assembled to discuss and assess Russian politics) with their catchy slogan of "peace, land, and bread," the Bolsheviks urged the Russians to revolt. The public was once again swept up in an uproar, supporting Lenin and his movement and bursting out onto the streets once again in October 1917.

These demonstrations were far more brutal, with armed protesters and the police violently clashing for days. In the end, the Bolsheviks triumphed. The demonstrators were able to storm the White Palace in St. Petersburg, arrest the members of the provisional government, and declare Russia as a socialist state led by the Bolsheviks.

The Bolsheviks suddenly gained the authority to rule Russia and influence its domestic and foreign policy decisions. One of the first things the new government did was negotiate a separate peace treaty with the Germans—the Treaty of Brest-Litovsk—which marked the end of Russian involvement in World War I. Prioritizing peace to please the upset public, Lenin and his government approved the Decree on Peace almost right away. Russia and the Central Powers agreed to an armistice in December.

After two months of negotiations at the German-controlled town of Brest-Litovsk, the two sides, with German, Austro-Hungarian, Bulgarian, Ottoman, and Russian delegations present, agreed to the terms of the peace treaty in early March 1918. Russia was forced to cede control of Lithuania, Latvia, Estonia, Ukraine, Belarus, and Finland, which were most of its European holdings. In addition, it returned the provinces gained from Turkey during the war in 1878, with the three Caucasian nations of Georgia, Armenia, and Azerbaijan declaring their independence and forming the Transcaucasian Democratic Federative Republic. In addition to territorial losses, Russia also promised to pay war reparations to Germany, which would amount to six billion German marks.

Just like that, in the span of two revolutions, Russia was out of the war. It was a massive victory for the Central Powers, as Russia's exit freed up the forces on the Eastern Front. Germany had largely incited the Russian Revolution by allowing Vladimir Lenin, who was in Switzerland in 1917, to pass through its territories to get to St. Petersburg and lead the revolutionary movement. In the end, Russia was left empty-handed, while the Central Powers had clearly gained a big advantage.

However, as we will soon see, the Central Powers were not able to capitalize on the results of the Russian Revolution, as the Allies managed to get a new ally on their side, which upset the balance of power once again.

The Zimmermann Telegram

We have barely mentioned the United States in this book. This is largely due to the fact that American involvement in World War I was not very prominent or impactful for the first two years of the war. The American government pursued isolationism, which had characterized US foreign policy since the early 19th century. In addition, due to the absence of a major imminent threat in North America, the US Army was significantly smaller than its European counterparts, with an estimated 400,000 active personnel compared to, for example, about 4 million British troops. However, the United States still contributed greatly to the Allied war effort, supplying Britain and France with all sorts of goods, including arms and ammunition. Despite this, at the beginning of the war, the US did not exactly view Germany as hostile, having had somewhat of a warm relationship with the Reich since German unification in 1871. The US also had a sizeable German diaspora.

So, the US, led by President Woodrow Wilson, tried to play the role of an intermediary between the Allies and the Central Powers, offering to lead peace negotiations on multiple occasions. At the beginning of the war, peace negotiations were not seen by either side as possible, let alone necessary, since both believed they had the upper hand. But as the war dragged on and millions of people died, the belligerents thought about stopping the war and diplomatically resolving the conflict.

For example, after talks with both sides in December 1916, Wilson proposed a "peace without victory" to the warring nations, something the British side, for the first time since the beginning of the war, viewed as favorable. It is likely that the French would have also been persuaded if the British and Americans had pushed for such a resolution. The Austro-Hungarians likely would have been on board since the war had been the most crushing for the dual monarchy. However, being the first to sue for peace would be regarded as a political defeat and a display of weakness. President Wilson soon discontinued his efforts.

Technically, Germany "wanted" peace, but the terms presented by the Germans in January 1917 were absurd, something akin to the Austrian ultimatums to Serbia back in 1914. Accepting them would have practically meant the ceding of German-occupied

France and Belgium to the Reich, something the Allies would have never accepted in the first place.

The situation dramatically changed after Germany decided to conduct unrestricted submarine warfare in January before declaring it to the rest of the world on February 1st. Germany gave itself the ability to interfere and engage with any foreign ship that entered the North Sea while warning countries to evacuate their civilians. It was perhaps an overly confident move from the Reich, as it restricted not only the movement of the Allied ships but also US merchant ships. Two days later, the Americans cut off diplomatic ties with Germany and decided to reinforce and arm all ships that were set to pursue trade with Britain and France. However, despite the unrestricted submarine warfare, the Germans were wise enough not to attack any passing US ships, knowing that it would create anti-German public sentiment in the US and risk war.

Despite this, the German high command made another inconsiderate move that did raise of anti-German sentiment in America. On February 24th, President Woodrow Wilson received a decoded telegram intercepted by British intelligence. The infamous message, which has come to be known as the Zimmermann Telegram, was directed to the newly elected Mexican President Venustiano Carranza by German Foreign Secretary Arthur Zimmermann. Zimmermann proposed German support to Mexico against the US if the Americans entered the war against Germany, something that was a sound possibility due to the recent rise in tensions between the two countries. In the event of victory, Zimmermann promised Carranza the return of territories Mexico had lost during the Mexican-American War, namely the US states of Arizona, New Mexico, and Texas. To the US, this proposal was a clear sign that Germany was a hostile nation, especially after taking into consideration the fact that the US was not on friendly terms with Mexico either.

After days of consideration, the telegram was published in the press, and the public response that followed was what Germany had feared all along. The whole nation had changed their views regarding the war, with the majority calling for America's entry into the war. Seeing the situation escalate, Mexico promptly declined to engage in any sort of military action against the US, while Germany resorted to increasing its submarine attacks, realizing that it had angered the US beyond the turning point. Throughout March, President Wilson observed the situation unfold and called for a joint session of Congress on April 2nd to discuss America's entry into the war against Germany. In his speech, the president referred to the prospect of US involvement as a highly undesired necessity and stressed that German actions had forced the United States to act decisively.

Four days later, on April 6th, 1917, the United States entered the war on the side of the Allies, although it only declared war on Germany and not all of the Central Powers.

Section Four – The End of the War

Chapter 13 – Last Chance for Germany

This chapter will focus on the German Spring Offensive of March 1918 and the events that led up to it, including the Nivelle Offensive on the Western Front. We will analyze these developments and paint a picture of World War I in its final and most decisive year, where an array of misjudgments and surprises greatly influenced the final outcome of the war.

The Allies Fail Again

The entry of the US into the war gave the Allies new hope and the drive to continue the fight, especially on the Western Front. By the time the United States had sent its divisions to France to reinforce the Allied efforts, Britain, France, and Italy all knew that it would only be a matter of time before Russia was forced to surrender or leave the Eastern Front. Thus, the Allies perceived the months following April 1917 as crucial, believing that only a sudden breakthrough of the German positions on the Western Front would ensure their victory. If the Allies did not emerge triumphant, Germany and Austria-Hungary would have the time to transfer their Eastern divisions to the Western Front, reinforcing their defenses and giving the Central Powers numerical superiority.

The plan of attack was drawn up before April by the new commander of the French forces, Robert Nivelle. It envisioned a combined Franco-British breakthrough of the German defenses in Champagne and the capture of the pivotal Chemin des Dames by the French forces, while the British divisions engaged simultaneously at Arras to try and gain the high ground and force the enemy to retreat.

The plan, as always, seemed sound and cohesive; however, just like in the past, officials were overly optimistic and refused to take all variables into consideration. Most importantly, the majority of the French Army was completely exhausted after fighting viciously at Verdun for months. Unlike most of 1915, when the newly entrenched forces rarely went on full-frontal offensives, the soldiers had no time to rest in between defensive and offensive operations. Thus, the Nivelle Offensive was a massive gamble. If the plan did not work as intended, the French soldiers' poor morale could result in disaster.

In the end, the plan was partially successful. It was launched in early April 1917, with the Germans aware of the general objectives of the Allies. The British saw better success at Arras than the French did at the Aisne. The British attack caught the Germans off-guard, inflicting many casualties and forcing them to fall back. In the battle, the Canadian corps heroically achieved victory at Vimy Ridge, which gave the British forces a massive advantage, as they were able to defeat the Germans. The French, on the other hand, despite carrying out the plan to the best of their ability and partially reaching the intended objectives, saw more losses than Nivelle had planned—about 135,000 casualties in total, with 30,000 of them deaths.

By late April, the Allied efforts had been largely successful, but to ensure a decisive victory, non-stop fighting was necessary. On May 3rd, in an unfortunate turn of events for Commander Nivelle, the French 21st Division, which had been ordered to go on the offensive, refused to carry out its orders. The French Army mutinied en masse, with most of the troops refusing to attack because of exhaustion and poor supplies. About twenty thousand soldiers deserted in May.

The Spring Offensive

The rest of 1917 went favorably for the Central Powers. Parallel to the failure of the Allies to achieve success on the Western Front, the Russian Revolution had effectively knocked Russia out of the war by late 1917. The German high command was optimistic. It believed that to ensure victory, Germany just had to hold out on the Western Front for as long as possible, giving the Eastern divisions enough time to join up and launch a final assault on the Allied positions in France. Germany's hopes were especially high after the Allies could not break through the Hindenburg Line, an extremely well-organized line of German defenses. It had been organized by General Paul von Hindenburg himself after the Nivelle Offensive.

Seeing that the bulk of the US forces was still on the way and that the French morale was low, General Erich Ludendorff drew up plans for the offensive, which was supposed to achieve a decisive German victory by splitting up the Allied forces on the Western Front. The Spring Offensive envisioned a rapid assault on the Allied positions while the Germans still had numerical superiority, thanks to their reinforcements from the Eastern Front. The German high command ordered assaults on five different Allied points to separate the enemy.

On March 21st, 1918, Germany started its advance, using a completely new method to overcome the Allied defenses. The new Hutier tactic, named after German General Oskar von Hutier, saw smaller, better-trained groups of troops bypassing the most heavily defended points to achieve victory at weaker points, mainly areas in charge of logistics or communications. After these troops infiltrated the points, the main infantry corps, with the support of artillery fire, would overwhelm the Allied positions. The Hutier tactic was fundamentally different from anything either side had done before, as the forces would focus on weakening enemy defenses with artillery barrages before trying to cross no man's land with everything they had. As it turned out, the tactic was extremely successful. The Allies could not find an effective answer, causing them to suffer many casualties in the first days of fighting. The Germans made significant advances of some forty miles into the Allied positions and started to close in toward Paris.

German artillery during the Spring Offensive.
https://commons.wikimedia.org/wiki/File:The_German_Spring_Offensive,_March-july_1918_Q8629.jpg

However, these quick, smaller-scale assaults meant that it took more time for the bulk of the German forces with their slower-moving artillery to follow and clean up the resistance. Thus, despite their advantageous position, the Germans could not capitalize on their gains and were forced to stop the offensive soon after its launch. After a month of suffering heavy casualties, the Allies started to retaliate, consolidating their forces. They were further motivated to fight after the increased arrival of American troops.

In July 1918, in a desperate effort to finally break through, the Germans started the Second Battle of the Marne, hoping to fully exploit their numerical superiority. But their efforts were thwarted, as they were confronted with reinforcements from the American Expeditionary Forces, which dissuaded them from continuing the attack. Thus, the Spring Offensive, albeit achieving some initial success, was effectively stopped in the summer of 1918. Throughout the campaign, Germany lost about 600,000 men, while the combined casualties of the Allies numbered more than 800,000.

Chapter 14 – The Fall of the Central Powers

The Spring Offensive was the final major attempt from the Central Powers to achieve a decisive victory and break the Allies. Since the offensive's intended objectives were not reached, the Allies realized that the momentum had swung back into their favor on the Western Front with the arrival of the AEF (American Expeditionary Forces). Thus, the Allies struck simultaneously both on the Western Front and on the Ottoman front in one of the largest campaigns of World War I. The Hundred Days Offensive produced remarkable results and eventually led to the Allied victory in the war.

The Fall of the Ottomans

The fighting between the Allies and the Ottomans never ceased, unlike what transpired in Europe. Because of the Ottoman Empire's massive size, the Allies were able to strike at different locations, stretching the Turkish forces thin and limiting their resources and cohesiveness. Over time, due to constant clashes with the Allies, who were getting reinforcements from their colonial territories, the Ottoman army became exhausted. The main leverage the Ottomans had over the Allies was their numerical superiority, but they were far less technologically advanced or disciplined than the British or the French. Their poor discipline showed as the fighting continued. After suffering humiliating defeats during the Gallipoli campaign, the Allies retaliated and broke the Ottoman Empire.

The Allies saw the most success in the Sinai and Palestine campaign, which lasted for over three years, from early 1915 to mid-1918. Over the course of the campaign, the Egyptian Expeditionary Forces (EEF) achieved victory after victory, fighting their way through the Palestinian lands after suffering some setbacks in the First and Second Battles of Gaza in the spring of 1917. The British then achieved a victory at the crucial Battle of Mughar Ridge in November 1917, as they were able to break out of the stalemate that had ensued after their defeats at Gaza. Seeing the low morale of the Ottoman troops, they pushed northward, capturing the city of Jerusalem in December. Taking control of Jerusalem, which held immense symbolic importance, was a reassuring moment for the Allies and a precursor to their following success.

In early 1918, to reinforce the Western Front against the German Spring Offensive, many of the EEF soldiers were sent right from the Ottoman front lines, causing the Allied efforts to slow down for a little bit. However, thanks to Britain's immense colonial holdings, it was able to swiftly transfer Indian corps to fill the ranks of the EEF and dissuade the Ottomans from launching a counteroffensive. After retraining and resting its soldiers in the summer, the British high command began organizing a new plan of attack to break the bulk of the Ottoman defenses at Palestine and push them back to Anatolia. In September, the Allies proceeded with their operations, crushing the Ottomans at the crucial Battle of Megiddo. Only six thousand of thirty-five thousand Turkish soldiers escaped capture.

The victory at Megiddo was followed by another series of Allied victories. In the ensuing battles of Tulkarm and Nablus, the Ottomans lost their military headquarters and, thus, much of their ability to continue an effective war effort in the Middle East. The Allies closed in from all directions, seeing success in Mesopotamia and the Transjordan. One of the final decisive moments of the Sinai and Palestine campaign was the capture of Damascus on September 30th, 1918, by the British XXI Corps and the Desert Mounted Corps. With Damascus and all of the Middle East under British control and the Allies slowly converging on Anatolia and threatening Istanbul from the Balkans, the Ottomans realized they had lost the war.

The Ottoman Empire's defeat was finalized with the signing of the Armistice of Mudros on October 30th, 1918. Since the war had unfolded unfavorably throughout all of 1918, the Ottoman government hid the news of their defeats back home to not incite an already upset public, which had been massively affected by the war. Ottoman Grand Vizier Talaat Pasha visited Germany and Bulgaria in September to personally inquire about the Central Powers' plans to continue fighting but left empty-handed. With no hope left, Talaat Pasha resigned from office in late October, urging the other members of the government to follow his example since he believed the Allies would punish them for conducting the war. Three days after his resignation, Ahmed Izzet Pasha, who replaced Talaat as the grand vizier, signed an armistice with the British Admiral Somerset Arthur Gough-Calthorpe on board the British HMS *Agamemnon.*

From the very beginning, the Ottoman entry into the war was a big gamble, based on the hopes of achieving quick victories and motivated by the public's irredentist sentiments. In reality, the Ottoman Empire was in no shape to contest the European powers, as it lagged behind them in all aspects, which clearly showed over the course of their time in the war. The Armistice of Mudros brought about the Ottoman Empire's end. The Ottomans removed their soldiers from all locations, including the Caucasus, the Middle East, and the Balkans, and surrendered to the Allies, who assumed control of Ottoman Anatolia and briefly occupied Istanbul before the end of the war. The armistice was later followed by the Treaty of Sèvres, which had even more detrimental effects on the Ottomans.

The Sinai and Palestine campaign was a historic demonstration of the British colonial forces acting together as one. The cooperation between the Egyptian, Indian, Australian, New Zealand, and Canadian troops brought victory to Britain and the Allies. Back in Britain, the public was largely unaware of the campaign's significance, as most of their attention was on the Western Front. However, the true scope and importance of the campaign were quickly realized by the British government, which praised the colonial troops for their bravery and contribution to the war effort.

The Hundred Days Offensive

Meanwhile, the situation was getting tense on the Western Front, where the Allies had finally welcomed the bulk of the American Expeditionary Forces and had high hopes to once and for all end the war. What ensued in the late summer of 1918 has come to be known as the Hundred Days Offensive, which was perhaps the most important campaign in World War I. Devised by Allied Supreme Commander in Chief Ferdinand Foch of France, it envisioned taking matters back into Allied hands after the failed German Spring Offensive and breaking through the infamous Hindenburg Line, which was heavily defended by the Germans.

Thus, the Allies got to work, initiating the Battle of Amiens on August 8th, 1918. In the battle, the British 4th Army led the attack, supported by ten Allied divisions, including troops from the colonies and the US. The British preliminary forces were able to deal a significant blow to the German line, and their strike was followed by tank reinforcements.

The element of surprise played a pivotal part in the Allies' success, who had switched from trying to soften the enemy's defenses with long artillery barrages to quick, concentrated attacks. In a single day, they managed to inflict about thirty thousand casualties on the Germans, who were forced to retreat, caught off-guard by the Allied attack. By the end of the battle, the Allies had gained significant ground, pushing into the German positions south of the Somme.

The events at Amiens were quickly followed by the Battle of Albert on August 21st, which was initiated by the British 3rd Army. Although smaller in scale, the Allied efforts were nevertheless successful, creating another gap in the German positions, which was swiftly exploited by the newly victorious 4th Army. The soldiers swept in from the flank and routed the Germans, who were again forced to retreat.

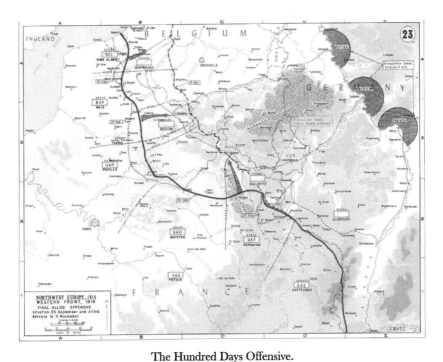

The Hundred Days Offensive.
https://commons.wikimedia.org/wiki/File:Western_front_1918_allied.jpg

Following these advances and the unrelenting pressure of the Allies on their positions, the German high command seemed, for the first time, pessimistic about continuing the war effort. On September 2nd, General Ludendorff ordered all the German forces to fall back to the Hindenburg Line, giving up any headway the Germans had made during the Spring Offensive. In fact, Ludendorff was one of the first to recognize the impending doom of the German army and tried to urge the Kaiser to engage in peace negotiations. With nearly 100,000 soldiers taken prisoner since the start of the Allied offensive, Ludendorff consulted with other high-ranking German officials, as well as the Austro-Hungarian high command, on the state of the war. Perhaps it was too late, as the responses from both were increasingly gloomy. Austria-Hungary even responded by saying they could only afford to continue fighting by the end of November. The pessimism showed after about two weeks when Emperor Charles I of Austria tried sending a letter to the Allies to express his wish to negotiate peace to avoid a total catastrophe. A day later, the Germans also followed through, offering a separate peace agreement to Belgium.

However, the Allies realized their comfortable position and their advantageous position in the war and declined both offers.

What followed was the total annihilation of the remaining German troops by the Allied forces on the Western Front. The confidence level of the Allies reached an all-time high, with thousands of American reinforcements arriving every day in France and being transported right to the front lines. On top of that, Germany had tried to sue for peace. Every positive thing mounted up and gave a huge morale boost to the Allied soldiers. The Allies did not take their foot off the gas pedal after their victories at Amiens and Albert, exerting continuous pressure on the Germans and never stopping their attacks. The British forces achieved multiple breakthroughs with the Battle of Mont Saint-Quentin on August 31st, while the French and American soldiers converged on the Hindenburg Line in the south.

Aiming to cut off German supply lines and communication, the French and the AEF initiated the Meuse-Argonne Offensive on September 26th. At the same time, King Albert I of Belgium commanded a united Belgian, British, and French army at the Battle of Ypres in Flanders, seeking to break through at two different positions. Both attacks were successful, with the Allies exploiting their numerical superiority and overwhelming the German positions. After securing the northern and southern flanks, the Allies then converged on the central stretch of the Hindenburg Line. Recognizing their advantage, the British 4th Army and the French 1st Army engaged at St. Quentin on September 29th and crushed the Germans, who were forced to retreat and abandon much of their equipment. On October 8th, the victory at St. Quentin was followed by yet another victory at Cambrai by the 1st and 3rd British Armies, which was the final straw. The Hindenburg Line had been overwhelmed, and the German mainland was exposed.

Victory in the Balkans

In addition to achieving success on the Western Front and the Middle East, the Allies were also able to finally break through against the Bulgarian defenses in the Balkan theater. The stalemate that had ensued after the events of the Salonica offensive had brought the conflict in the Balkans to an almost complete standstill, something that resembled the stalemate on the Western Front in 1915. The Central Powers did not wish to advance since they did not have any valuable objectives to take in the Balkans after the fall of Serbia, despite the fact that Greece entered the war on the side of the Allies in mid-1917. In addition, the Central Powers lacked resources and preferred to transfer troops after Serbia's defeat to other conflict zones, especially to Romania, whose short-lived participation actually held up a sizeable Central Powers' army for months.

After months of inactivity and small-scale fighting, the Allied troops decided to launch an offensive in September 1918, perhaps motivated by their success in other theaters. The Vardar Offensive, which was launched on September 15th, mainly envisioned overwhelming the Bulgarian trenches in Macedonia. The Allies had correctly recognized that the Bulgarians had exhausted their resources after years of prolonged fighting and believed that a breakthrough would be decisive enough to force the complete collapse of the Bulgarian forces.

From the beginning of the attacks, it was evident that the Allies would emerge victorious, as their artillery bombardments significantly softened up the Bulgarian defenses in the trenches, resulting in a relatively easy Allied victory at Dobro Pole. Two days later, another Allied force, consisting of French, British, Serbian, Greek, and Italian troops under the command of French General Louis d'Espèrey, achieved another victory near Lake Doiran, which shattered the Bulgarians' morale and forced them to retreat. However, unlike other instances when the Allies were reluctant to push their advantage right after achieving victories, d'Espèrey ordered his troops to chase down the fleeing Bulgarians, something that proved to be extremely effective. Although the Allied advance was stretched somewhat thin by September 20th, the Bulgarians had virtually nothing to answer them with.

The word of the defeat spread quickly in Bulgaria, as well as to the rest of the Central Powers. Since all of the Allied advances were largely simultaneous, it resulted in a massive domino effect. The Ottoman Empire, for example, had suffered defeats in the Middle East and was increasingly wary of Allied advances in the Balkans, which threatened the safety of Istanbul. Bulgaria was swept up in a nationwide protest, resulting in the Radomir

Rebellion, which blamed the monarchy for the recent defeats. By September 29th, the Allies had made even more progress, taking Skopje and threatening to encircle and capture the remaining Bulgarian forces.

On the same day, the Bulgarian delegation, having already deemed the continuation of the war impossible, arrived in Salonica to meet with the Allies and sign an armistice. It was yet another defeat for the Central Powers, which now had their southern flank and the heart of Austria-Hungary's territories exposed to the Allies. The instability and rebellion in Bulgaria forced Tsar Ferdinand I to abdicate and go into exile. Meanwhile, the Allies split up their forces to close in on Budapest and Istanbul.

Chapter 15 – The War Ends

With the Ottoman Empire and Bulgaria forced to sign separate armistices with the Allies, the rest of the Central Powers—Germany and Austria-Hungary—knew their days were numbered. The Allies had also overwhelmed the German defenses at the Hindenburg Line and threatened to advance through the heart of Germany, while Austro-Hungarian clashes on the Italian front had produced a disastrous stalemate and demoralized the Austro-Hungarian soldiers. Faced with crisis after crisis, the Central Powers realized they had lost the war.

The Final Surrender

By October of 1918, all of Germany knew that the war had been lost. There was no possible way in which the Central Powers could recover from their losses. The German high command felt humiliated, as they could not effectively end the war in their favor, despite the initial success they had seen in the first two years of the war. In a desperate move, the German naval command ordered the High Seas Fleet to engage in a final decisive battle against the British Royal Navy, which had choked out the former in the North Sea and had clearly asserted its dominance over the seas throughout the course of the war.

However, after receiving these orders in late October, the German sailors refused to leave the ports to fight, believing that the battle would have no value since the war was already lost. The word of the mutinies of Wilhelmshaven and Kiel on October 29th and November 3rd quickly spread throughout the desperate, war-torn country. Eventually, it amounted to something much bigger than soldiers disregarding orders.

Participants of the sailor's revolt took to the streets, inciting similar anti-war protests throughout Germany. In Berlin, thousands of people protested the war, believing that their lives had been negatively affected by years of conflict. Things were not looking great for the monarchy and the government, which decided to proceed somewhat peacefully by not trying to violently crush the revolts. On November 9th, 1918, the protesters, led by the leaders of the German Social Democratic Party, proclaimed a republic instead of the imperial monarchy, forcing Kaiser Wilhelm II to flee the country and abdicate in the coming weeks. Prince Maximillian von Baden, the chancellor who had been appointed in early October, ceded his office to Friedrich Ebert. The revolutionaries had triumphed.

Protesters in Germany during the revolution.
https://commons.wikimedia.org/wiki/File:Germany_at_the_End_of_the_First_World_War,_Including_Scenes_of_the_German_Revolution,_1918-1919._MH34191.jpg

The new government's first move was to sue for peace. The negotiations of a potential armistice and peace terms were already being discussed in October in Germany and among the Allies, who were confident they had won. Two days after the revolution's success, the German delegation, led by Matthias Erzberger, arrived at the front lines and met with the Allied high command. The two sides started to discuss terms, although the Germans had nothing to negotiate with. The German high command had made it clear to accept all terms of the armistice to immediately stop the fighting and avoid any more casualties. On November 11th, the Germans accepted the terms of the armistice presented. It was a humiliating display, as the Germans were forced to demobilize their army, surrender all of their military equipment and guns, and evacuate their forces from all locations. Germany was out of the war. It had been defeated and torn apart, but it still had to await the final consequences.

Parallel to the events of the revolution, a separate armistice was signed by Austria-Hungary on November 3rd with the Italians. After months of stalemate, the decisive battle that decided the fate of the war was the Battle of Vittorio Veneto, where the Italians, supported by other Allied divisions, finally achieved a significant victory, inflicting more than 500,000 casualties on the Austro-Hungarians. This marked the end of fighting on the Italian front.

The Austro-Hungarians, much like their German allies, had exhausted all of their resources, and the toll of the war had been evident on the population. Pietro Badoglio and an Austro-Hungarian delegation led by General Viktor von Webenau signed the armistice at Villa Giusti, which was outside of the small town of Padua in northeastern Italy. The armistice was put into effect the very next day. Austria-Hungary was forced to retreat back to the pre-war borders and evacuate all of its troops. Italy moved in to occupy Innsbruck and North Tyrol with about twenty thousand men.

The Paris Peace Conference

With the separate armistices signed by all four of the Central Powers, the war was finally over. The fighting stopped in November on all fronts, and soldiers from both sides abandoned their positions. As the defeated countries started carrying out the terms of the different armistices, the Allied nations rejoiced. For France and Britain, the successful end of the war brought a much-needed sigh of relief. After millions dead, different towns and settlements destroyed, and the landscape torn apart from years of heavy artillery fire, the Allies expected their victory to have been worth it. Thus, in order to formally end the war, the victorious nations organized a conference in Paris to start peace negotiations with the defeated countries and decide what was next for the world, which had just experienced the bloodiest conflict in history so far.

In the ensuing Paris Peace Conference, which started in January 1919, representatives from thirty-two nations around the world assembled to create a new world order, something that was very much reminiscent of the Congress of Vienna after the defeat of Napoleon. Although the formal peace negotiations would last until 1923, the outcome of the talks was based on the Paris Peace Conference.

The beginning of the conference was stalled until January, mostly by British Prime Minister David Lloyd George, who wanted to wait for the results of domestic elections before engaging in negotiations. The "Big Four" presided over the negotiations and had largely agreed upon the outcome by privately consulting with each other. The "Big Four" consisted of Britain, represented by a delegation led by Prime Minister David Lloyd George; President Woodrow Wilson of the US, whose unfortunate illness caused Robert Lansing to assume his position; Prime Minister Georges Clemenceau of France; and Italian Prime Minister Vittorio Emanuele Orlando. Japan, the other major Allied power, is often excluded from the "Big Four" by historians, despite the fact that it was well represented during the conference and achieved favorable gains from the talks.

Representatives also assembled from the British Dominion, including Canada, Australia, India, South Africa, and New Zealand, although they were regarded as "supporters" of British views and assigned the status of minor powers due to their heavy contribution to the overall war effort. Delegations were present from the remaining belligerents of the war, like Greece and Romania, while the Serbs were represented together with the Croats and Slovenes. In addition to those nations, delegations were present from South and Central America, as well as from Asia. Finally, some delegations represented countries that sought international recognition and sovereignty, such as the Baltic states, Ukraine, the Caucasus, and so on. All in all, the Paris Peace Conference included nearly all of the existing sovereign countries in the world, something that stressed the importance of the conference even more.

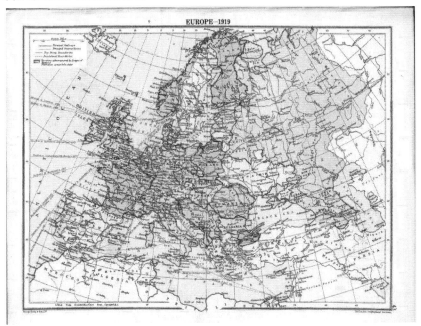

Europe after the Paris Peace Conference.
https://commons.wikimedia.org/wiki/File:Europe_map_1919.jpg

As expected, the negotiations were led by the victorious nations, which sought to maximize their gains while also weakening the defeated belligerents as much as possible to avoid another war from breaking out on the same scale and magnitude. The five official peace treaties that would be signed by the Allies and members of the Central Powers were prepared over the course of the conference. These included the infamous Treaty of Versailles with Germany, signed on June 28th, 1919; the Treaties of Saint-Germain and Trianon, which were signed separately by the two monarchies of Austria and Hungary on September 10th, 1919, and June 4th, 1920, respectively; the Treaty of Neuilly with Bulgaria, signed on November 27th, 1919; and, finally, the Treaty of Sèvres with the Ottoman Empire on August 10th, 1920, which would be replaced by the Treaty of Lausanne three years later.

In addition to these treaties, an important outcome of the Paris Peace Conference was the formation of the League of Nations, the first international organization that sought to establish and preserve world peace. The creation of the League of Nations was largely influenced by President Woodrow Wilson in his efforts to spread what is now referred to as "Wilsonian idealism," an approach to international relations that endorses demilitarization, cooperation, and a peaceful resolution. President Wilson had propagated the idea of international cooperation since his famous "Fourteen Points" speech in January 1918, where he proposed the fourteen terms that should be reached for an effective conclusion of World War I. Throughout the Paris Peace Conference, America's decisions were largely shaped by this concept, which envisioned the creation of a peaceful international community and the pursuit of a united plan of action, one based on mutual friendship rather than rivalry.

Aftermath

The Paris Peace Conference had an immense impact on the world, as it decided the lives of millions of people. The Allies, finally having achieved victory after four years of brutal fighting and experiencing hardship after hardship, made sure to leverage their privilege as the victors. Out of the five treaties that were agreed upon in the conference, the Treaty of Versailles was undoubtedly the harshest and had massive implications for decades to come. It was signed in the Palace of Versailles almost fifty years after the formal creation of the German Empire.

The Allies made Germany suffer the most out of the defeated nations. According to the humiliating terms of the agreement, Germany agreed to take all the blame for causing World War I and the subsequent damage and loss of life that had transpired during the conflict. It clearly outlined Germany as the main aggressor in the war. The Allies also made Germany sign off on the complete demobilization and dissolution of its army. In addition, Germany had to make substantial territorial concessions, giving up about 10 percent of its European territories and all of its overseas colonies, which were swiftly divided between Britain, France, and Japan. Germany was also forced to pay an absurd amount in war reparations for the damages it had caused to the Allied nations. the total amounted to about 132 billion German marks, which is equivalent to about 270 billion USD today.

All of these measures were taken to make sure that Germany would never rise up again and contest the Great Powers' superiority on the continent. The French were exceptionally hard on the Germans, as they had a personal score to settle with the Germans. They took back control of the Alsace and Lorraine provinces they had lost in 1871.

All in all, the Treaty of Versailles had a devastating effect on Germany. The economy was in ruins after the war, and massive international and domestic debt meant there was little room to improve the situation. The newly established Weimar Republic—a name temporarily adopted by Germany after the revolution—had no way of dealing with the problems that cropped up after the Paris Peace Conference. Germany's international role was reduced beyond belief, and to ensure that Germany stayed pacified, the Allies occupied the Rhineland for the next fifteen years, with troops present at all times.

The German public had lost all hope of retaliation and was faced with extreme poverty, hunger, and tough living conditions. This, in turn, incited a sense of hatred toward the Allies, something that would finally be exploited in the 1930s by the Nazi Party and the rise of Hitler. Germany's humiliation made it possible for radical nationalist movements to become prominent in the country as time passed by, with more and more people being upset over the fact that the whole war had been blamed on them by their enemies. It would have been interesting to see how Germany would have developed if the international community had actually helped Germany recover instead of overly punishing it after the war.

The German Empire was not the only one that saw disastrous outcomes after the war. Austria-Hungary, as a single political entity, was disbanded, and in the lands previously controlled by the dual monarchy, new democratic nation-states were established. Some parts were absorbed by Italy, as promised by the Allies. With Austria-Hungary's dissolution, the political landscape of Europe was completely altered, and a new power dynamic emerged. All of those nations that had previously been under the control of the Habsburgs finally achieved freedom, and their sovereignty was internationally recognized, giving these young states new hopes and aspirations to pursue. Among the newly formed nations were

Poland (for the first time in over a century), Ukraine, Belarus, Czechoslovakia, the separate states of Austria and Hungary, as well as a new Yugoslavian state, which had been predominantly inhabited by Serbs, Croats, and Slovenes.

It was also an end for the Ottoman Empire, which was reduced to only its Anatolian territories, as well as the small European part of Constantinople (Istanbul). It lost all of its Middle Eastern and Mesopotamian territories, with France and Britain seizing control of the region and dividing it between themselves. There, the two European powers organized "protectorates," two separate spheres of influence, something which, in hindsight, further contributed to the rising tensions in the region during the rest of the 20th century. The Ottoman Empire was formally reestablished as the Republic of Turkey following the Paris Peace Conference.

This was the political landscape that emerged from the ashes of World War I. It completely changed Europe, with four fewer empires than there had been in 1914: the German Empire was now the Weimer Republic; Austria-Hungary had been divided into multiple smaller nations, including the separate republics of Austria and Hungary; Turkey replaced the Ottoman Empire; and, finally, the Russian Revolution of 1917 had seen the Russian Empire reorganized as a soviet state. A new world order was established, with clearly defined, internationally recognized state boundaries that were, in most cases, in line with the national boundaries of different peoples. Nationalism and liberty had triumphed, an outcome that seemed inevitable even before the start of the war.

Conclusion

The League of Nations was supposed to lead the new world into a period of peace and prosperity. While the mission of this first intergovernmental organization was noble and respectable, as time would show, it would not be able to achieve its goals. The League of Nations could not hold a firm grip over the actions of sovereign nations, which were still motivated by self-interest and pursued their national goals instead of what was best for the international community. Other members of the League of Nations watched these states from a distance, reluctant to intervene on multiple occasions and reassert the organization's dominance. Thus, over time, the League of Nations lost its role and importance. A peaceful and prosperous world, one built on cooperation and mutual understanding as perceived by President Wilson, was challenged by individual actors that destroyed the organization's credibility. The inability of the League of Nations to act eventually manifested itself in World War II, which broke out just twenty-one years after the end of World War I.

The Great War had brought destruction on a previously unseen scale, with an estimated forty million casualties on both sides. About ten million civilians around the world were lost, in addition to about the same number of military personnel. While it is difficult to know the exact number of people whose lives were affected by the war, it is clear when observing the post-war states of the belligerents that the effects of the war lasted for years. Those soldiers who survived relentless, non-stop fighting on the front lines suffered from severe anxiety, PTSD, and other psychological problems. Living in such harsh conditions for months on end, under the threat of constant shelling by enemy artillery and in muddy, overcrowded trenches with low supplies, had certainly taken its toll on the survivors. As they returned back from the war to their homes, they had to pass through miles of destroyed terrain and hundreds of ruined towns.

In the end, the First World War only became "the First" after the events of the 1940s, which saw the world plunge into turmoil again, although the Second World War was far more catastrophic. The First World War did not "stop all conflicts," as many had predicted, including the winners. What emerged from the ruins was a more complex global system, in which the war's winners enjoyed various privileges while the losers were purposefully isolated and made to feel guilty for the world's problems.

The victorious nations attempted to enact policies that would maintain peace and stability throughout the period of recovery, but their efforts were in vain, as the international order formed immediately after World War I would only continue for thirty years. Their efforts failed terribly, and the world's rapid collapse into yet another world war in 1939 made everyone recognize that the paradigm adopted after 1918 was fundamentally flawed. It had been based on the redistribution of power at the expense of millions of people living in the defeated nations. The losers' suffering was effectively exploited by the winners, but no one anticipated that their efforts would result in another conflict that would eclipse the First World War in nearly every way.

Part 2: World War II

An Enthralling Guide to the Second World War

WORLD
WAR II

AN ENTHRALLING GUIDE TO THE SECOND WORLD WAR

ENTHRALLING HISTORY

Introduction

More often than not, World War II is associated with the Holocaust and Hitler.

While this is not *untrue*, it is also not quite so simple. In the 1930s, by the time Adolf Hitler came along with a desire to conquer Europe, there were already many complex issues at play. The rise of Nazism and Hitler's power grab in Europe served to create the perfect storm, unleashing a chain of events that is now known as World War II.

Hundreds and thousands of books, articles, and journals have been written about the war, the Holocaust, and how the events from those six critical years continue to influence the world we live in today. With so much information available, it can be difficult to decipher the important points and events. The purpose of this book is to provide an accurate, concise, and comprehensive account of the key events of World War II in an easy-to-understand and enjoyable manner.

The book will begin with a brief look at how less than a quarter of a century after the end of one major global conflict, the world became embroiled in a second, perhaps far more disastrous one. It will also provide a clear understanding of the background to determine what led to the Second World War, as well as a look at the major events of the war.

Section One: The War Summarized (1939–1945)

Chapter 1: Invasion and Attack (1939–1941)

Starting as early as 1931, a global crisis was brewing. There were already rumblings of disquiet and tension in many parts of Asia and Europe. The United States withdrew completely from European affairs, choosing to take an isolationist stance.

However, when discussing World War II, the focus is often on Hitler's "rise and fall." As such, historically, World War II is officially said to have begun with Nazi Germany's invasion of Poland in 1939.

To understand why Hitler's Germany invaded Poland and why this act dragged most of the world's major players into the fray, we need to go back to 1919, to the end of the First World War.

After four years of war, on November 11th, 1918, an armistice was signed by the Germans and the Allied countries, officially bringing World War I to an end.

Brief Overview of World War I

World War I, also known as the Great War, started in 1914 with the assassination of Archduke Franz Ferdinand of Austria by Serbian nationalist Gavrilo Princip. With the support of German Kaiser Wilhelm II, war was declared against Serbia.

Serbia turned to Russia for help, and within a week, major European players were picking sides and joining the war. The Great War was fought between the Central Powers (Austria-Hungary, Bulgaria, Germany, and the Ottoman Empire) and the Allied Powers (France, Russia, Italy, Great Britain, Canada, United States, Romania, and Japan).

Technological advances in weapons and the use of poisonous gas led to a no-holds-bar type of war. The loss of lives was catastrophic. Over sixteen million civilians and soldiers lost their lives.

By 1918, it was evident the Central Powers were losing the war, and one by one, they began to surrender; Germany was the last hold-out. When it finally signed the armistice on November 11th, 1918, World War I officially came to an end.

Once the dust settled, it became apparent just how shocking the events of the war had been and what a trail of devastation it had left around the world. The carnage was so horrific and devastating that the Allies were determined that such a thing would never happen again.

Reshaping of Europe

After the war ended, four of the world's empires collapsed. As part of the peace talks, the Allies reshaped Europe and distributed territories that formally belonged to the Russian Empire, the German Empire, the Ottoman Empire, and the Austro-Hungarian Empire. Countries like Poland, Czechoslovakia, Hungary, Lithuania, and Turkey were created, while German colonies in the continent of Africa were divided between the Allies as part of the League of Nations' "mandates."

The redrawing of the European map would have far-reaching consequences and play a pivotal role in the Second World War.

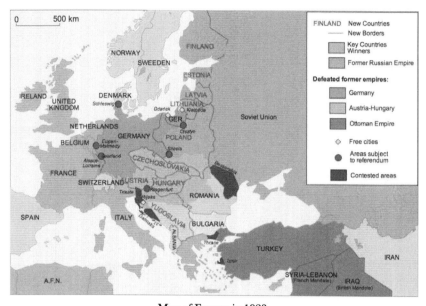

Map of Europe in 1923.
Paris Peace Conference – Fluteflute;
https://en.wikipedia.org/wiki/File:Map_Europe_1923-en.svg

Divisions also happened in Asia, with Japan gaining control of Shandong Province. This was unacceptable to China since Shandong was part of its mainland. China also refused to sign the Treaty of Versailles.

What Was the Treaty of Versailles?

When the Allied leaders met in 1919 at the Paris Peace Conference, they decided the Great War had to be the "war to end all wars." The leaders expressed their intention of putting measures in place to prevent a future world war.

In June 1919, leaders from Great Britain, the United States, and France, among other nations, met at the Palace of Versailles in Paris and signed the Treaty of Versailles.

The four big leaders at the Treaty of Versailles
https://commons.wikimedia.org/wiki/File:Big_four.jpg

The treaty's main purpose was to outline the terms of peace at the end of the war. It was also designed to be punishing and humiliating for Germany. The treaty placed the blame of the war squarely on Germany's shoulders and imposed numerous penalties on the country.

For instance, Germany had to pay reparations, give up territories it had seized, and demilitarize, which limited Germany's land and naval forces (its air force was completely disbanded). The treaty did not try to understand or resolve the main issues or tensions that had led to the war. Instead, the Allies hoped severe punishments would ensure peace throughout Europe.

The Treaty of Versailles also set the stage for the creation of the League of Nations. The league was Woodrow Wilson's brainchild, and its purpose was to create an international organization that maintained world peace by mediating and resolving any conflicts before they got out of hand.

The League of Nations was a great idea in theory, but it suffered growing pains. The countries were not always good at putting aside their own self-interest, while key players, such as Germany, were forbidden from joining the organization. The League of Nations was disbanded during World War II (a war it had failed to prevent) and eventually evolved into what we know today as the United Nations.

Ironically, the Treaty of Versailles, the very thing designed to promote peace in Europe, indirectly led to the start of World War II since none of the long-simmering issues had actually been addressed or resolved.

The humiliating terms of the treaty crippled Germany's economy and caused growing resentment among the Germans. Many saw it as a punishment rather than an attempt at finding peace and harmony. This unrest gave Hitler the ideal platform to garner support for the Nazi Party and rise to power.

Causes of the Second World War

Anschluss

Trouble had been brewing in Europe long before the start of the Second World War. One of the issues at play was an *Anschluss*. The term refers to the creation of a "Greater Germany" where Austria and Germany would be united together.

After the end of WWI, the Republic of German-Austria wanted to unite with Germany but was not allowed to do so under the terms of the Treaty of Versailles. In fact, some of Austria's territories, like the Sudetenland, were taken away.

When Hitler, who was born in Austria, came to power, he dreamed of a unified Germany.

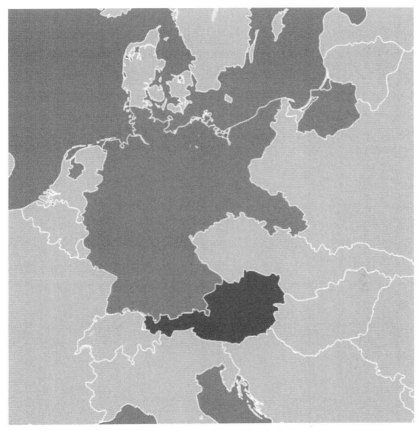

A map of the Anschluss, March 1938.

In 1920, after Hitler joined the National Socialist German Workers' Party (NSDAP), he stressed the importance of unifying "all Germans in the Greater Germany on the basis of the people's right to self-determination."[1] This sentiment and desire to unite Austria and Germany were reiterated by Hitler in his book, *Mein Kampf.*

Austria had also suffered greatly after WWI due to its unstable economy and high unemployment rate. A combination of Hitler coming into power and Nazi propaganda led to the Austrian Nazi Party's growing popularity in the country. The desire to join

---

[1] Hamann, Brigitte (2010). *Hitler's Vienna: A Portrait of the Tyrant as a Young Man.* Tauris Parke Paperbacks. p.107. ISBN 9781848852778.

Germany also grew as slogans like "One People, One Empire, One Leader" gained traction and swept through the nation.

Had things continued in this fashion, it is almost certain that the *Anschluss* would have happened. However, the Austrian Nazis began to use terrorist tactics to attack the Austrian government. They attempted a coup in July 1934. The coup failed, and power was taken by an authoritarian right-wing government.

In the meantime, during the 1930s, as Germany began rearming, Austria had become a rich source of both labor and raw materials. Germany desperately needed its resources. When Austrian Nazis began to make plans for a second coup, Austrian Chancellor Kurt von Schuschnigg set up a meeting with Hitler. He wanted to ensure Austria could remain an independent country. But under pressure from Hitler, he ended up appointing high-ranking Austrian Nazis to his government and calling a national vote to settle the matter of the *Anschluss*.

This was not enough for Hitler, though. Schuschnigg was faced with an ultimatum of an invasion, and he resigned from his position on March 11th, 1938. The national vote never took place.

Before resigning, Schuschnigg asked for help from countries like France, Italy, and Britain, but nobody wanted to interfere in the matter. During his resignation, Schuschnigg advised the Austrian people not to fight back against Germany should they advance into Austrian territory. He was arrested by the Nazis and taken away as a prisoner soon after.

On March 12th, German troops marched into a cheering Austria. Hitler established a Nazi government and declared *Anschluss* on March 13th. The country became a part of the Reich, and Austria ceased to be an independent nation.

As Hitler annexed Austria, the other powers did nothing, even though this was a direct violation of the Treaty of Versailles. Buoyed by his success, Hitler turned his sights on Czechoslovakia.

Invasion of the Czech Provinces

Within months of annexing Austria, it was clear to the world that Hitler's next move would be to occupy Czechoslovakia.

France and Great Britain had both promised to help the country; however, they did not wish to enter into another war.

They instead decided to compromise with Germany to maintain the peace.

After several back-and-forth messages between France, Germany, Britain, and Italy, the Sudetenland was handed over to Germany under the Munich Agreement. In exchange, Hitler pledged not to wage war in Europe. Czechoslovakia was not consulted in the matter and was told it could accept the decision or take on the German Army alone.

Ethnic Germans in the Sudetenland greet German troops with the Nazi salute.
Bundesarchiv, Bild 146-1970-005-28 / CC-BY-SA 3.0, CC BY-SA 3.0 DE
<https://creativecommons.org/licenses/by-sa/3.0/de/deed.en>, via Wikimedia Commons;
https://commons.wikimedia.org/wiki/File:Bundesarchiv_Bild_146-1970-005-
28,_Anschluss_sudetendeutscher_Gebiete.jpg

Czechoslovakia had no choice but to accept. Great Britain and France believed they had averted a crisis and prevented another war. They were wrong. Not even six months later, on March 15th, 1939, Hitler violated the terms of the Munich Agreement and sent his troops into Bohemia and Moravia, annexing the provinces to the Reich.

Once again, the powers in Europe said nothing. They made some faint protests, but there were no real repercussions for Germany from breaking the Munich Agreement.

Invasion of Poland

Hitler's ultimate dream and goal was to create one unified German Empire and conquer Europe. Six months after annexing the rest of Czechoslovakia and receiving little more than a slap on the wrist, Hitler invaded Poland on September 1st, 1939.

Poland had a weak military, and Hitler knew if he moved quickly, he could easily gain control of the country. He correctly assumed that none of the European powers would intervene in time to stop him.

When Hitler invaded Poland, the Soviet Union was already on his side. The two nations had made a secret agreement called the Hitler-Stalin Pact, Nazi-Soviet Pact, or Molotov-Ribbentrop Pact (named after the foreign ministers of the countries who signed the pact). The pact essentially guaranteed that neither country would declare war on the other. It also included some secret provisions to divide up some of the smaller countries, including Poland, between them.

Hitler's troops invaded Poland soon after the pact was signed, and the Soviet Union made no protests. Instead, Stalin began preparing his own troops for an invasion of Poland.

And now the world leaders began to get a little worried.

Blitzkrieg

When Germany invaded Poland, the country put up a valiant effort to resist Hitler's troops. However, the under-equipped and unprepared Polish forces were no match for Germany's calculated bombarding and blitzkrieg strategy. Within a month of German forces advancing on Warsaw, the Polish army surrendered.

The blitzkrieg approach is how Hitler intended to win the war in Europe. This approach basically meant immobilizing the enemy as quickly as possible via whatever means necessary. For Hitler's troops, this involved the Luftwaffe (the German air force) relentlessly bombing the country they were invading so that communication lines, railroads, important landmarks, offices, and other key areas were completely destroyed and rendered useless.

A German dive bomber.
https://commons.wikimedia.org/wiki/File:Henschel_Hs_123_in_flight.jpg

The bombing was followed by tanks and troops moving in to take whatever they could. The final step was for the infantry to come through and do a final sweep, removing any final obstacles along the way.

Within days of an invasion, the troops were ordered to set up a base to control the country and gather intelligence. The security forces were given orders to get rid of anyone who opposed Nazi ideology. Concentration camps were also quickly set up.

By 1939, the Nazis had become something of an expert in the creation of concentration camps. The very first one, Dachau, had been built six years prior, soon after Hitler became chancellor of Germany. Although that camp was used for political prisoners, it would later be used as a model for the other concentration camps that were built during the Holocaust, most of which were built for a very different purpose.

The concentration camps were managed by the SS (the Schutzstaffel or "Protection Squad"). Within a day of his troops invading Poland, Hitler had already organized SS regiments whose sole purpose was to ignite fear and obedience among the Polish people.

While Germany took control and annexed eastern Poland, Stalin sent his troops in to annex western Poland.

With the invasion of Poland, Hitler had finally overstepped. Great Britain and France, which had done everything they could to stay out of another conflict, declared war on Germany on September 3rd, 1939.

World War II had begun.

Beginning of the Holocaust

When German forces took over Poland, Nazi ideologies and beliefs began to be enforced almost immediately. Hundreds of thousands of Polish people were sent away, allowing ethnic Germans to settle in their homes instead, while Nazi policies began to be introduced.

On November 23rd, 1939, the Nazi governor general in Poland decreed that Jewish people had to wear a white armband with a blue Star of David on it. This helped the Nazis identify and separate the Jews from the rest of the population.

An armband seller in the Warsaw ghetto.
https://www.timesofisrael.com/new-book-dredges-up-warsaw-ghetto-police-who-sent-fellow-jews-to-their-deaths/

Jewish people were also enlisted to work in camps as slaves. As the war progressed and Hitler's power grew, the fate of the Jewish people would become far worse. The Nazi Party would devise the

"Final Solution" to solve the Jewish problem.

Hitler's European Conquest: An Overview

After Poland, Hitler and his troops were like a war machine, rapidly sweeping through parts of Europe and invading and conquering country after country. And they found victory every time.

Poland was defeated and occupied within weeks in September 1939. The following year in April 1940, Hitler took over Denmark and Norway just as easily. A month later, Belgium, Luxembourg, the Netherlands, and France were occupied by Nazi forces.

When Hitler tried to invade Great Britain, the British navy protected the English Channel while the Royal Air Force defended the skies. Hitler's German forces were unable to defeat either and had to turn back.

After abandoning his plans to invade Great Britain, Hitler set his sights elsewhere instead. In April 1941, he took Yugoslavia and Greece. Two months after this, Hitler suddenly and without provocation decided to go after the Soviet Union.

This would be the beginning of the end.

But before we get to that, let's take a closer look at some key battles and events.

The Battle of Dunkirk

A small coastal town in northern France near the French-Belgian border, Dunkirk (or Dunkerque) had been the site of many battles long before Hitler's troops invaded. However, it is most associated with WW2 and the critical role it played in the war effort. The Battle of Dunkirk was fought for less than two weeks and signified the end of the "phony war." It would be a turning point in the war for the Allies.

The seven months between September 1939 and April 1940, when Hitler was rapidly moving around Europe collecting countries like trophies with little fighting, is often referred to as the "phony war." Even though war had been declared, the fighting hadn't started in earnest.

This changed as soon as Hitler began a blitzkrieg attack on Belgium, the Netherlands, and Luxembourg. It didn't take his forces long to occupy all three countries, and within a period of three weeks, Hitler had taken over all three.

France was expecting to be invaded next, so it was prepared. However, Hitler sent his troops not along the Maginot Line (a line made by the French consisting of concrete barriers and fortifications) but by the Somme Valley, near the English Channel.

The French were not expecting this.

As the German forces continued to advance, the British and French forces were pushed back and left trapped on the French coast. It soon became apparent to the Allied forces that they had to evacuate Dunkirk since they had no hope of winning against the German forces.

Thankfully, Hitler ordered his troops to stop advancing because he was worried about a counterattack from the Allies. By stopping his troops, he inadvertently gave the British and French forces enough time to prepare for an evacuation.

A couple of days later, when Hitler urged his troops forward again, plans were already in place for Operation Dynamo. Despite the vicious German bombing attacks on the shores of Dunkirk, the Allied forces were able to evacuate over 338,000 troops.

Approximately ninety thousand troops were left behind. They were unable to push back the German offensive. The German forces continued with their blitzkrieg invasion. Dunkirk surrendered to German troops on June 4th, and the country collapsed on June 22nd.

Why was Dunkirk so important to the Allied forces when they had been so soundly defeated? Even though the Allies did not win the battle, it was seen as a success and referred to as the "Miracle at Dunkirk" because the vast majority of the troops had been rescued.

Hitler believed the blitzkrieg attack of France would lead to Great Britain bowing out of the war, clearing the path for him to take over Europe. However, this did not happen.

The Battle of Dunkirk was a symbolic win for the Allies and strengthened their resolve, determination, and perseverance to continue the war effort.

The Battle of Britain

Following the fall of France, Hitler believed it would only be a matter of weeks before he gained control of Great Britain as well. In fact, he believed the war was over and that he had won. When Great Britain did not crumble or bow out of the war, instead making it very clear the war would continue, Hitler started to reconsider his options.

But before this big loss, Hitler was dreaming of a quick victory. On July 16th, 1940, Hitler declared his intention to invade the country and started preparing for it. The invasion was given the name Operation Sea Lion.

Despite all of the German Army's previous victories and successes across Europe, it was woefully unprepared for the invasion. The German forces had not received any training; they did not have enough aircraft and had very little experience with crossing a sea while waging a war. German admirals felt their best option for a successful invasion would be to attack via the skies.

Hermann Göring, one of Hitler's most trusted military leaders, felt confident the Luftwaffe could take on the Royal Air Force (RAF) through an air offensive. They decided the goal would be to simply wear down the country's air defenses and deplete its resources until German forces could gain control.

On July 10th, the Germans started bomber attacks on ports and convoys. This continued for nearly a month until August 13th, when the main offensive called "Eagle Attack" began. Air bases, factories, and radar stations were all targets. Germany had larger troops and more fighters than England. But the British had Chain Home, a far superior radar system. Chain Home allowed for early warnings of Luftwaffe attacks, which allowed the British forces to be prepared.

Britain also had better aircraft. The twin-engine German bombers didn't have the capability to render utter destruction, and their dive bombers were easy to shoot down. Some of their other jets couldn't fly long distances. The RAF did not have these issues.

The inferiority in the Germans' equipment led them to lose almost half their aircraft within a month of invading Britain, while the British only lost about a third. Germany was also carrying out the invasion in an inconsistent manner and dropping bombs in civilian areas of London. The Germans said this was done accidentally, but Britain, nonetheless, retaliated by bombing Berlin, much to Hitler's fury.

Following the raid on Berlin, Hitler ordered the Luftwaffe to start attacking other cities. For nearly two months, London was subjected to nightly raids. But Britain held strong, and by the middle of September, German bombers were being shot down at an alarming rate.

The RAF was so deadly and precise that the Luftwaffe changed tactics and began to carry out their attacks at night only. These attacks were known as the Blitz and resulted in tens of thousands of civilian deaths.

German forces made no major headway or advancement through these raids. They were unable to dominate the British skies, and it quickly became clear to Hitler that he was fighting a losing battle.

In early September, he decided to cut his losses and announced the invasion of Britain would be pushed back by a few weeks. By October, he had decided to halt the operation since winter was coming.

The German troops withdrew, and by the time spring arrived, Hitler was looking at Russia with renewed interest. Plans to invade England were put on the back burner.

Whether Germany wanted to admit it or not, Great Britain had soundly defeated them.

Invasion of Russia

Even though Hitler had signed a non-aggression pact with Stalin prior to invading Poland, he never intended to honor the pact and only saw it as a temporary measure while he focused elsewhere. Getting rid of the communist Soviet Union and expanding his empire into Eastern Europe had long been cherished dreams for Hitler. In fact, going back as early as the 1920s, some core Nazi ideologies included eradicating communism and seizing land in Russia for German settlement.

The invasion of the Soviet Union was codenamed Operation Barbarossa. It was an enormous military operation involving over 3,500,000 troops. The order for the invasion had been planned well in advance, and Hitler signed the directive in December 1940.

The following year, on June 22nd, 1941, German troops officially invaded Russia.

The invasion took Russia completely by surprise. For months, the Allies had warned Russia that this was coming their way, but they did not believe it. And it did not take Hitler long to destroy Russia's air force, which was stationed on the ground.

A significant portion of the Soviet Army was trapped by German forces and forced to surrender. The army was followed by the Einsatzgruppen (SS death squads), whose role was to identify threats, eliminate the threat, gather intelligence, and establish intelligence networks.

The Einsatzgruppen was also known as "mobile killing squads." They played a key role in the extermination of Jews. Mass shootings were conducted by the mobile killing units. Anyone who was viewed as a threat to Nazi Germany was shot dead by the SS. While mass killings took place, millions of other citizens were deliberately starved by the Nazis and eventually died due to mistreatment.

The Soviet Union began to be used as a place to send German Jews and eventually evolved into the "Final Solution."

Although the Soviet Union was initially overwhelmed by Hitler's invasion, the country did not collapse. Halfway through August 1941, they started to push back, making the invasion anything but an easy victory.

Nonetheless, the German forces continued to make strides. By December, they had finally made it to the outskirts of Moscow. But they were unprepared for the Russian winter. Hitler had expected to gain full control of the Soviet Union by fall and had not planned ahead for the cold months. As a result, the army was exhausted, ill-equipped, and half-starved. When Russia launched its counterattack, it was able to easily drive the Germans away from Moscow.

The Tripartite Act

While Hitler was focused on invading European countries, Japan and Italy were busy waging wars and signing agreements to benefit their interests.

Several years before invading Poland, on October 25th, 1936, Germany and Italy signed the Rome-Berlin Axis. In November of the same year, Japan signed the Anti-Comintern Pact and joined the Axis powers. This pact was basically an anti-communist pact and was also signed by Italy in 1937. The pact fell apart when Hitler and Stalin signed their non-aggression pact in 1939 so that Germany could invade Poland without Soviet interference.

In 1940, the Axis powers (Germany, Italy, and Japan) held a meeting in Berlin with the intention of creating a defense alliance. This became the Tripartite Pact.

Under the terms of the Tripartite Pact, each country had to "assist one another with all political, economic and military means." The attack had to be by a power "at present not involved in the European War or in the Sino-Japanese Conflict."

It was deliberately worded in this manner to warn the United States to stay out of the war. Some other European countries, like Hungary, Croatia, and Romania, would go on to sign the pact as well, but most of them were forced or threatened to do so.

For the most part, the Tripartite Pact served no real purpose since the Axis countries were each pursuing their own interests and agendas. It was only invoked once, after Japan bombed Pearl Harbor on December 7th, 1941.

Why Japan Bombed Pearl Harbor

Japan attacked the United States partially due to mounting tensions and partially as a preventative measure. While Europe was busy fighting with each other, Japan was quietly working away at building its own empire near the turn of the 20th century.

After waging two wars with great success and fighting in WWI with the Allies, Japan now had bigger dreams. The biggest challenge to the country's expansion was the lack of natural resources.

The solution was simple: invade Manchuria. The League of Nations frowned upon this invasion of China, so Japan withdrew from the league.

Following the invasion and capture of Manchuria and an altercation on the Marco Polo Bridge near Beijing, Japan and China were embroiled in the Sino-Japanese War. The Japanese forces quickly captured Nanjing (Nanking). Over a period of six weeks, they carried out mass killings and other atrocities against the Chinese living there.

While the United States had steadfastly refused to engage in any more European conflicts, it wanted to put a stop to these atrocities and put a stop to Japan's plans of global expansion. The US started to impose economic sanctions on the country, including embargoes on oil and other goods.

After months of negotiations, Japan and Washington were unable to resolve their disputes or accept each other's terms. The US maintained its decision to continue with the economic sanctions, which Japan found unacceptable. It was further incensed by the US sticking its nose in and interfering with Asian affairs. Japan knew it needed to do something to retaliate, especially if it wanted to be taken seriously as a major player.

Since the US had such a powerful military, Japan knew its only shot at winning would be to take the US by surprise. The decision was made to bomb Pearl Harbor and destroy the US Pacific Fleet in Hawaii. It was seen as an easy target, and the United States would not be expecting an attack there. Japan hoped the preventive action would stop the US from getting in Japan's way as it continued to advance in Southeast Asia and other overseas territories. The Japanese also hoped to negotiate a peace treaty once they had the upper hand.

Early on the morning of Sunday, December 7th, 1941, at 7:48 a.m., the Japanese began attacking the US base. Three hundred fifty-three Imperial Japanese aircraft were launched from half a dozen aircraft carriers in two separate waves.

A photo of the attack on Pearl Harbor.
https://commons.wikimedia.org/wiki/File:Pearl_harbour.png

Over 180 US aircraft were destroyed, almost twenty ships were either destroyed or damaged, and thousands of Americans were killed and wounded.

Initially, Japan believed its attack was a success. But the Japanese failed to completely destroy the Pacific Fleet since they missed important ammunition sites, oil tanks, and other facilities. Furthermore, not even one US aircraft carrier was at the base at the time of the attack. The attack ultimately turned the tide of the war.

On December 8th, both the United States and Great Britain declared war on Japan and officially entered the war.

Between December 11th and 13th, Germany and its Axis partners declared war against the United States.

The "phony war" was well and truly over. The early stages of Hitler advancing upon Poland and other European countries would seem like child's play compared to the bloodshed and violence yet to come.

With all the major powers of the world declaring war on each other, all bets were off. The world once again found itself plunged right back into the same kind of global conflict the Allies had tried so hard to prevent twenty-five years prior.

Chapter 2: The War Expands 1941–1943

War in the Pacific

Hitler's dream of a European conquest turned into a global war once Japan and the United States entered the picture. Japan was on the side of the Axis, while the US sided with the Allies.

To understand how these countries came to join the war, we have to go back to the early 1930s, a time when there were already grumblings of dissatisfaction quietly spreading around the world.

The conflicts in Asia began years before Hitler's invasion of Poland. They began, in part, because Japan needed raw materials like fuel to keep its industries running. So, on September 18th, 1931, Japan invaded Mukden, a city in the Chinese province of Manchuria.

The Japanese military moved forward ruthlessly and was no match for the Chinese army. By September 21st, with help from Korea, the Japanese army quickly began to take control of the entire province of Manchuria. In a matter of three months, Japanese troops could be found all over the province. The occupation of Manchuria continued until 1945.

The resistance from China was minimal, as Chiang Kai-shek, a Chinese military leader and politician, was busy pursuing his own agenda of gaining control of China. He advised the army not to resist and left the matter up to the League of Nations. The league's investigation found that Japan had behaved in an aggressive manner, but they did not place any sanctions on the country. Japan retaliated by withdrawing its membership from the League of Nations. In 1937, Japan attacked China, beginning the Second Sino-Japanese War.

Second Sino-Japanese War (1937–1945)

When China finally began to resist Japanese expansion by mounting a full-scale resistance, an undeclared war broke out between the two countries.

Historically, the war is divided into three separate phases:

1) Japan's invasion of Manchuria and rapid expansion from 1931 to 1938

2) A stalemate from 1938 to 1944

3) Involvement of the Allies during the Second World War and Japan's surrender

When the United States started to impose sanctions on Japan as a way of curtailing its plans for expansion, Japan sought to gain the upper hand by attacking Pearl Harbor. While there were many factors at play behind the scenes, Pearl Harbor ultimately led to both countries entering the world war on a bigger scale.

The Battle of Midway
(June 4th, 1942, to June 7th, 1942)

Japan saw the United States as a hindrance on its path to expanding its control over East Asia. The Japanese desperately wanted to remove US influence from the Pacific. By attacking Pearl Harbor, they were hoping to do just that. With one swift move, Japan could cripple the US military base and set itself up as the dominant power in the region.

Unfortunately, while Pearl Harbor had been a successful campaign for Japan, it also resulted in the US entering the war.

Undeterred, Japan continued its efforts to claim dominance in the Pacific. This led to the Battle of the Coral Sea in May 1942, where they were soundly turned away by the US Navy.

Believing this to be a minor setback, the commander of the Japanese Navy was determined to have another success like Pearl Harbor. Six months after attacking Pearl Harbor, the Japanese forces were planning another sneak attack, this time on Midway Island, which sat between the two countries. The Japanese hoped this would destroy the remainder of the US Navy located in the Pacific.

They expected this to be a quick and efficient victory; unfortunately, it would become the beginning of the end for Japan's expansion goals.

What Japan did not know was that starting in 1942, US Navy cryptanalysts were secretly breaking the Japanese Navy's JN-25b code. They were privy to messages and communications sent by Japan and knew about Japan's plans to attack a location it named "AF" in the US.

The cryptanalysts suspected the location might be the base at Midway, and this was confirmed when the Americans set a trap for Japan. A fake message was sent out saying that Midway was "short of fresh water."[2] A code was sent out by Japan saying that "AF was short of fresh water." By breaking this code, the US Navy was able to confirm the location. They were also confident the attack would occur on June 4th or 5th.

As a result of breaking these codes, when Japanese aircraft carriers swooped over Midway to begin their attack, the US was ready. Carrier forces were hidden away, and when the Japanese aircraft headed back to refuel and get more arms, the US Navy attacked the fleet and destroyed them.

Only one Japanese carrier survived: the *Hiryu*. It was able to retaliate and cause considerable damage to one of the US ships. Later that day, a scout plane found the *Hiryu* and attacked. The *Hiryu* burned and eventually sank.

An all-out war between the two countries broke out over the next few days as they continued to attack each other relentlessly. The Japanese suffered heavy losses, losing over three thousand men, while the US lost just under four hundred men.

---

[2] "The Battle of Midway." https://www.nationalww2museum.org/war/articles/battle-midway

Mikuma at Midway.
https://commons.wikimedia.org/wiki/File;Japanese_heavy_cruiser_Mikuma_sinking_on_6_June_1942_(80-G-414422).jpg

Although it was fought over just a few days, the Battle of Midway played a very critical role in the war. The US emerged victorious and halted Japan's plans to expand control in the Pacific, leaving the Axis power in a weakened position.

Executive Order 9066

Following the attack on Pearl Harbor, it was not surprising that anti-Japanese sentiment was on the rise. Some of the largest Japanese communities were based in close proximity to the Pacific coast, which was also where many American war assets were located. These communities and Japanese Americans began to be viewed with deep suspicion and mistrust by other Americans.

Military commanders felt nervous about having the "enemy" so close and asked Henry Stimson, the Secretary of War, to do something about it. Henry Stimson turned to the president, Franklin Delano Roosevelt (FDR), who issued Executive Order 9066.

Without making specific mention of the Japanese, President Roosevelt issued the executive order on February 19th, 1942, essentially giving the secretary of war carte blanche to move or evacuate any individual or groups of individuals the government deemed a threat to America's national security.

Even though Japan was not mentioned, the directive was clear. Under this order, Japanese Americans' rights under the Fifth Amendment were denied and revoked. They received no trials and were not given due process. It didn't matter if the individual was a citizen or American by birth. Simply being of Japanese descent was enough.

Within days of the order being issued, over 1,500 leaders in the Japanese community were arrested. Thousands of other Japanese-born individuals had their assets frozen by the government. In southern California, Japanese immigrants began to be forced out of their homes with only a few belongings.

Proclamations establishing military areas were issued, and it was determined that any and all individuals with a Japanese background would have to leave California. The War Relocation Authority was created with the signing of Executive Order 9102 on March 18th, 1942. This was signed to allow a civilian-led agency to help move the immigrants.

Camps were set up across the country to house them. The first group was transferred to the Manzanar War Relocation Center, which was located in the desert in California. The center basically consisted of a series of barracks surrounded by barbed wire. It was guarded by armed troops and would become home to the displaced Japanese for three years.

In total, ten internment camps were set up, and over 120,000 Japanese Americans were incarcerated at these camps.

For all intents and purposes, they had become prisoners and were kept at these camps until the end of the war. Many people's lives were uprooted forever, while others lost everything they had ever worked for.

On December 18th, 1944, nearly two years after the signing of Executive Order 9066, the United States Supreme Court found the government did not have the right to detain any American citizens without just cause. The ruling, while a positive step, did not change the situation of the incarcerated Japanese overnight. It would take over four years for the government to remove everyone from the internment camps.

Three years after the war ended, the Evacuation Claims Act was signed by US President Harry Truman. The act allowed Japanese Americans who had lost their properties and belongings during the relocation to submit claims.

It's deeply unsettling that while fighting the Nazis and the atrocities they were committing against Jewish people, the US government approved the internment of Japanese Americans. Some of the similarities are difficult to ignore. In fact, these centers were initially referred to as "concentration camps." However, after Hitler's concentration camps were discovered, the term was no longer used in America. What's equally shocking is that it would take over three decades for the order to be fully rescinded! It was done so formally on February 16th, 1976, by President Gerald Ford.

The injustice faced by Japanese Americans was officially recognized in 1988 when the Civil Liberties Act was passed by Congress. Approximately $1.6 billion was paid out in reparations to the victims or their surviving families.

War Expands to Africa

Abyssinia (Present-day Ethiopia)

The Second World War even touched Africa! As Hitler moved around Europe with his expansion plans, Benito Mussolini, the fascist dictator in Italy, was considering his next steps with an eye on Africa.

Mussolini decided to expand his empire in Africa and boost Italy's image. In 1895, Italy had unsuccessfully tried to invade and occupy Abyssinia (present-day Ethiopia), so Mussolini wanted to try for it again, planning to add it to East African territories already under Italian control.

In October 1935, Mussolini attacked Abyssinia, igniting a conflict in North Africa and eventually bringing Africa into World War II. While the League of Nations rebuked his actions, no meaningful sanctions or penalties were imposed. Mussolini had anticipated this reaction and continued with the invasion. By June of the following year, the capital of Addis Ababa was successfully captured by Italy, and the Italian ruler was named king of Abyssinia.

The League of Nations continued to do nothing save to make a few protests. Meanwhile, Italy continued to control and occupy Abyssinia until 1941, when British and South African troops liberated the country while fighting in the Second World War.

First Battle of El-Alamein (July 1ˢᵗ–July 27ᵗʰ, 1942)

Another country in Africa to become embroiled in World War II was Egypt.

Egypt became involved in 1940 when Italy decided to invade one of its colonies, Libya. Italy was not successful in its invasion; however, they were saved from defeat by its ally, Germany.

A German officer named Erwin Rommel was charged with leading Germany's Afrika Korps during the war.

A photo of Erwin Rommel.

The Afrika Korps was established by Hitler in January of 1941 in order to help Mussolini maintain control of the territories he had gained in North Africa. According to Hitler, Germany had to provide support to Italy for "strategic, political, and psychological reasons."[3]

The British Army was already engaged in a number of battles and skirmishes with the Royal Italian Army in Egypt, and in a matter of months, Italian troops had mostly been pushed out of the country.

So, to help his friend and ally, Hitler commanded General Rommel to go to Libya and handle the situation. Unfortunately, taking control proved more difficult than anticipated. Rommel met resistance from Italian troops who didn't like taking orders from a German officer. They also had a difficult time adjusting to the weather. In short, they were not as organized or as prepared as they should have been.

While Rommel was in Libya, British forces pushed him into a defensive position. However, this was short-lived.

Hitler's gamble initially paid off, and the Axis forces, under Rommel's leadership, were able to recapture Libya. In early 1942, Axis troops defeated British troops at Gazala and took over Tobruk. By using the Panzer divisions, Rommel forced the British to retreat into Egypt.

The First Battle of El-Alamein would take place between July 1st and July 27th, 1942. Rommel's arrival saved the Italian troops from total defeat, and the Axis powers felt confident about their victory. Britain's naval base, which was located in Alexandria, Egypt, was only sixty miles away, and they had no doubts that they would be able to capture it. Mussolini and Hitler felt it was only a matter of time before Egypt became a part of their empire.

However, the British troops received supplies from the United States and troops from South Africa, India, and New Zealand, assuring the Axis powers did not get their anticipated victory. Instead, the First Battle of El-Alamein resulted in a stalemate, with the Axis once again on the defensive.

---

[3] "German General Rommel Arrives in Africa." https://www.history.com/this-day-in-history/rommel-in-africa

The Second Battle of El-Alamein (October 23rd--November 11th, 1942)

The Allies were determined to bring an end to the Axis powers' ambitions in the Middle East. They took the summer to regroup and plan under the newly appointed Lieutenant General Bernard Montgomery.

A photo of Bernard Montgomery.
https://commons.wikimedia.org/wiki/File:Bernard_Law_Montgomery.jpg

British Prime Minister Winston Churchill wanted the battle to be fought immediately. However, General Montgomery wanted to take it slow and steady and ensure his troops were adequately prepared, both physically and mentally.

Montgomery had 190,000 men under him. These men came from places like Greece, France, Poland, and British colonies, to name a few. He wanted to ensure everyone was trained properly and had all the necessary equipment and reinforcements.

By late October, Montgomery was feeling confident and ready to head out. He had trained a powerful and capable Allied force and was now eager to go head-to-head with the brilliant and infamous Erwin Rommel, who earned the nickname "Desert Fox" because of his skilled and cunning tactics on the battlefield.

Three months after the First Battle of El-Alamein ended in a stalemate, the second battle began. On October 23rd, 1942, artillery barrages were unleashed by the Allied forces.

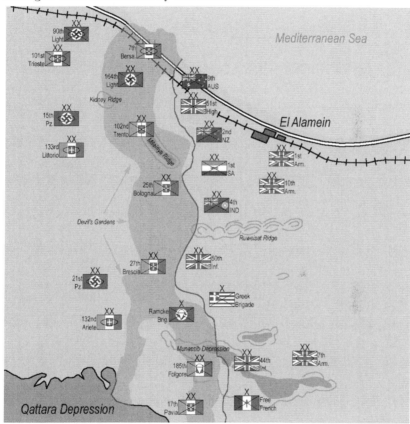

Deployment of forces before the second battle began.

The first phase of the battle was called Operation Lightfoot, and it began with the creation of two channels through minefields. The Allied forces used these channels to advance on the Axis forces and begin fighting them in a relentless assault.

Although the Allied forces were able to hold up successfully against counterattacks from the Axis forces, they did meet with some challenges when tanks got stuck in the minefield corridors. But the Allied troops held on, and the final attack was launched a week after the battle began on November 1st.

By November 2nd, Rommel told Hitler he had lost the battle. By November 4th, the Axis troops were retreating. In just over ten days, the battle was over. It had resulted in a resounding defeat for the Italian and German troops.

The Second Battle of El-Alamein would prove to be critical. In fact, the battle is historically viewed as the climax of what was happening in North Africa between the Axis and the Allies. It was a very clear and definitive victory for the Allies. After years of setbacks and defeats on the battlefield, they had finally found their groove.

Symbolically, the battle would signal the beginning of the end for the Axis powers. It provided a great boost in morale for the Allies and was heavily celebrated. Montgomery's reputation was also firmly cemented after this victory, something he capitalized on heavily.

The Atlantic Conference (August 14th, 1941)

While these battles were being fought across Europe and North Africa, the United States was still keeping itself out of the war, preferring to maintain a neutral stance.

While publicly there was no question about who the US sided with in the war, the country was reluctant to formally enter it. The American people were very firmly against getting involved in something they viewed as a "European problem." This was a sentiment Franklin Delano Roosevelt was hoping to change with the Atlantic Charter.

On August 9th and 10th, 1941, British Prime Minister Winston Churchill and American President Franklin D. Roosevelt met on a US warship called *Augusta*, which was docked in Placentia Bay off the coast of Newfoundland, Canada. Over a period of several days, they discussed what they wanted and envisioned for a post-war world.

Roosevelt and Churchill on the quarterdeck of HMS Prince of Wales during the conference.
https://commons.wikimedia.org/wiki/File:President_Roosevelt_and_Winston_Churchill_seated_on_the_quarterdeck_of_HMS_PRINCE_OF_WALES_for_a_Sunday_service_during_the_Atlantic_Conference,_10_August_1941._A4816.jpg

One of Churchill's main goals in attending these meetings was to convince the US to join the war effort or at the very least increase the amount of aid and support to the United Kingdom. Roosevelt was hoping for the same. He hoped the public would see why it was important for the US to enter the war and help out the Allies.

To both leaders' disappointment, the Atlantic Charter meetings did not result in the US formally declaring war. The American people were still not behind the move, and FDR was reluctant to declare war without greater support. The US would join the war, but that would not happen until a few months later with Japan's attack on Pearl Harbor. However, even without formally joining the war, the US was already looking toward the future and what the world would like after the war ended.

There were doubts in the minds of some of the Allied nations that Hitler would be defeated. The US and the UK wanted to be prepared for the post-war world, placing a strong emphasis on global peace. What the Atlantic Charter *did* do was present a united front to the world, which was something the Axis powers did not take kindly to.

Following Roosevelt and Churchill's meeting, a joint declaration was released by them on August 14th, 1941. The declaration was called the Atlantic Charter, and this pivotal policy provided an overview of what they hoped to achieve from this war.

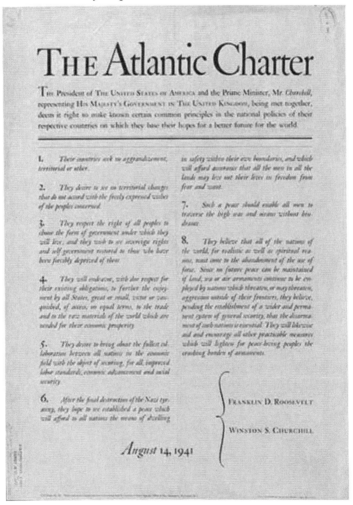

The Atlantic Charter.
https://www.pc.gc.ca/apps/dfhd/page_nhs_eng.aspx?id=1042

Eight points were highlighted in the charter. They are as follows:

1) The US or the UK would not seek to gain any additional territories or aggrandizement;

2) Any changes or adjustments to territories could not be made without the consent of citizens and the peoples living on the land in question;

3) Self-determination of nations, meaning every person had the right to choose the type of government they wanted; this would be respected by the UK and the US;

4) The UK and the US would help countries gain equal access to raw materials and trade;

5) Encourage global collaboration to improve economic progress amongst all countries, promote safety and security, and maintain a similar labor standard;

6) Destroy the Nazis and look at how all countries and their citizens could live in peace;

7) This peace should also include peace on the seas so ships could travel without fear of attack;

8) Any country tagged as a potential aggressor had to be dealt with and disarmed.

The document and the eight points were approved by the Allied countries.

The Atlantic Charter was a significant piece of legislation since it would later (January 1st, 1942) be signed by the countries as the Declaration of the United Nations. It became the foundation of what we know today as the United Nations.

In addition to providing the foundation for the United Nations, the Atlantic Charter also heavily influenced the post-war fight for independence for many colonies and inspired international agreements, such as the General Agreement on Tariffs and Trade (GATT).

Siege of Leningrad
(September 8th, 1941–January 27th, 1944)

With the Holocaust and the plight of the Jewish population often emphasized when discussing World War II, the atrocities suffered by the Soviets at the hands of Hitler's armies are often forgotten.

One of the most surprising events from the war—though maybe it should *not* have been surprising—was Hitler's decision to launch Operation Barbarossa. This was the codename for Hitler's invasion of the Soviet Union, which, as you know, was a German ally.

On June 22nd, 1941, Germany's Army Group North, which was made up of over three million troops, swarmed through the Soviet Union and began attacking. The invasion effectively ended the non-aggression pact Hitler had signed with Stalin a few years earlier, in 1939.

Historians widely believe that Hitler had always intended to invade the Soviet Union and that the signed pact had simply been a stalling mechanism.

Hitler was keen to capture Leningrad for strategic reasons. As the former capital of Russia, Leningrad was politically symbolic. Home to over six hundred factories, including arms factories, the potential for industrial output in Leningrad was enormous. Also, the city played a very important role as a base for the Soviet Navy along the Baltic Sea.

Within a matter of weeks, the Red Army was defeated, leading to the start of the long and infamous Siege of Leningrad (present-day St. Petersburg).

When the Axis forces first entered the Soviet Union, their main target was Leningrad. The plan was to encircle it with the help of Finnish allies. The two armies worked efficiently and methodically. The town of Chudovo was reached by August 20th, while Tallinn was taken eight days later. Rail links were severed whenever necessary.

While the Germans attacked Leningrad from the south, the Finnish forces invaded from the north. Their goal was to encircle Leningrad and cut it off completely from the rest of the Soviet

Union.

By August 31st, the town of Mga was seized by the Germans. Shlisselburg was captured a mere week later. Mga had the last rail connection to Leningrad, while Shlisselburg had the last roadway open to Leningrad. Both connections were promptly severed by German troops as they took over the cities.

After that, Leningrad's only connection to the world beyond was through a water route near Lake Ladoga. This route was used by the Soviets to bring whatever food, supplies, and fuel they could get their hands on into the city. Relentless bombing and shelling over Leningrad by the Luftwaffe killed and wounded over fifty thousand civilians.

By late September, Hitler had decided that his army would settle at Leningrad. But what was he going to do with the people inside the city? Surrender was not an option, and he commanded that all such requests had to be denied. Accepting the population's surrender would mean having to ensure their safe passage to another city, keep them safe from harm, or worse, feed them. Lack of food was a significant problem faced by the Germans and the people of Leningrad alike. In addition, he could save his men by starving out a population he deemed "undesirable."

Hitler had no desire or interest in dealing with the citizens of Leningrad. Initially, he wanted to raze the city to the ground. In a memo, he stated his desire to *"...encircle the city and level it to the ground by means of artillery bombardment."*[4] However, the fighting was tougher than he had anticipated. The best way to deal with people at Leningrad, he decided, was simply to wait for them to die of starvation.

During the winter of 1941/42, known as the "Hungry Winter" in Leningrad, Hitler's wish began to come true. An average of one hundred thousand people died of starvation *per month*, with most deaths occurring during the first winter. The lack of food had become so extreme that people ate anything that could be considered edible, including petroleum jelly and animals. Cases of cannibalism also rose.

---

[4] "The Siege of Leningrad.".

Coupled with the food shortage, the people of Leningrad also had to deal with the extreme cold. In early 1942, the Soviets managed to get nearly half a million civilians out of Leningrad through the water route of Lake Ladoga.

Once the winter passed, Leningrad focused on surviving and defying the Germans in any way possible. Food and supplies continued to be an ongoing problem; however, the people banded together to try and clean up the city and even planted gardens. When Dimitri Shostakovich performed a symphony he had written at the start of the siege, Leningrad acted as the host. The concert could be heard all over Leningrad on loudspeakers, which were defiantly positioned toward the German camps.

Since the beginning of the siege, the Red Army had tried on numerous occasions to break through Germany's blockade. Each attempt had been unsuccessful and resulted in the loss of many lives. By early 1943, however, things began to look up for Leningrad.

At the start of the year, the Red Army tasted a tiny slice of victory when they managed to take a land bridge away from the German troops. The bridge was used to build a special railway, and by the time 1943 rolled to an end, millions of tons of food and other vital necessities had been brought into Leningrad. The factories were up and running and doing extremely well, producing tons of ammunition and arms.

Even though Germany continued to bomb the city, Leningrad was feeling more positive. The city was determined to fight back and reclaim what was theirs.

Just a couple of months later, in early 1944, the tide had definitely turned. It was becoming increasingly clear the Axis powers were fighting a losing battle.

The Red Army managed to mobilize over one million men and launched an offensive against the German troops, forcing them to retreat. Hitler's Army Group North soon had to follow suit. Eight hundred seventy-two days after the siege, Leningrad was finally free!

But the price of freedom had been steep.

It is estimated that approximately 800,000 civilians were killed during the siege, with some numbers going over a million. The

Siege of Leningrad is one of the longest blockades in history. Due to the number of deaths, some say it was one of the deadliest sieges. In fact, some historians argue that if we consider the atrocities that occurred during the siege and the number of lives lost, the siege should be classified as genocide.

Due to heavy censorship by the Soviet Union, the true extent of what happened during the siege may never be known. While many details were released after the end of the Cold War, there is much that remains unknown.

The Battle of Stalingrad (August 23rd, 1942–February 2nd, 1943)

While Leningrad was under siege and completely blocked off from the rest of Russia, the Red Army was continuing its fight elsewhere in the country.

As the Germans continued to overrun the Soviet Union, Russian troops were able to successfully stop them from taking over Stalingrad. Like Leningrad, Stalingrad was an industrial city and would have been a huge boon for Hitler and his army if they had managed to capture it.

Unfortunately for the Germans, they failed.

The Battle of Stalingrad was hugely successful, and many agree that it was one of the greatest battles fought during the war.

During the battle, the Russian troops stopped the Germans from advancing. In a war marked by several significant, history-making victories, this was one of them. The outcome of the battle helped to turn the tide of the war against the Axis powers.

The Battle of Stalingrad will be discussed in more detail in the next chapter, where we will examine how, after a string of losses, the war suddenly shifted in favor of the Allies.

When we look at some of the key events that took place between 1941 and 1943, it's clear it was a very stressful period. Within two years of Poland being invaded, Hitler and his Nazis had become a global problem. Altercations, existing tensions, and political leaders' ambitions to create empires all came to a head during this time and turned a European skirmish into a world war.

The period between 1941 and 1943 was especially nerve-wracking since nobody had any way of predicting which way the war would go. It often seemed as if victory for Hitler and his allies was assured. If he had won some of these key battles, where would we be today?

Chapter 3: The Turning Tide — Resistance and Surrender 1943–1945

The period between 1941 and 1943 was riddled with anxiety for the Allies, but when the Allied forces masterfully turned things around, it was like a domino effect. When one enemy was defeated, another swiftly followed.

The Allies were winning battle after battle, tasting victory at nearly every corner.

One of the major turning points in the war for the Allies was the fall of the Italian regime and Benito Mussolini's resignation. Knocking down this fascist regime was a significant victory and left Germany in a weaker position.

Benito Mussolini

Long before Hitler came into the picture, fascism was already in existence in Europe. Since 1925, Italy had been ruled by a fascist dictator named Benito Mussolini, also known as Il Duce.

A photograph of Benito Mussolini.
https://commons.wikimedia.org/wiki/File:Duce_Benito_Mussolini.jpg

Hitler greatly admired Mussolini. Many Nazi ideologies were based on Mussolini's fascist ideologies. Mussolini, for his part, helped the Nazi Party by providing financial help and allowing Nazi troops to train with his squad of soldiers, the Blackshirts.

The two countries and leaders shared a lot in common and were military allies. However, their relationship was not always the strongest.

While Mussolini publicly applauded Hitler's rise to power in the early 1930s, he did not think much of him and even expressed his disapproval of Hitler's ideas and beliefs. While Mussolini firmly believed in the superiority of "white Europeans," he did not have the same type of hatred for Jewish people as Hitler did. Mussolini also did not agree with Hitler's extreme views on Aryan supremacy.

Mussolini and Hitler's first meeting, which took place in the summer of 1934 in Venice, did not go well. Neither Hitler nor Mussolini understood each other well due to a language barrier (Mussolini refused to use a translator), and both of them came away from the meeting disappointed in each other.

However, if there was one thing both men understood well was the power of propaganda. A carefully curated image of solidarity and friendship was presented to the world, making everyone believe the two were much closer than they actually were.

Slowly, over time, the two men did forge something akin to a friendship. More importantly, even as they prioritized their own agendas, they became allies and partners.

For example, when Italy invaded Ethiopia in 1935, Germany became one of the first countries to recognize and acknowledge Italy's legitimacy over the country. When Hitler terminated Germany's membership in the League of Nations, Mussolini also pulled out as a show of support.

As time went on, Hitler's influence on Mussolini grew to the point where Mussolini issued a decree in July 1938 called the Manifesto of Race. This manifesto was geared toward Jewish Italians. It called for them to lose their Italian citizenship, which meant they had to leave their government positions and could not be employed by the Italian government.

Pact of Friendship – May 1939

The relationship between Italy and Germany was further solidified in May 1939 when Hitler and Mussolini signed the Pact of Friendship or "Pact of Steel."

In the agreement, both nations pledged to help each other with economic and military support if one became engaged in a war. The pact also included a secret agreement that they would prepare for a war in Europe. However, they also agreed not to do anything to trigger a war until at least 1943.

Of course, Hitler broke this part of the pact in a matter of months. He had already set the ball in motion to start a second world war.

When Hitler invaded Poland in September of 1939, Mussolini chose to remain neutral, going against the pact. He refused to support Hitler or the Nazis by saying Italy simply wasn't ready for a war.

Mussolini's Resignation and Italy's Surrender

By the time Italy joined the war almost a year later in June 1940, Hitler's troops had invaded and occupied almost all of Western Europe. So, Mussolini set his sights elsewhere, namely in Africa.

Almost from the beginning, Italy began to fail, doing so first in Africa, where they were defeated and ousted by the Allies. In 1940, Italy also invaded Greece. Hitler did not approve of the move, thinking it to be a mistake. Not wanting his ally to lose face, Hitler came swooping in, overtaking the Allied forces in Greece. He pinned the failure of Operation Barbarossa on Mussolini.

In July 1943, the Allies invaded Sicily, and the fascist regime collapsed. On the night of July 24th, the Grand Council of Fascism met under cover of darkness to figure out Italy's next steps.

Dino Grandi, Italy's former Minister of Justice, turned on Mussolini, expressing his frustration with Mussolini's leadership style. Grandi proposed that some of Il Duce's powers as leader be transferred to King Victor Emmanuel III. The motion passed quickly, and Mussolini was forced by the Grand Council to resign. He did so on July 25th, 1943.

After his resignation, Mussolini, who was somewhat in a daze over everything that had happened, went to keep his regularly scheduled meeting with King Victor Emmanuel, where he was advised that Pietro Badoglio would now be taking over the duties as prime minister.

Mussolini had nothing to say about any of this. After he left his meeting, the police arrested him. Mussolini quietly accepted his fate and did not protest when he was sent to Ponza. Ponza was an island that Mussolini had used for decades to imprison his enemies. And Ponza would now become his prison.

Mussolini's fall from power had been swift and rather pitiful. As word spread around the country about Il Duce's arrest, a sense of relief washed over the population. Nobody, not even the most die-hard fascist, fought to save him. Italy's chief concern was where to go from there. Should they continue fighting alongside Hitler and the Nazis? Or should they wave the white flag?

Ultimately, Italy made the decision to bow out of the war, and it surrendered unconditionally to the Allies on September 8th, 1943.

Less than two years after the surrender, when the war ended, Mussolini was executed.

Tehran Conference
(November 18th–December 1st, 1943)

Historically, the United States and the Soviet Union have not always had the warmest relationship, and leading up to the Second World War, the relationship between them was quite strained. The idea of an alliance or cooperation was laughable. The relationship had worsened significantly after Joseph Stalin signed the non-aggression pact with Germany in 1939.

However, Hitler had since turned on Stalin. Faced with the idea of destruction at the hands of a common enemy, the countries came together to forge a partnership.

This alliance between the "Big Three" is commonly known as the Tehran Conference.

By the time the US joined the war, the British were already providing assistance and support to the Russians, so it was only natural for the Soviet Union to become an ally of the United States.

From November 18th to December 1st, 1943, US President Franklin D. Roosevelt, British Prime Minister Churchill, and Soviet Premier Joseph Stalin met in Tehran, Iran, to discuss military strategies that would help them invade Nazi-occupied France and defeat both Germany and Japan.

The Tehran Conference was a significant moment in history as it was the first conference to be held between the three most powerful Allied leaders during World War II.

The three leaders in Tehran: Stalin, Roosevelt, and Churchill (left to right).
https://commons.wikimedia.org/wiki/File:Tehran_Conference,_1943.jpg

During the conference, key decisions about the post-war world were made. Of course, each leader had his own objectives, but they were all united in their determination to get rid of Hitler once and for all.

At the conference, the Western Allies agreed to invade France and launch a western offensive against Nazi Germany. The three leaders agreed to support Reza Shah's government in Iran while Stalin promised support to Turkey if the two countries, which had remained neutral during the war, would pledge to enter the war on the side of the Allies.

It was decided at the conference that the invasion of France by the American and British troops would take place in May 1944. Once Nazi Germany was defeated, the Soviet Union would then join in to attack Japan.

There can be no doubt that without the Soviet Union's cooperation and help, the Allies would have had a much harder time winning the war. It is widely believed and accepted that without the Soviet Union, World War II would have had a very different outcome. Russia was at the forefront of some of the most significant battles, pushing the Nazis back from further advancing. Hitler's army was far more ruthless and savage with the Russians than with the Western powers.

Among the three big powers, the Soviet Union suffered the most casualties, with approximately twenty-six million Soviets dying during the war. Just over eleven million of them were soldiers. President Dwight D. Eisenhower himself wrote in his memoir that when visiting Russia in 1945 he "did not see a house standing between the western borders of the country and the area around Moscow...so many numbers of women, children, and old men had been killed that the Russian Government would never be able to estimate the total."[5]

The country also paid a steep price in the sheer amount of industrial capacity lost to the Nazis. Because of the Cold War that followed and the continued tensions with Russia after, it's often easy to forget the critical role the Soviet Union played during the war. But it is a role that must be acknowledged.

The Tehran Conference was a highly significant event. The Siege of Leningrad ended within a month of the meeting, and the outcome of the discussions played a major role in the liberation of France and steered the war in the right direction.

End of the Siege of Leningrad

The siege of Leningrad began in September 1941, but Soviet forces made repeated attempts to break through the blockade. However, with all roads and railway connections leading out of Leningrad cut off and destroyed, Soviet forces had a very difficult time making progress.

By cutting all connections, the Nazis ensured that civilians would have no access to food or other resources. What they were not able to touch, however, was Lake Ladoga. It became the only route available to the Soviet forces. It was especially useful in the winter when the lake froze over, creating an actual road.

This route was also known as the "Road of Life," as it allowed the evacuation of nearly one million civilians and literally saved the lives of the remaining people in Leningrad since troops were able to pass along some food and other necessities.

---

[5] Tharoor, Ishaan. "Don't Forget How the Soviet Union Saved the World from Hitler." https://www.washingtonpost.com/news/worldviews/wp/2015/05/08/dont-forget-how-the-soviet-union-saved-the-world-from-hitler/

The Soviet troops' determination to get through slowly began to pay off. By early 1943, they had managed to breach the German encirclement and were able to bring in more food and supplies to the civilians. And on January 12th, 1944, after the successful launch of a counteroffensive, they were finally able to force the Germans to retreat.

Soviet forces kept pushing forward until the German troops ended up on the outskirts of the city. The siege of Leningrad was over at last.

Often referred to as the 900-day siege, the Siege of Leningrad lasted for a total of 872 days. Approximately one million lives were lost, and hundreds of thousands were uprooted and displaced forever, torn away from everything they had ever known.

The bittersweet victory was celebrated with a gun salute as civilians poured out onto the streets, laughing, crying, and singing.

For the remaining civilians of Leningrad, the nightmare was finally over.

In 1945, the city received the Order of Lenin, an award from the government to highlight their bravery, endurance, and fighting spirit. Twenty years later, in 1965, the city was also given the title of "Hero City."

The Liberation of Paris

One of the most enduring images of victory during World War II is soldiers on the beaches of Normandy. When we read about winning the war, it is invariably tied to D-Day or the Battle of Normandy.

While D-Day was by no means the only decisive battle, it has become synonymous with winning the war. This is, in part, because the liberation of Paris *was* a huge deal. When the Germans were finally ousted from Paris, it truly felt like the end was in sight.

Germany invaded France soon after the start of the war, so rescuing the country from Nazi occupation was like seeing the light at the end of a very long and dark tunnel. And for the French, who had been occupied by the Nazis for nearly the entire duration of the war and forced to submit to the rule of Hitler's army, it *was* freedom.

Whether the war was over yet or not, they were finally free.

During the Battle of France, which took place between May 10th to June 25th, 1940, Germany invaded France, Belgium, Luxembourg, and the Netherlands. In just a matter of six weeks, German troops drove out the British forces. By June 14th, 1940, Paris had fallen. After the invasion and occupation of the city, the French Third Republic had little choice but to dissolve itself. They surrendered to Germany on June 22nd, 1940.

Power was handed over to Marshal Philippe Pétain, a soldier and hero of the First World War. Under Pétain, an armistice was signed with Germany. An authoritarian government was established in the town of Vichy, France.

French General Charles de Gaulle, however, refused to bow down to the Germans. Days before the country's surrender, he fled to the UK, where he received support and assistance from the British government.

Charles de Gaulle.
The National Archives UK, no restrictions;
https://commons.wikimedia.org/wiki/File:General_Charles_de_Gaulle_in_1945.jpg

While the puppet government in Vichy was "running" the country, the exiled Charles de Gaulle was busy setting up his own government called Free France, which was funded by the British government.

Free France refused to accept the puppet government and was determined to resist and fight back. They urged and encouraged the people of France to put up a fight against the German invasion. Charles de Gaulle, in the meantime, sought support from the French colonies. It took several years, but by 1943, French Chad and other French colonies had pledged their support to him.

Over four years of Nazi occupation followed the invasion of France. The Allies' top priority was getting rid of the Germans from the Soviet Union and France. During the Tehran Conference, the liberation of Paris became one of the key points of discussion.

The Allied Army

After the conference, it was decided that American and British troops would mount a cross-Channel invasion into France and try to get the Nazis out.

Hitler had long been anticipating such a move and put Erwin Rommel in charge of reinforcing France and building an Atlantic Wall. The Atlantic Wall was meant to act as a 2,400-mile-long line of defense along the French coastline. It would be filled with obstacles, mines, pillboxes, and bunkers. However, the Nazis had neither the money nor the resources to undertake such a massive project, so they concentrated on fortifying existing ports instead.

While the Allies had been talking about a cross-Channel attack since 1942, the lack of resources and a clear strategy kept getting it delayed. It was clear to the Allies that the best way forward was to stretch the German forces thin. This could be achieved by opening up the Western Front in Europe. The tricky part was deciding which location should be targeted and, most importantly, when.

Preparations for the attack only began in earnest in December 1943, with a record number of American troops landing in the United Kingdom. British soldiers had been undergoing intense training for the invasion since 1942 and felt fully prepared.

As they planned for the invasion, the future president of the United States, Dwight D. Eisenhower, was appointed as commander of the Supreme Headquarters Allied Expeditionary Force (SHAEF). He would work with Bernard Montgomery, the man who had fought against and defeated Rommel back in Africa.

General Dwight D. Eisenhower.
https://commons.wikimedia.org/wiki/File:Dwight_D._Eisenhower_as_General_of_the_A rmy_crop.jpg

Eisenhower's chief of staff was an American named Walter Bedell Smith. His other subordinates, Air Chief Marshal Arthur Tedder, Admiral Bertram Ramsay, and Air Chief Marshal Trafford Leigh-Mallory, were all British. Charles de Gaulle's Free France also sent a delegate named Marie-Pierre Koenig to act as a liaison between de Gaulle and the Allied Expeditionary Force.

By the spring of 1944, over 1.5 million American soldiers were in Britain, ready for action. Lieutenant General J. C. H. Lee was responsible for overseeing logistics. By May 1944, he had 6,500 ships and landing crafts ready. The landing crafts would assist with the landing of approximately 200,000 vehicles and 600,000 tons of supplies during the first few weeks of the invasion.

Air support was also given a key role in the campaign to combat the Luftwaffe. The Allies had over thirteen thousand bomber, fighter, and transport aircraft. Prior to the actual invasion, Allied troops dropped more than 195,000 tons of bombs at key locations in France, including German airfields, military bases, and rail centers. The aircraft destroyed all the bridges crossing the Seine and Loire Rivers.

These preliminary attacks were very important since they helped to completely isolate the area that would be invaded by the Allies from the rest of the country. It was also meant to deceive the Germans and make them believe Allied troops would land in Pas-de-Calais instead of Normandy. The Allies did so by dropping the bulk of their bombs in the wrong area.

An added bonus of the air campaign was that it left the German troops feeling a little rattled. They were forced to concede that the Allied troops were far superior when it came to aircraft.

It had taken the Allies years to prepare for the invasion, but it was time well spent because they were extremely well prepared. Aside from launching a very successful air campaign, the Allies had also become adept at decrypting German codes and thus had a fairly good idea of where Nazi forces were situated and what their next steps would be.

One of the more brilliant moves by the Allies was creating phantom armies using false radio transmissions. They based the phantom army at Dover, England, directly across from Pas-de-Calais.

Montgomery's Plan

D-Day was an extremely complicated military operation. It required precise coordination, meticulous planning, and a dash of luck.

While Eisenhower was assigned to direct SHAEF, General Bernard Montgomery was the ground commander responsible for leading the 21st Army Group and organizing Operation Overlord, the codename given for the Battle of Normandy. The 21st Army Group was made up of Allied ground forces and was the group that would put Operation Overlord into action.

What's interesting and rather amusing about Montgomery's plan is that it was laid out on *one* solitary sheet of paper. He marked the document as "Most Secret" on the very top and wrote, "The key note of everything to be SIMPLICITY," at the very bottom.

In the end, his battle plan *was* rather simple, as so many brilliant things are.

For the invasion, Montgomery requested five divisions to land at five different beaches instead of three. He also asked to have the landing area include the Orne River.

Each of the five beaches was given a codename. They were as follows:

- Utah
- Omaha
- Gold
- Juno
- Sword

The plan had two parts to it. The first part, called NEPTUNE, required Allied troops to cross the English Channel, land on the beaches, and provide support with gunfire. The second part of the plan, called OVERLORD, was the actual invasion and battle.

The goal was to gain complete control of the Normandy coast. Once this was done, the troops would continue inland.

Montgomery felt confident that with all the preparations and resources they had readied, the Allies would be able to mount a successful attack and push the Germans out of France.

German Troops' Preparation

Meanwhile, Hitler, who was starting to sense that something may be coming, warned his troops that the Allies might land at Normandy even though they had believed all along the invasion would happen at Pas-de-Calais. It seemed the natural choice for a location given its proximity to Dover just across the English Channel. To prepare, three enormous gun batteries were situated on the coast of Calais by German troops. The cannons were pointed directly at Dover.

The message was clear and menacing. Calais was off-limits.

While working on the Atlantic Wall, Rommel laid out about four million mines and other traps on the beaches of Normandy, as well as in inland marshes. He also wanted the German tank divisions placed near the beaches, but German Field Marshal Karl Rudolf Gerd von Rundstedt disagreed and felt the tank divisions should be kept as a reserve. Hitler had the final say in the dispute and settled it by splitting the divisions between the three of them.

Mismanagement and disputes were not Hitler's only problems. The Allies had come up with a brilliant campaign of deception by creating a "dummy army," and Hitler fell for it completely. The campaign was given the codename Operation Fortitude, and its entire purpose was to make Hitler and the Nazis believe the Allied invasion would take place in Calais. German spy planes entailed keeping an eye on southeastern England and saw what they believed was an enormous army ready to invade. In reality, what they were looking at were mainly decoys.

England had also managed to capture almost every German spy in the country. They were either imprisoned or began working for the Allies as a double agent. The double agents were used to pass along messages to the German troops, confirming that the invasion would indeed take place in Calais.

The Allies even passed this fake message on Allied radio traffic, knowing full well that the Nazis would listen to it. When the Allies did attack, it took the German troops aback. They had not expected to be so completely wrong!

What saved the Nazis from facing total destruction immediately after the invasion was Rommel's preparation and fortification of the Atlantic Wall in Normandy. The mines, traps, and guns he had so carefully positioned gave the Germans a fighting chance and were the main reason Allied troops suffered terrible casualties.

Rommel had been adamant that Panzer tank divisions needed to be positioned and ready for an attack on the coastline, but Hitler did not agree with him. He wanted most of the Panzer divisions closely guarding Paris. The rest were scattered sporadically throughout the southern coastline. As a result, only one division was close enough to attack and defend Normandy.

Ironically, had Hitler heeded Rommel's advice and warnings, D-Day might have turned out very differently for the Allies.

Thankfully for the world, he didn't.

D-Day or the Normandy Invasion

The Normandy invasion was planned out in such a way that British, American, and Canadian forces would all land at five separate locations on the beaches of Normandy, France, at the same time.

Operation Overlord or D-Day was initially planned for May 1944, but it kept being delayed due to problems with the assembly of landing crafts, rough seas, and bad timing. It was pushed to June instead, and Eisenhower fixed June 5th as the new date for the invasion. He was adamant the date would remain firm and that there would be no more changes.

However, as June 5th approached and the Allied troops readied themselves to cross the English Channel, the weather took a turn for the worst. A violent storm swept along the French coast. The weather was so bad the Nazis were convinced they didn't need to keep watch at their posts since it would be foolhardy to brave such a stormy sea. Rommel and a few other military commanders took leave to return to Paris and Germany.

A heated debate among the Allied leaders followed, and it was decided the crossing and landing would be too dangerous under such conditions. The invasion would be delayed an additional twenty-four hours. The ships that were at sea were already brought back.

When June 5th rolled around, the Allied weather beacon indicated the weather would clear up around midnight, at least enough to go forward with the plan. The troops jumped into action.

The troops were told by Eisenhower, "You are about to embark upon the Great Crusade, toward which we have striven these many months. The eyes of the world are upon you."[6]

---

[6] Fitzgerald, Clare. "The Powerful Speech Dwight D. Eisenhower Delivered to Allied Troops Invading Normandy." https://www.warhistoryonline.com/world-war-ii/dwight-eisenhower-d-day-speech.html?chrome=1.

And indeed they were! It would be a battle that would go down in history.

In a matter of a few hours, the Allied squadron, which was made up of 2,500 ships, 3,000 landing crafts, 500 naval vessels, and other bombardment ships and escorts, began their journey from the English ports toward Normandy.

US soldiers preparing for the landing at Normandy.
https://commons.wikimedia.org/wiki/File:Omaha_Beach_Landing_Craft_Approaches.jpg

Shortly after midnight, 822 aircraft—just a small fraction of the actual number of aircraft set aside for D-Day—carrying soldiers ready to land via parachutes, gliders hovering over the Normandy landing zones, and paratroopers, began landing.

Just before the landings were completed, British and American troops bombed the five beaches with the intention of destroying any gun bunkers that may have been positioned by the Germans. And by the early morning of June 6th, 1944, approximately 160,000 Allied troops had crossed the English Channel and landed on the beaches by ship and aircraft, ready to invade France. There were some casualties during the landing, as some soldiers drowned at sea or went missing, but overall, the landings were deemed a success.

The thousands of glider troops and paratroopers who had landed and were positioned behind enemy lines began working to secure roads and bridges. At 6:30 a.m., the invasions began, and Allied troops made up of British and Canadian forces were able to easily overcome the unprepared Germans and quickly capture the beaches of Sword, Gold, and Juno.

Things were not as easily managed at Utah or Omaha Beach, where things started off badly for the American troops. The force that was supposed to land on Utah ended up landing miles away because they were blown off course. But once they organized themselves, they were able to take control of Utah.

Omaha, unfortunately, faced the most challenges. The aerial bombings by the Allies didn't hit many of the targets at Omaha due to the cloudy weather, and American troops faced intense resistance from German troops. As soon as American soldiers began landing on the beach, Nazi machine guns began firing at them. More than two thousand Americans died or were wounded by the Nazis at Omaha.

By the time night fell, some 156,000 Allied troops were left. The beaches of Normandy had been stormed and were taken over with great success. Within a week, by June 11th, over 326,000 troops had swarmed the beaches and secured them completely. Meanwhile, 50,000 vehicles and over 100,000 tons of equipment arrived on the beaches.

The surprised Germans, who had been taken aback by the location of the attack, continued to deal with confusion and mismanagement. They were without the guidance of Rommel, who was on leave, while Hitler was fast asleep on the morning of the attack, having left strict instructions that he was *not* to be woken up. When he did finally wake up just before noon to absolute chaos, he refused to immediately release divisions positioned nearby for a counterattack. He was convinced the landings in Normandy were nothing more than a diversion tactic designed to shift focus from the real place of attack near the Seine River. He wanted his troops in place for that invasion.

The hugely successful Allied air campaign proved to be another sore point for the Germans. The destruction of the bridges forced the Nazis to take detours, which was time-consuming and inefficient. Allied navy troops also played a critical role in providing support and protection for the advancing ground troops.

Over the coming weeks, the Allied troops continued their advance into the Normandy countryside, undeterred by German resistance. Within weeks, the port of Cherbourg was seized successfully by the Allies and used to land nearly one million men and 150,000 vehicles. The British forces, in the meantime, gained control of Caen.

Two months later, toward the end of August 1944, Allied troops reached the Seine River. By this time, Nazi troops had been ousted from northwestern France. Paris was liberated at last. The Battle of Normandy was over.

The simple plan that had been written on one sheet of paper had been a huge success. One major goal of the Allied war effort had been achieved.

The war was not yet over, but Paris was free. The tide was definitely turning against Hitler and the Nazis. With his troops out of France, he was unable to fortify the Eastern front against the Soviet troops. This was an extremely low point for the Nazis, and things were only going to get worse.

For the Allies, however, winning the Battle of Normandy provided a much-needed boost to their morale. Although they had been winning smaller battles, this was one of the first major victories that truly signaled the end of the war. The end of the Nazi regime was near.

The estimated casualties from the Battle of Normandy are as follows:

- Germany
  - 30,000 killed
  - 80,000 wounded
  - 210,000 missing
- United States
  - 29,000 killed
  - 106,000 wounded and missing

- United Kingdom
  - 11,000 killed
  - 54,000 wounded and missing
- Canada
  - 5,000 killed
  - 13,000 wounded and missing
- France
  - 12,000 civilians killed and missing

Battle of the Bulge
(December 16th, 1944–January 25th, 1945)

Hitler's Strategy

The last major battle against Hitler took place in the Ardennes region when German forces sprang a surprise attack against the Allies who were stationed in the forest in southeastern Belgium, close to Luxembourg.

The Battle of the Bulge or Battle of the Ardennes would be Hitler's last-ditch effort to win the war and Germany's last major offensive against the Allies. Hitler's goal was to split the focus of the Allies who were advancing into Germany.

After liberating Paris, Allied forces continued to travel across northern France toward Belgium, which had been occupied by the Nazis since May 1940. Soon after the invasion of Normandy, the momentum for the Allies was at a high, but as the months passed, the momentum dwindled.

In mid-November, the Allied forces launched an offensive on the Western Front, which yielded little success. The troops were exhausted, the battles were long, and no major victories were secured in the months since the liberation of France.

Hitler, in the meantime, was working hard to strengthen his troops by bringing new reserves from where he could. He was preparing to launch a new offensive. The location he chose was the woodsy, forested region of the Ardennes.

He calculated that the Allies would not expect an attack there since the terrain was difficult to work in. Hitler also liked the region because the dense woods provided the perfect shelter to conceal his forces. In addition, he timed the attack for December, deciding to use the weather as a weapon. He was banking on winter storms, blizzards, freezing rain, and cold weather to further hamper American efforts.

In Hitler's ideal world, the surprise offensive would be launched through the Ardennes, with the final aim being the crossing of the River Meuse, allowing them to recapture Antwerp, Belgium.

Along the way, the Germans would force the British Army to split from the American forces and all their supplies. In this weakened position, the German Army would swoop in to destroy the defenseless British.

Field Marshal Gerd von Rundstedt was put in charge of commanding the offensive. While this was happening, the plan was for the Fifth Panzer Army to attack the US forces in the Ardennes. The Sixth Panzer Army would move northwestward to create a strategic barrier. Hitler was well aware and wary of the Allies' superior air power, so he decided to only launch the attacks when the weather was guaranteed to keep the Allies grounded.

When the Germans began their offensive early on the morning of December 16th, 1944, in their traditional blitzkrieg style from the beginning of the war, the Allies were taken by surprise and left scrambling to mount a defense.

German divisions swept out through the dense woods of the Ardennes to attack battle-weary American troops who were stationed across a stretch of seventy-five miles to rest and regroup. As predicted by Hitler, for the first little while, the Allied air force could do absolutely nothing to retaliate due to heavy rain and mist.

Taking advantage of the general confusion from the Allies, the Nazis moved quickly and made great strides. As the Germans pressed on into the Ardennes, spilling out and around the forested area, they created a sort of "bulge" on the map. That's how the term "Battle of the Bulge" came to be.

Chaos soon descended into the Ardennes. It looked like a tornado had swept through it. Both armies blasted, hacked, and dug through the forest. As Hitler had hoped, the cold weather did not help. Over fifteen thousand American troops got sick or died just from the weather alone, suffering from pneumonia, frostbite, and trench foot.

The Nazis perhaps took notes from the deception tactics used by the Allies during the Battle of Normandy, as they attempted to deceive the Allies by sending imposters to infiltrate the troops. Road signs were changed to deliberately divert Allied troops, while German soldiers who spoke English were dressed up in American uniforms and placed in strategic locations to cause further confusion and send the real American troops to the wrong places.

These soldiers were handpicked because of their superior English skills and were trained in American slang language, which was picked up from Americans who were imprisoned in German camps. When the Allies got wind of this, they began asking American trivia questions to anyone they suspected of being a German spy.

All in all, the early days of Hitler's last great offensive were marked by confusion, chaos, heavy losses, and fear of the Allies. Was all they had so dearly gained now lost?

Allied Response and the Meuse River

But since the Allies had come so far, they would not give up so easily at this critical stage. They carried on with grit and determination, trying to find humor where they could and facing every horrifying situation with bravery and courage.

Word soon spread of the German attack, and fear gripped the hearts of people and nations who had been quietly confident that the Allies would prevail. In Belgium, the terrified civilians replaced the Allied flags with Nazi swastikas, and a curfew was imposed in Paris again. It was a sobering moment for the world at large and the United States, which had believed that victory was already within its grasp.

In the meantime, British generals quietly moved troops around to protect the crossing at the Meuse River. This river was one of the most important rivers in Europe. The majority of the Meuse River can be navigated by ships and barges and connects France to Belgium and the Netherlands.

The Albert Canal stretches from the Meuse River all the way to Antwerp, while the Juliana Canal runs parallel to the Meuse and reaches the southern tip of the Netherlands. Back in 1940, when Germany first invaded Belgium, the troops crossed the Meuse

River and were able to break into France after forcefully breaching the Meuse-Albert Canal line.

The British wanted to avoid a repetition of that at all costs.

By December 24th, the Fifth Panzer Army was just over five kilometers away from the Meuse River. But the German troops' luck was finally about to run out. The Allies had finally found their groove and were starting to fight back ferociously while the Germans were facing problems with the frigid weather and gasoline shortages.

German progress was gradually slowing down.

Siege of Bastogne (December 20th–December 27th, 1944)

But before Christmas Day and the clearing of the weather, things were starting to look very bad, especially in the small town of Bastogne. The Germans needed to capture the town as part of their push toward the Meuse River.

After a few days of intense battling between the Germans and the Allies, the German troops managed to completely surround the famous 101st Airborne Division, trapping them and others within the town. But the Americans did not allow the setback to break their spirits and instead defied their captors cheerfully.

On December 22nd, 1944, the Germans demanded that the 101st Division surrender. This was flatly refused by Brigadier General Anthony McAuliffe, the commander of the division. Instead, to help them out of the situation, Eisenhower sent more troops.

Rather poetically, on Christmas Day, the weather finally cleared up. The ground was frozen solid. The Allied air force was ready for action and began a relentless campaign of air attacks, while tanks were finally able to move.

Meanwhile, as the troops continued to hold Bastogne, they suffered many casualties and waited for reinforcements. Reinforcements finally arrived on December 26th when General George Patton's Third Army arrived at Bastogne and, in rapid order, pierced through the German line, ending the siege and saving the trapped American troops.

Over the following weeks, the 101st Division and the Third Army faced off against the German forces. By January 17th, 1945, after a series of battles, the Allies had managed to push the

Germans back.

End of the Battle of the Bulge

While Patton's troops were detached to Bastogne, Montgomery took the northern flank in hand. He assembled a force of whoever he could get and headed southward to stop the Germans from crossing the Meuse River.

With the Germans mere miles away from the Meuse River, the Allies successfully halted their advance. On Christmas Day, the German tanks were forced to stop and could not advance any farther toward the river. They were just six kilometers away from reaching their goal.

By this time, the Germans were nearly at the end of their rope. They had run out of supplies and were dealing with fuel and ammunition shortages. Facing resistance and pressure at every turn, on January 8th, 1945, the Germans began to slowly withdraw from the battle.

The Americans pressed on with their counteroffensive, often fighting against snow drifts and blizzards as well as the enemy. But little by little, over the coming weeks, the Allied forces' grit paid off. The German bulge shrunk, and the Allies managed to eliminate all of Germany's gains. On January 25th, 1945, the Battle of the Bulge officially ended with the Allies as the clear victors.

The Battle of the Bulge had come at a heavy price. It was the costliest battle ever fought by the American army. According to the numbers collected by the US Department of Defense, approximately 19,000 soldiers died during the battle, another 47,500 were wounded, and over 23,000 went missing. On the German side, around 100,000 soldiers were either captured, killed, or wounded.

After the battle was declared over, the Allied forces finally celebrated Christmas, doing so a month after the actual holiday. They enjoyed frozen beer shipped from the United States. But their celebration was short-lived as they now had to move on to Berlin.

End of Germany

When we consider the events in the years between 1943 and 1945, we can see a definite shift in favor of the Allies. Although Germany only officially lost in 1945 when they surrendered, some historians argue that Hitler started losing the war as early as 1941.

What went wrong with Germany's strategy and Hitler's leadership?

At first glance, Germany had it all. Better weapons. Better equipment. A better army. Better everything. The Nazis were dubbed a war machine.

But much of Germany's successes and victories in the early years were due to their blitzkrieg tactics, and their efficiency and speed fizzled out halfway through.

For all Germany's bluster and confidence, it had several weaknesses that proved fatal in the end. These included a poor economy and poor productivity during the war, fighting wars on several fronts, a lack of leadership, and weak supply lines.

Germany simply did not have the resources, such as oil, steel, and food, to launch invasions in multiple countries on such a massive scale. The country's economy did not have the prowess or production power to supply the goods the army required for their numerous invasions. And as the war wore on, these issues only got worse, and Germany's situation became increasingly desperate.

Their supply issues only started to get better in 1942 when Albert Speer, the newly appointed Minister of Armaments and War Production, began to mobilize Germany's entire economy for war. It wasn't the perfect solution, but it did start to make a difference by 1944. Unfortunately for Germany, by then, it was too late.

According to James Holland, the author of *The War in the West,* given the Nazis' supply issues, they would have needed to entirely destroy their enemies right away if they wanted to come out as winners of the war. As you know, that is not what happened. While the Germans invaded and occupied several European countries, they were unable to beat Great Britain. Hitler had arrogantly believed his Luftwaffe would easily be able to crush Britain. When this didn't happen, he was stuck fighting Britain while starting his invasion of the Soviet Union.

Holland argues that Hitler *had* to invade the Soviet Union to survive and get more resources. The invasion led to Germany overextending its resources, leaving it scrambling for supplies later.

Whether Hitler invaded the Soviet Union for survival or whether it's because that was his plan all along, the invasion did not help his or Germany's cause. When he backed out of the non-aggression pact he had signed with the Soviet Union and invaded Leningrad, he instantly made an enemy.

And not just that, by invading the Soviet Union, Hitler's troops become embroiled in a long, costly, and tedious battle on the Eastern Front, using up precious resources.

The invasion had a domino-like effect around the world. One battle led to another. Countries began to make and break pacts and agreements and look out for their own interests. Eventually, rising tensions in other parts of the world led to Japan attacking Pearl Harbor, which, as we know, would become the final straw for the United States, which had already publicly sided with Great Britain but had been reluctant to declare war.

Once the United States joined the war on the side of Great Britain, which was allied with the Soviet Union, it was a foregone conclusion that the three countries would band together to defeat their common enemy. And this was where it began to cost Hitler even more because now he was forced to divide his troops and split all his resources so that two defensive battles could be fought: one on the Western Front against the British and Americans and the other on the Eastern Front against the Soviets.

Finally, Hitler's leadership and power over the people and his troops started out strong. He ruled with an iron fist, and his followers blindly believed every word he spewed. But as the war waged, the support and faith from the German people and his own troops began to wane. There was mismanagement at every level, and many of his advisors had their own agenda.

The Battle of Normandy is a perfect example of how the lack of leadership and lack of unity among Hitler's commanders resulted in a catastrophic loss. Rommel wanted to pursue things a certain way as Germany prepared for a possible Allied invasion, but Hitler and Rundstedt disagreed with him and did not support him. On D-Day itself, while the Allied forces were landing on the beaches in

Normandy, Hitler was sleeping, having left instructions that he should not be disturbed. Meanwhile, his commanders were on leave. This may have been the decisive battle that fully tipped the balance in favor of the Allies.

Even though the Allied forces had steadily begun to gain ground and win some battles, a complete victory was not within their grasp. At any moment, the war could have gone either way. The "either way" happened at the Battle of Normandy.

Another huge, decisive moment for the Allied troops was the end of the Siege of Leningrad. The Soviets' successful counteroffensive ended another long German occupation and was a huge blow to their operation. Due to the loss of France, coupled with the loss of the Soviet Union, Germany knew the end was in sight. It also knew the war would not end in their favor.

Hitler's arrogance and his refusal to admit defeat also contributed to Germany's losses. In the later years of the war, Hitler began to retreat more and more. He was seen in public very rarely and spent most of his time in his bunker in Berlin.

The other thing Germany hadn't counted on was the Allies' strength, not just in the sheer number of troops but also in resources and financial aid. A policy called the Lend-Lease Act was drafted by the United States in 1938. Under this program, the Allies were entitled to receive aid in a number of different ways. As the war went on, the program was expanded.

Through this act, Great Britain was given over thirty billion dollars of aid in supplies like weapons, aircraft, and medicine. The Soviet Union also received eleven billion dollars of aid through this program.

Because the Americans joined the war much later, the Allies had the advantage of millions of additional soldiers who were strong, healthy, and full of energy.

By the time the American troops arrived, German troops, who had been fighting non-stop for years, were tired, weak, and exhausted. It would not be surprising if they were just tired of it all.

All of these challenges and weaknesses combined proved to be too much for Germany to overcome. However, luck and fate may have also had something to do with it.

Although the war was over in Europe, the war continued on in the Pacific. Japan was a strong contender, but the Allied forces could now direct all of their attention on it. The fighting went on for another four months, but Japan eventually surrendered after the atomic bombing of Hiroshima and Nagasaki. More information on the Pacific theater can be found in Chapter 5.

Chapter 4: The Cost of War

The Second World War was one the bloodiest and deadliest military conflicts ever fought, wiping out between 3 percent and 3.7 percent of the world's entire population.

While the true numbers will never be known, historians estimate that forty to fifty million people died during the war. They died in battle, in concentration camps, and in forced labor camps. People died because of bombings, raids, famine, disease, and violence.

What was it all for? Was it worth it? The answer would likely depend on where you are currently situated in the world.

While the war was a *world* war and had a significant impact on many countries and nations, for the purpose of this book, we will examine the cost of the war for the main Allied and Axis powers. What happened to them after the war ended? What were the consequences they faced? What were the losses? The gains?

The Allied Powers

The United States

Early in the war, after Hitler began to invade countries in Europe, the United States refused to get involved. It was clear its allegiance was with the United Kingdom, but it was reluctant to formally declare war or take a position.

However, this changed when the war hit close to home. In early December 1941, Japan attacked America's naval base in Pearl Harbor.

Casualties of War and Reparations

The US joined the war in December 1941 and fought alongside the British and the Soviets until the very end. In total, the US lost 419,000 lives. The majority of these deaths were military deaths. Very few US civilians were impacted by the war in Europe because of where the US was located. The Nazis could not subject the US to air raids as they could to the European countries. As a result, the total number of civilian deaths was around 12,100.

As part of the treaty with Germany, the United States was a recipient of reparations from the country. This will be discussed below in Germany's section.

The Post-war United States

While the loss of life cannot be viewed in a cavalier manner, in some ways, the war turned out to be a very good thing for the United States, as it reaped the most benefits.

After the First World War ended, the US went through a period of jubilance and fun called the Roaring Twenties. Money flowed freely, and the people just wanted to live and enjoy their lives.

It seemed as if things changed overnight when the stock market crashed in October 1929. The Roaring Twenties faded away, and the United States entered the Great Depression. It began in 1929 and lasted for an entire decade.

By 1939, things had started to look up, and when war broke out in Europe, it radically transformed the American economy. At that time, the country's gross national product was at $88.6 billion; by 1944, that number had increased to $135 billion.

How did this happen? The United States was a big country with a large population. It had the skills and available technology and money needed to increase its industrial productivity, which it did by a staggering 96 percent!

Businesses and industries began to recover, and profits began to double. After a decade of unemployment and no wages, people were working full-time again with better pay. Seventeen million jobs were created because of the war, along with new industries and technologies.

Because men were fighting in the war, women and African Americans had to take over their jobs. This would lead to social reforms and better rights for women and minorities in later years.

After the war, America's economy and global influence only got stronger. The United States had not been devastated and laid to ruin like parts of Europe. Once the war ended, the Americans had minimal rebuilding to do; instead, they focused on strengthening their industries.

Because of the role the US played during the war, the country also emerged as a global superpower.

In every way, the US came out on top after the war. By providing aid and support to the European countries ravaged by war, the US exerted a lot of influence and control over those countries, which, in turn, benefited them.

Today, the US continues to be one of the world's superpowers and is looked up to by many countries in the world as the ideal model of democracy, freedom, and rights.

Great Britain

Great Britain was on the winning side of World War II, but it had been embroiled in the war with Germany since the very beginning. British troops fought bravely and valiantly for six long years.

Although the British came out as winners, they suffered a lot of casualties and lost a great deal in the process of fighting for freedom.

Casualties of War

Great Britain lost approximately 450,900 lives during the Second World War. More than half of those deaths (383,700) were military deaths; the remaining 67,200 were civilian deaths related to military actions or activities.

Reparations

England did not have to pay any reparations and instead was the recipient of reparations from Germany as outlined in the Yalta Conference and finalized during the Potsdam Conference.

Post-war Britain

The war cost Great Britain and its colonies dearly. Even with support and aid from the United States, the war had an enormous impact on the country's economy and led to it losing the grand empire it had spent centuries building. Great Britain also lost its prestige and prominence as a global superpower, a title that was claimed by the United States.

Nazi bombing had left many parts of England in shambles and ruins. After six long years of war, the people were exhausted and mentally wrecked. The end of the war brought joy and happiness, but it also meant the start of rebuilding efforts. Reconstructing the country was a difficult task since most of Europe had to deal with shortages in goods, materials, and labor.

Great Britain's economy was a mess, and its industries were struggling. Railways and coal mines needed materials and equipment to function, but there was no money to import anything. Because the country wasn't producing much of anything, it also was not exporting anything. It seemed like a vicious, never-ending cycle.

Things were so bad that even bread had to be rationed. There seemed to be a crisis at every turn. The people faced economic and housing crises and lacked basic necessities.

But the Labour Party, under the leadership of Clement Attlee—who had been elected at the end of the war—soon established some measures, such as nationalizing the coal mines, road transport, railroads, electrical power, docks, and harbors.

Decolonization

As the war went on, it became evident to the British that holding on to their territories and colonies was becoming too costly. The colonies themselves were fueled by ideas of nationalism and wanted their independence. They no longer wanted to be ruled by the British. People from British colonies fought fearlessly alongside the British during the war and felt they deserved and had earned their freedom.

The turmoil and simmering unrest resulted in India gaining its independence from Britain in 1947. One year later, in 1948, Great Britain moved out of the Middle East. Palestine was becoming a point of contention, and the British government no longer wished to deal with it. It would go on to become an even bigger problem in later years.

What England had not considered was the loss of their African colonies. They had banked on using Africa's wealth to help rebuild England and bring back its affluence. This meant they would need to increase British presence in the continent.

However, as is so often the case in life, things did not go as planned.

Africa

A coup led by Colonel Gamal Abdel Nasser in Egypt on July 23rd, 1952, overthrew the monarchy, and a nationalist government was put in its place. When Nasser became Egypt's president, one of the first things he did was take control of the Suez Control and nationalize it. He believed the Suez should be owned by the Egyptians. As a result of the nationalization, Great Britain lost its shares of the canal.

Wanting to get them back and put Nasser in his place, France, Britain, and Israel hatched a plot and invaded Egypt in late 1956. They eventually regained control of the canal.

The attack angered the United States, and when the matter was taken to the United Nations, the British and French were forced to withdraw from the area. This international scolding further solidified the fact that Britain was no longer an international power. It appeared as if it no longer had international authority.

As nationalism swept through Africa, Great Britain began to find it increasingly difficult to maintain power in the continent. The continued unrest and fighting began to get costly, and the profits the British had hoped to gain didn't seem worth it. It was clear they had to withdraw.

In 1960, British prime minister Harold Macmillan visited South Africa. While speaking at Cape Town, Macmillan acknowledged that Britain understood that African countries were keen to gain their independence.

Between the late 1950s and 1975, nearly two dozen African colonies fought for and gained their independence. For Great Britain, this and the loss of its international authority are perhaps the biggest repercussions of WWII. The war triggered calls for independence and led to a dramatic shrinking of the British Empire.

Present-day Britain

Of course, Britain did not allow these setbacks to defeat it, and within a few years, the country was making significant progress in its rebuilding efforts.

From 1945 to 1979, the British government basically went back and forth between the Labour Party and the Conservatives. The Labour Party worked hard to establish initiatives designed to create a welfare state and introduced other social reforms. When the Conservatives came into power, they focused on foreign policy and oversaw the crisis with the Suez Canal.

Over the decades, each party contributed something to help rebuild the UK. Assistance from the United States under the Marshall Plan also provided much-needed relief and helped the country deal with its economic crisis. Withdrawing from its colonies also helped.

While the United Kingdom never got back its global empire or former status, it is one of the most developed nations in the world today. It is closely allied with other democratic nations and continues to wield considerable influence socially, culturally, politically, and economically around the world.

The Soviet Union

Rather ironically, the Soviet Union, which was a powerful ally to Britain and the US during the war, ended up becoming the new global enemy almost as soon as the war ended.

However the world may feel about the Soviet Union after the world war or even today, there is no doubt that without its help, Hitler and the Nazis would have been nearly impossible to defeat. The Soviet Union played a crucial role in helping the Allied powers end the war, but unfortunately, they paid a hefty price for it.

Casualties of War and Reparations

It is estimated that the Soviet Union had the highest number of casualties during World War II. Approximately 13,950,000 lives were lost.

- 6,750,000 were military deaths;
- 4,100,000 were civilian deaths caused by military action;
- 3,100,000 were civilian deaths as a result of famine and disease.

The actual number of deaths may be much higher since the Soviet Union was not keen on sharing statistics from the war, only doing so after the end of the Cold War. Historians believe that the number of deaths in the Soviet Union could be as high as twenty-seven million! They estimate that approximately 11.4 million troops died in battle, 10 million civilians died as a result of military activity, and 8 to 9 million civilians died of starvation and illness.

Over twenty-five million Soviets became homeless, and the ratio of women to men became greatly imbalanced since so many young men died during the war. An additional fourteen million soldiers suffered injuries and were wounded through the course of the war.

In terms of reparations, under the Paris Peace Treaty (1947), the Soviet Union was a recipient of reparations and entitled to receive compensation from the Axis powers. They were owed the following:

- $100 million USD from Italy;
- $300 million USD from Finland;
- $200 million USD from Hungary;
- $300 million USD from Romania.

Germany paid its reparations by sending the Soviet Union factories (which were taken apart in Germany and then shipped to the Soviet Union), industrial products, goods, and food.

After the war, the Soviet Union kept the eastern part of Poland, making it part of the Ukrainian Soviet Socialist Republic. Moldova and the three Baltic states (Estonia, Latvia, and Lithuania) also stayed under Soviet control. The USSR also took control of the governments in Bulgaria, Czechoslovakia, East Germany, Hungary, Albania, Yugoslavia, and Romania.

The Post-war Soviet Union

Within a year of the war ending, famine, epidemics, and illnesses spread through the country, lasting until 1947. On top of this, the people were struggling with drought and the repercussions of the war. The civilians suffered a lot, and it must have felt like a never-ending battle for them.

However, the exceedingly resilient population did not give up. Joseph Stalin's first priority for the Soviet Union was to rebuild. He accepted some credits from Great Britain but refused any other financial assistance, especially from the United States. Instead, they turned to the countries in Eastern Europe they were occupying for raw materials and machinery.

Emphasis was placed on modernizing their industries and arms production. By 1949, the Soviet Union had even created and successfully tested its first nuclear weapon. The German factories and supplies they received as reparations went a long way toward helping them achieve their goals.

Once the Soviet Union was able to stand on its feet, it expanded the economy and strengthened its control over Eastern Europe. In the meantime, greater control and influence were also being exerted on the population.

Under Stalin's reign, the country quickly overcame its struggles and emerged as a powerful military and industrial superpower with the goal of expanding its influence around the world. The British had ruled the world for a long time, but the war had left Great Britain weak, and its global influence had diminished significantly.

The United States, on the other hand, had come out of the war as the new superpower. Within a few years, the Soviet Union would join ranks with the US as another global superpower.

The two countries, which never had a great relationship to begin with, would go on to frequently butt heads, giving rise to an entirely new conflict.

If we consider the matter objectively, World War II helped the Soviet Union become a powerful force. Although the country suffered the most casualties and its civilian population suffered greatly from the war, the steps the government took after the war helped to establish the nation as a global power. Regardless of how many feel about the Soviet Union's politics, views, or beliefs, it has to be acknowledged that for a country that suffered such great losses, it did a remarkable job of picking up the pieces of devastation and becoming a country that nobody wanted to mess with.

It is unfortunate that, in the process, its tenuous friendship with the West came to an end, turning them from allies to foes.

The Axis Powers

Germany

Consequences of the War

Days before Germany surrendered to the Allies, Hitler shot himself and died by suicide on April 30th, 1945. Everyone who was left behind had to pick up the pieces of the carnage he instigated.

Much like the Allied powers did after World War I, Germany was punished severely for instigating World War II. In addition to suffering a humiliating defeat for the second time in less than a century, Germany also suffered enormous casualties. The country was devastated by war *and* had to pay a lot in reparations.

Basically, after nearly six years of fighting endless battles, Germany lost everything and gained nothing in return.

Casualties of War

It is difficult to have an exact number of German casualties because the numbers provided by the German High Command don't go past January 31st, 1945. However, several major battles took place after this date.

The official numbers that have been used by historians state that approximately four million German soldiers either died or went missing. However, in the 1990s, Rüdiger Overmans, a German historian, challenged this number after he dug into the military records. He conducted a study sponsored by the Gerda Henkel Foundation and discovered that the total number of dead German troops was closer to around 5.3 million. Nearly one million of them were men conscripted from countries in east-central Europe and Austria.

The final number for civilian deaths is also debated, with some believing that the number of people who died as a result of forced labor and war crimes by the Soviets and their expulsion by the Germans ranges from half a million to over two million.

It is estimated that between 350,000 to 500,000 civilians died as a result of air raids and Allied bombings. An additional 300,000 people died in Germany as a result of religious persecution, racism, and politics.

And finally, approximately 200,000 German people who suffered from disabilities were killed as part of the Nazis' euthanasia programs.

The Yalta Conference

The question of what should be done about Germany was a point of discussion for the Allied powers months before the war actually ended. When they met in February 1945 in a city called Yalta, along the coast of the Crimean Peninsula, they were confident the war was already won.

The meeting of the three major Allied leaders—US President Roosevelt, British Prime Minister Churchill, and Soviet Premier Stalin—was aptly titled the Yalta Conference.

Churchill, Roosevelt, and Stalin (left to right) at Yalta.
https://commons.wikimedia.org/wiki/File:Yalta_Conference_1945_Churchill,_Stalin,_Roosevelt.jpg

When the three powers had met previously in November of 1943 in Tehran, they had discussed strategies on how to liberate Paris and defeat Germany. By the time of the Yalta meeting, Paris had been liberated, and Germany was on the verge of being crushed.

Now, they needed to figure out what to do about Japan, which was still going strong at that time. Roosevelt was certain that without a clear strategy, the war in the Pacific would continue. He wanted to make sure the Soviet Union would support the US, and he also wanted them to join the United Nations.

Churchill wanted to discuss how to bring about democracy in Eastern and Central Europe. Stalin was plotting how best to expand the Soviet Union's influence.

After much discussion, some key points were agreed upon.

- Germany would have to surrender unconditionally, and the country would be divided into four zones to be occupied by the four Allied powers.

- All of Germany, including civilians and prisoners of war, would be punished severely for what they had done. This would be done via reparations.

- Poland would be allowed free elections.

- The Soviet Union would take a seat in the UN Security Council as a permanent member and would go to war against Japan once Germany was dealt with.

The leaders left the conference feeling confident about their next steps. However, it would soon become apparent that Stalin wouldn't do what he said he would.

Another meeting was held between July 17th and August 2nd, 1945, called the Potsdam Conference. This conference would decide Germany's post-war fate.

The Potsdam Conference

At one point, Germany was on an unstoppable high. Nazi troops were stealing from countries, demanding forced labor, and taking whatever they wanted with little care about the destruction they were leaving behind. The end of the war was a sobering moment for Germans, especially when it came time to discuss how they would repay the damage, chaos, and catastrophe they had caused around the world.

Since the initial discussion in Yalta couldn't be relied upon, a new conference was organized. In the five months since the Yalta Conference had taken place, some major changes in personnel had happened. Roosevelt had died just three months earlier, so President Harry Truman attended the conference. Churchill came, but he lost an election halfway through the conference and was replaced by Clement Attlee, the new prime minister. On the Soviet side, nothing had changed, and Stalin was in attendance.

During the Potsdam Conference, the Allies decided Germany would pay $23 billion USD, the bulk of which would be paid with factories and machinery. We will discuss some of the key highlights of the conference below.

Annexation

It was agreed that all the countries that had been annexed by the Nazis would be returned to their pre-war borders, including Hungary, Czechoslovakia, and western Poland.

Occupation

Austria and Germany were divided into four zones that would be occupied and controlled by four of the Allied powers: Great Britain, France, the Soviet Union, and the United States.

All costs and expenses incurred by the occupying countries would need to be paid for by Germany. By the time the occupation of the four zones ended in 1950, these expenses had amounted to several billion dollars.

The German Military

The treaty demanded the demilitarization of Germany, as well as its democratization and denazification.

Industries and Rail Infrastructure

When the four Allied powers began to occupy the four zones, whatever was left of German industries was dismantled. Factories, plants, railroad systems, machinery...everything.

After taking them apart, they were taken to Allied countries. Germany's ships and merchant fleet were also taken. Whatever industries were left and still producing had to give a share to the Allies. Industrial productions, including steel and coal, were all taken out of the country as well.

Germany had foreign stocks that had a value of approximately 2.5 billion dollars. This, too, was confiscated.

Double track railways in the zone occupied by the Soviet Union were dismantled and turned into one track. The Soviet Union took away the rest of the materials.

In short, Germany was stripped bare of every salvageable good and material. Almost everything of value was taken away. However, after a few years of doing this, the Allied powers, with the exception of the Soviet Union, backed off a little and implemented the Marshall Plan. The Soviet Union, however, continued to take goods and materials from Germany until 1953.

Victims of the Holocaust

Germany agreed to provide compensation to the Holocaust victims. The treaty also outlined the intent to prosecute Nazi war criminals and hold them accountable for their actions during the war, especially in concentration camps. (More details about the Holocaust and the atrocities the Nazis perpetrated will be talked about in Chapter 9.)

Other Terms

Germany was in possession of around ten billion dollars' worth of intellectual property. These were in the form of trademarks, copyrights, patents, and other things. Like the stocks, this was taken away by the Allies.

Another condition in the treaty demanded that Germany provide forced labor to the Allies for a number of years. The laborers would be required to work in mines or industries or on farms or camps.

Reparations from Germany

In addition to the conditions outlined in the Potsdam Conference, Germany had to pay reparations to several countries that had been left in shambles due to either Nazi aggression or occupation.

Poland

In 1953, pressured by the Soviet Union, the People's Republic of Poland waived any reparations from Germany. In exchange for waiving this right, Poland and Russia wanted Germany to accept the Oder-Neisse border. Accepting this border meant that Germany would have to give up a quarter of its borders to the two countries.

In 1990, after German reunification, Poland asked for reparations. The Foundation for Polish-German Reconciliation was established in 1992, and around 4.7 billion zlotys were paid to the Polish people by Germany. Compensation continued to be paid by Austria and Germany to surviving Polish victims until 2006.

Even today, it is still widely debated whether Germany actually owes Poland any reparations or not, given the Polish had waived that right in 1954.

Greece

The Nazi occupation of Greece resulted in enormous losses and the destruction of the country. Greece was even forced to take out large sums of money from its banks and hand them over to Nazi Germany as a "loan."

Under the Paris Reparation Treaty, Greece received a share of the reparations taken by the Allies. When the Paris Peace Treaties were finalized in 1947, Greece was awarded an additional share of reparations.

In 1960, 115 million German marks were given as compensation to Greek people who had been victims of the Nazis. The Greek government later demanded more money and claimed the payment before was simply one of many payments to come.

A final treaty was signed in 1990 between Britain, France, the US, the Soviet Union, and East and West Germany. It was called the Treaty on the Final Settlement with Respect to Germany, and it put an end to any and all questions about Germany after the war. Based on this treaty, Germany considers all questions regarding reparations to be resolved.

Greece did not agree. In 2015, it began to call on Germany to pay the reparations still owed to them. The current balance of the reparations, according to Greece's calculations, stands at 279 billion euros.

Israel

Reparations for Jewish property confiscated by Germany and the Nazis were made to Israel by West Germany. Payments totaling approximately $14 billion USD were made until 1989.

The Netherlands

Initially, the Netherlands asked Germany to pay them twenty-five billion guilders. This demand was later changed, and they requested to annex a part of Germany instead. In 1949, around sixty-nine square kilometers were annexed by the Netherlands.

Nearly fifteen years later, in 1963, West Germany paid the Netherlands 280 million German marks and bought the territory back.

Yugoslavia

Germany paid Yugoslavia around $36 million USD in equipment and material taken from their factories. An additional eight million German marks were paid to Yugoslav citizens as compensation for forced experimentation.

The Soviet Union

The Soviet Union received reparations from Germany through machines, factories, industrial production, raw materials, food, and other supplies. The Memel Territory from Lithuania, which was annexed by Germany prior to the start of the war, was annexed by the Soviets after the end of the war.

To this day, many of the reparations have not been paid in full to the recipient countries, and it is unlikely that they ever will be. Most countries have moved on from their desire to punish Germany and demand payback. However, the question of reparations occasionally rears its head, but whether anything will come of these requests remain to be seen.

Post-war Germany

After Germany collapsed and surrendered to the Allies, one of the treaty's conditions was that the Allied powers would occupy the country.

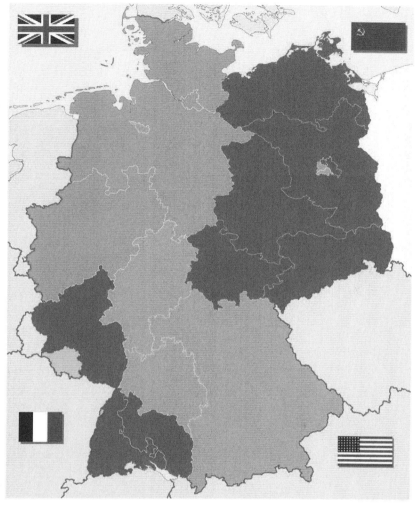

Post-war occupation of Germany.

The country was divided by the four powers in the following fashion:

- Great Britain took over the northwest part of the country.

- France was put in control of the southwest portion.

- The United States had its zone in the south.

- The Soviet Union got the east.

In addition to this division, territories that fell to the east of the Oder and Neisse Rivers were shifted under the Polish. This led to a great displacement; nearly fifteen million people of German ethnicity were made to leave the area. The expulsion was not a seamless and successful process and resulted in a huge number of civilian deaths. People froze, became ill, starved, were abused, or were forced to work in labor camps.

By 1949, West Germany organized itself and established the Federal Republic of Germany. This was occupied by the UK, France, and the US. In the meantime, East Germany, which was occupied by the Soviet Union, established the German Democratic Republic.

East and West Germany would go on to have very different futures. The divide was both physical and ideological, with two differing beliefs. West Germany followed a Westernized model of government, while East Germany was subjected to communist rule.

What's interesting is that Berlin was also divided between the four occupiers. This would become hugely significant in less than two decades when the Berlin Wall went up, resulting in a physical barrier separating the two ideologies and two different ways of life.

West Germany

When the rubble from the war was cleared, it unveiled a striking truth: Germany, for all its victories and triumphs, had been left decimated and crippled. Large portions of the country were in utter ruins. And since Germany faced harsh reparations, its prospects for the future did not look promising.

Therefore, it was shocking and unexpected when within four decades, the country emerged as not just *a* global economic power but one with the third-largest global economy. This is often referred to as the *Wirtschaftswunder* or "economic miracle."

How did Germany do it?

Significant credit is owed to the internationally renowned economist Walter Eucken. He fought during the First World War and eventually became a professor at the University of Freiburg. While teaching, he began to develop economic theories. These theories were rooted in the concept of free-market capitalism with input from the government to prevent monopolies by any one company or group of people. He also believed the government would consider the interests of all people instead of a select few.

Eucken also developed theories on a social welfare system to provide assistance to those less fortunate and promoted the idea of a central bank that was not tied to the government. He argued that a centralized financial institution would help keep the economy stable by using monetary policies.

The theories he put forward are essentially the way most Western or developed countries operate, but when they were initially proposed, they seemed like an entirely foreign concept. Emphasis was instead placed on the idea of socialism.

In the middle of the socialism vs. free-market capitalism debate, a man named Ludwig Erhard, who was mentored by Eucken, began to gain a certain reputation and caught the attention of US intelligence forces. After Germany's surrender, he became the finance minister of Bavaria. He eventually worked his way up to director of the economic council in Allied-occupied West Germany.

Under his direction, a new currency was created, reducing the amount of money available by nearly 93 percent! This resulted in a dramatic reduction of wealth for affluent Germans and companies. He also implemented large tax cuts designed to help people spend and invest their money. The new money came into effect in late June 1948. Price controls were also removed, which left Erhard's superiors questioning his decisions. But Erhard held firm, and the gamble paid off—big time.

When people realized the money had value, they began to shop again. Black market dealings ceased, and people were filled with a desire to earn gainful employment once more because they actually had an incentive to work.

This shift in mentality led to increased productivity. For example, in June 1948, the country's industrial production was half of what it had been over a decade prior in 1936. Within five to six months of the new currency being introduced, industrial production had reached nearly 80 percent! And by 1958, industrial production had quadrupled.

The Marshall Plan, which was created by George Marshall, the US Secretary of State, also helped Germany turn things around. Under the Marshall Plan, around $15 billion USD was distributed to European countries that had suffered enormous losses from the war. A large portion of this aid was given to Germany.

It was also lucky for West Germany that it was occupied by the UK, France, and the US. The influence of these powers and having America as a close ally helped the rebuilding process.

The perfect comparison can be found just on the other side of the ideological border in Soviet-controlled East Germany.

East Germany

Unlike West Germany, East Germany did not enjoy the same benefits and prosperity. Its economy continued to lag, and political freedoms diminished substantially. Things became so bad that people from East Germany became desperate to leave, willing to defy the stringent travel restrictions.

As a way of preventing East German residents from leaving, the Soviet Union began constructing a concrete barrier. The Berlin Wall went up in 1961, and it became a global symbol of the Cold War and a divided Europe.

The residents of East Germany would remain trapped on the other side of the wall until November 9th, 1989, when large crowds swarmed the wall and began to dismantle it. The wall's dismantling came about after the East German Communist Party told the people that they were allowed to cross the border if they wished. The Berlin Wall fell that day. In 1990, the two parts of Germany reunited. The following year, the USSR was officially dissolved.

Today, Germany is a democratic developed nation. It is considered to be a superpower and is one of the most technologically advanced countries. It has a strong military and has one of the largest trading blocs in the world. It is also part of the European Union.

Germany put the events of WWII behind them while still remembering the destruction it had caused. The nation is a strong ally in the West and is focused on maintaining global peace and stability. The country belongs to both the North Atlantic Treaty Organization (NATO) and the United Nations (UN).

Italy

Consequences of the War

Italy paid a steep price for its role in the war. They got almost nothing out of it, and until their surrender in 1943, the war was just a series of military disasters for the country.

Casualties of War and Reparations

Not only did Italy lose its empire in East Africa, but it also lost approximately 492,400 to 514,000 troops in battle. A further 150,000 civilians are estimated to have died during the war.

Under the terms of the 1947 Treaty of Peace with Italy, Italy had to pay reparations to several countries.

- $125 million USD to Yugoslavia
- $105 million USD to Greece
- $100 million USD to the Soviet Union
- $25 million USD to Ethiopia
- $5 million USD to Albania

Under the treaty, Italy had to give up all its African colonies. Some of its Alpine territories went to France, while the Dodecanese, a group of Greek islands, was given to Greece.

During the war, many factories in northern Italy were completely destroyed due to Allied bombing. Production capacities in these factories dropped dramatically, leaving them unable to produce any weapons or other items.

Italians around the world also faced repercussions. Italian immigrants living in Great Britain and the United States were automatically assumed to have fascist ties or beliefs. Thousands of immigrants found themselves rounded up and displaced. They lost their citizenship and their properties and were treated like the enemy even if they were not.

By the time Italy had surrendered to the Allies, the country was in utter shambles. They had lost their empire in Africa, their cities had been destroyed, they were barely producing anything, and they couldn't see a way out of the mess. Surrender seemed like the best and only option available to them.

Within days of Mussolini's arrest, the Fascist Party and other fascist institutions dissolved. The interim government that was put in place was made up almost entirely of ex-fascists. Soon after, Italy broke ties with Germany, ending their alliance. Germany invaded Rome almost immediately. Within months, in a complete reversal from the start of the war, Italy had declared war on Germany. Now it was the Allies helping them out!

Post-war Italy

When the war finally came to an end in May 1945, a strong anti-fascist movement spread over the country. Before the end of the war, in 1943, all the political parties that were strongly opposed to fascism had joined together to form a political umbrella organization called the National Liberation Committee (*Comitato di Liberazione Nazionale* or CLN). The CLN began a resistance movement against the Nazis and was backed by the Allied powers and Italy's monarchy.

Once the war ended, Ferruccio Parri, the leader of the political party Party of Action, led the government.

Throughout Italy, thousands of fascists were found and killed, and a special committee was even set up to purge the country of fascists. This caused significant concern amongst the population, especially among people who held positions in the public sector. A backlash followed, and Ferruccio soon resigned. A more moderate and democratic leader named Alcide De Gasperi replaced him. He stopped the purges and brought order to the country.

One year after the end of the war, King Victor Emmanuel III abdicated in favor of his son, King Umberto II. He didn't hold the position for too long. The country held a referendum and decided they no longer wanted a monarchy and wanted to become a republic. The entire royal family was forced to leave Italy.

When the Cold War began in 1947, De Gasperi went to the United States. In order to keep the Vatican and the United States happy, he had made sure to exclude communists and socialists from his government. His visit to the US proved very fruitful, as he returned with $150 million USD in aid. It was understood that if any communists came to power, the aid would be revoked.

Italy was left off in a better situation post-World War II. The country became a republic and more democratic. Italy developed closer ties with the United States, relying on them for much-needed financial aid. Joining the war effort on the side of the Allies also put Italy on the "right side" of history. Joining the North Atlantic Treaty Organization (NATO) also went a long way to solidifying its position as a Western ally.

In the years after the war, with the help of the US, Italy was able to rebuild many industries and see economic growth. Its currency stabilized, and it joined the European trade, becoming known for its luxurious brand names and fashionable clothing.

Over time, Mussolini and his fascist regime became a thing of the past and are seen as a bump in the road to Italy's long and colorful history.

Japan

The consequences and losses for Japan post-WWII were catastrophic.

During the war, Japan was one of the main enemies of the Allies and paid for it dearly. The atomic bombs dropped on Hiroshima and Nagasaki brought utter devastation to the country. Their effects would last for decades to come.

Japan lost lives, money, and infrastructure. It would take years to reconstruct parts of the country that had been destroyed by atomic bombs and countless air raids.

Casualties of War and Reparations

Japan lost over 3,100,000 people in the war. Approximately 2,300,000 soldiers and troops died, while the remaining 800,000 deaths were civilians. These numbers don't take into account the thousands of people who died in the years since due to the long-term effects of the atomic bombs. Many civilians who survived the bombings would go on to become sick from cancer, leukemia, or other health issues related to radiation.

Japan paid dearly financially as well. Based on the Treaty of Peace with Japan (1951), which was signed by forty-nine nations, it was agreed that the Allied powers would receive reparations from Japan for the damage the country inflicted.

In total, fifty-four bilateral agreements were included in the treaty. Some of the reparations requested include:

- $550 million USD to the Philippines
- $39 million USD to South Vietnam
- $4.5 million sterling pounds to the International Committee of the Red Cross in order to provide compensation to prisoners of war
- $20 million USD to Burma
- $300 million USD to South Korea
- $223.8 million USD to Indonesia
- $5.5 million USD to Spain

Japan started paying these reparations in 1955. The payments ended in 1977. The complete document outlining all the reparations can be found in the Treaty of Peace with Japan.[7]

Occupation of Japan

While the Japanese surrender officially brought the Second World War to an end, it wasn't really the end. The question of what to do with Japan was discussed at great length during a number of conferences held between the Allied leaders. There were questions about Japan's army, its colonies, its economy, etc.

Soon after the war ended, the US led a mission of Allied forces to occupy and rehabilitate Japan. For eight years, they occupied the country under the direction of General Douglas MacArthur, who was the Supreme Commander for the Allied Powers (SCAP). The United Kingdom, China, and the Soviet Union were also involved in the rebuilding plans as advisors.

Sweeping and dramatic changes were brought into the country in three phases. The bulk of the changes took place in the first phase, which roughly lasted from 1945 to 1947. Japan's government was completely dismantled, and military officers were forbidden from any kind of leadership or political role in the new government. War crime trials were held in Tokyo.

---

[7] https://treaties.un.org/doc/publication/unts/volume%20136/volume-136-i-1832-english.pdf

The empire was gone. While the emperor of Japan was kept on as a figurehead, he had no political power or control. The government was overhauled and replaced by a democracy, and a parliamentary system was established.

Land reforms were introduced, which significantly reduced the amount of power and influence wielded by wealthy landowners. MacArthur also made it his mission to convert Japan's economy into a free market. Rights, privileges, and equality for women were also promoted.

The second phase between 1947 and 1950 was characterized by an economic crisis and growing concerns about communist ideologies spreading through the country. MacArthur felt strongly that a weak economy would make Japan and its population more vulnerable to communist tendencies. With China already headed down the path of communism, the Allied forces realized they had to change course.

Fixing the economy became a priority. Tax reforms were introduced, but the war in North Korea became Japan's saving grace. When the United Nations joined the war, Japan supplied everything the UN forces needed. This also helped secure Japan's position and safety on the world map.

In 1950, the third and final phase began. Five years into the occupation, the Allied forces were starting to feel confident that they had laid out a solid foundation for Japan's economic and political success.

The process of drafting a formal treaty that would officially end the war and the occupation began. Faced with the threat of communism and the Soviet Union, the idea of Japan having an army no longer made the United States nervous, nor did they see the country as a threat any longer.

In the final treaty, the two countries signed a bilateral security pact, although the US base in Okinawa was allowed to remain. The occupation officially ended in 1952.

Post-occupation Japan

All things considered, Japan came out stronger at the end of the war and occupation. In many ways, the occupation by the Allied forces was the best thing that could have happened to the country. Instead of being left to deal with their post-war mess on their own, the US helped to rebuild the country into a much stronger one. The country became democratic, and women were given privileges, such as the right to vote, something they did have before.

Today, Japan is a very prosperous country. It is one of the most developed and most educated countries in the world and has a fairly wealthy population. The country boasts low unemployment rates and has the second-largest economy in the world.

Today, the US and Japan share a very close relationship; their former enmity is a thing of the past. They are allies, friends, and great supporters of one another. To many, the US occupation of Japan can be considered a success story.

Section Two: Theaters of War

Chapter 5: The War at Sea

Battles on land, such as the Battle of Normandy or the Battle of the Bulge, are often talked about and written about when discussing the Second World War. While land wars made up the majority of the battles, naval warfare played a crucial role in how the war unfolded and the direction it went in.

In this chapter, we will look at a few significant battles that took place at sea and discuss what the repercussions of these battles were and how they contributed to the war effort.

Battle of the Atlantic (1939–1945)

The Battle of the Atlantic started at the beginning of the Second World War. It played out on the Atlantic Ocean, where German submarines launched a campaign of viciously attacking ships and convoys that were carrying supplies to the Allied forces.

The Battle of the Atlantic started in 1939 and was a continuous battle that lasted for the entire duration of the war. It ended in 1945, making it the longest battle of the war. The battle resulted in over seventy thousand deaths on the Allied side. The Germans lost about thirty thousand people.

It officially began on September 3rd, 1939, several hours after Great Britain declared war on Germany. The SS *Athenia* was headed to Montreal with over 1,400 passengers when it was attacked and destroyed by a German submarine, leading to the deaths of 112 people.

With the attack on the SS *Athenia*, the war on the sea had begun, with Germany fighting for control of the shipping routes through the Atlantic Ocean. The Germans believed that destroying ships carrying critical supplies like food, equipment, and oil would cripple the Allied forces and leave them in a weaker position.

Days later, on September 10th, Canada, a former colony and close ally of Great Britain, declared war on Germany as well. Canada is credited with playing a key role in the battle. Overnight, the Canadian Armed Forces were given the responsibility of escorting convoys to Europe. The convoys were also protected by the Royal Air Force (RAF). Through the course of the battle, the RAF sank nineteen German U-boats, while the RAF Coastal Command sank about two hundred U-boats.

At the beginning of the war, the Nazis were tasting victory after victory in their battles on land. A similar type of success was being seen at sea.

German Admiral Karl Dönitz was the man in charge of leading the naval side of the war, and he put in place a highly successful and extremely deadly strategy. The Allied convoys were hunted and cornered in groups; it was as if the Nazis were acting like a wolf pack. Dönitz assigned groups of submarines to cover a certain area on the route. As soon as a convoy was visible, the message was passed along to the other U-boats nearby, and they all gathered together. Under cover of darkness, the "wolf pack" would strike the convoy simultaneously.

Dönitz's strategy was first used on October 18th, 1940, when a total of seven German submarines attacked a convoy heading for England. A battle ensued, lasting for three days. The German submarines sank 20 of the 35 merchant ships, killing 140 sailors.

The Black Pit

A specific stretch of the Atlantic Ocean that fell beyond the aerial coverage of the Allies was called the Black Pit. The Black Pit would become the scene of many naval battles and attacks.

The German commanders gained confidence from the success of their attacks and decided to go a little further by sending U-boats along the coast of the United States and Canada. The U-boats destroyed the oil tankers and ships headed toward Nova Scotia, where they would have formed part of a convoy that would then go to Europe.

By May 1942, the U-boats were on the St. Lawrence River, sinking a total of twenty-one ships, including a ferry. For six months, from March to September, German U-boats were sinking roughly one hundred ships a month! By this point, around two thousand merchant ships had been destroyed by the Germans, killing several thousand sailors in the process. Millions of tons of supplies headed for the Allied forces fighting in Europe never reached them and were sunk instead.

The Turning Tide

Again, like the battles on land, the tide also turned for those battling at sea.

The British were able to crack the Germans' secret code, which went a long way toward helping the Allies. They were no longer flying blind and were able to have a better idea of what the Germans would do next.

Cracking the Enigma code also allowed the Allies to monitor the movements of U-boats. In addition to this, due to the development of long-range aircraft, the Allies were able to cover more ground (or rather water) when it came to the Atlantic.

The British navy took a more aggressive approach toward the German U-boats and actively began to track them down. They were also on the constant lookout for convoys that needed immediate assistance.

Additional support and assistance arrived from Canada in the form of ships. Canada's navy also began to hunt German U-boats and helped sink additional boats. This mighty combination began to pay off, and the tide began to turn.

In 1942, the Germans were sinking an average of one hundred merchant ships a month; in 1943, they managed to sink less than three hundred ships throughout the year! When the Germans began to suffer huge losses and lose their own U-boats at an alarming rate, they pulled back for a few months.

Canada's support resulted in all of the northwestern Atlantic falling under its command. It was up to Canada to keep the Germans in line at sea.

Although the Germans were struggling, they were not ready to give up just yet and still had a few more cards to play. Five years into the war, technology had greatly improved. The Germans now had much better submarines and were getting increasingly desperate, which meant Allied convoys on the Atlantic were still in danger.

Toward the end of the war, the Germans torpedoed the HMCS *Esquimalt* near Halifax, Canada. Forty-four people died. Three weeks after the attack, the U-boat that had carried out the attack, *U-190*, finally surrendered, bringing the battle to an end.

Although the Battle of the Atlantic is not discussed exhaustively, it played a critical role, as it helped the Allied forces that were fighting in Europe. The naval forces kept the sea safe, allowing for the passage of precious goods and supplies to Europe and contributing hugely to the Allies' eventual victory.

The long, drawn-out battle was draining and relentless and claimed the lives of over seventy thousand merchant seamen. Most of whom never made it back home. Their bodies were never recovered as they sank into the Atlantic Ocean.

Black Sea Campaigns (1941–1944)

The Black Sea campaigns took place in the Black Sea and its surrounding coastal regions. It was fought by the Axis powers and the Soviet Union between 1941 to 1944.

The Soviet Navy, called the Black Sea Fleet, was completely taken aback when Hitler broke his non-aggression pact with Stalin and invaded the country.

The Axis forces in the Black Sea campaigns were made up of Germans, Italians, Bulgarians, and Romanians. The Croatian Naval Legion also joined after it was established in July 1941.

The Soviet Navy was far superior to what the Axis had to offer. However, things started badly for them because not only had they been unprepared for the attack, but Germany's Luftwaffe was also very efficient and powerful. A series of bombings destroyed most of the Soviet ships.

Hitler's invasion of the Soviet Union, codenamed Operation Barbarossa, began on June 22nd, 1941. The Soviet Union suffered devastating losses on every front, but they were beginning to resist and fight back.

On August 8th, the Germans besieged the port of Odesa, which is located on the Black Sea. A battle ensued between the Axis and the Soviet forces, lasting for seventy-three days. By mid-October, the Black Sea Fleet decided to evacuate the garrison to the city of Sevastopol. It also evacuated nearly 350,000 civilians and military personnel.

During the start of Sevastopol's invasion, the Black Sea Fleet did everything in its power to defend the city. Soviet submarines sank thousands of tons of Axis supplies, while the southern Black Sea was scattered with minefields placed there by both the Axis and the Soviet Union. The minefields sunk several submarines on both sides.

Most of the Black Sea campaigns in 1942 were related to the Siege of Sevastopol. Supplies and other support were provided by Soviet warships during the winter and spring.

In February of 1942, while active Soviet submarines were monitoring the western part of the Black Sea, *Shch-213*, a Soviet submarine, torpedoed *Struma*, a ship that was sailing with the Red Cross flag. It was carrying around eight hundred Jewish refugees from Romania and taking them to Palestine. Everyone on board except for one person died.

By the following year, the Black Sea Fleet had been greatly reduced and was in poor condition. The Romanian Naval Forces had also suffered some losses but were performing admirably.

During 1943, most of the operations on the Black Sea were offensive campaigns launched by the Soviet Union. In July, the Soviet submarine *M-31* was sunk by a Romanian destroyer.

By this time, it was clear to the Axis that things were not going well for them as a whole, so Germany decided to evacuate the "Goth's head position," also known as Kuban Bridgehead. The bridgehead was located on the Taman Peninsula, which was situated between the Black Sea and the Sea of Azov. It was created after Germany was driven out of the Caucasus. The Germans had heavily fortified the area and had military personnel stationed there so they could start attacking the Caucasus when needed.

But when things started to go badly with the Red Army, the Germans decided to cut their losses and evacuate from the area. As they evacuated, they made sure to sink several Soviet destroyers with their Stukas (German dive bombers).

When the Second World War entered its fifth year, the Soviet fleet was almost in shambles and non-functioning. They were badly in need of repairs, and it seemed as if there was no way forward. As a result, they began to use smaller vessels in most of their offensive campaigns. The naval air force also lent its support.

But by 1944, things were looking very bad for the Axis. They were losing land battles on almost every front, with Axis troops trapped in the Crimea after Odesa's liberation. Axis forces near Sevastopol had also surrendered while Soviet submarines carried on with their attacks on Axis ships.

The Red Air Force was also playing an active role by raiding Axis bases located in the Black Sea and sinking U-boats and other targets. Their efforts reduced the number of German submarines by half!

As things continued to deteriorate for the Nazis, the Soviets gained more ground, bringing the Black Sea campaigns to an end.

Baltic Sea campaigns (1939-1945)

While the Soviets were busy fighting the Axis powers along the Black Sea, Allied forces were battling the Axis on the Baltic Sea. Although the main participants on the Allied side in this theater were the Soviet Union and the Polish Navy, the Swedish Navy also played a crucial role in the campaigns. On the Axis side, the German Navy was supported by the Finnish Navy.

The Polish Navy had first entered the picture in 1939 when the country was invaded by Germany during the Battle of Danzig Bay and the Battle of Hel.

The Battle of Danzig would be the first battle of WWII involving both naval forces and air forces. While the Polish flotilla was sailing across Danzig Bay, they were attacked by the Luftwaffe. The Polish warships managed to avoid most of them, suffering some damage. When they finally arrived at Hel, they were met with additional air raids on September 1st, 1939.

Within days, the Luftwaffe had severely damaged or destroyed the Polish ships, which were either abandoned or sank. The few remaining light vessels, such as tugboats and gunboats, that had survived were taken by the Germans.

In 1941, the Soviet Red Banner Baltic Fleet was in a good position. It had the Baltic Sea's largest navy with bases scattered all along the coast. But when Germany invaded suddenly and with no warning, the unprepared Soviet fleet began to evacuate frantically from Finland and the Baltic states.

In the process, they lost their naval bases at Liepaja and Riga, as well as a significant part of their navy. They took refuge in Tallinn, but it didn't remain a refuge for long since they were soon surrounded by German troops.

The Soviets were now scrambling to evacuate everyone from the sea while being attacked relentlessly by German bombers. During the evacuation, the Soviets suffered heavy losses at the Juminda Peninsula, which had been packed with mines by the Germans and Finnish.

A similar story unfolded at Hango, another Soviet naval base. While evacuating Hango toward the end of the year, the Soviet Navy again suffered massive losses.

What the Soviet Navy had been able to do was save Leningrad from Germany's first assault back in the fall. Of course, that, too, would be short-lived, as German troops went on to blockade Leningrad.

In 1942, the Oranienbaum Bridgehead was maintained by the Soviets. They sent out submarines to attack German and Finland and were able to successfully sink eighteen ships. However, in the process, they lost twelve of their submarines.

Even though it wasn't the most successful campaign, the Soviet Navy made the Axis navies uncomfortable and forced them to use longer alternate routes. In order to get rid of the Soviet Navy, the Germans began to use more aggressive tactics, leading to increased losses for the Soviets.

In January 1942, the Soviets recaptured Suursaari from the Finnish, but within a couple of months, the Finnish managed to drive them out. This set off a series of battles that would last until April, with both sides fighting to regain control of the island.

When the Soviets tried to capture another island, Someri, they were forced back but managed to damage two Finnish gunboats in the process.

In the fall of 1942, Finland sent out its improved and updated submarines to the Sea of Aland to search for Soviet submarines. They destroyed three Soviet submarines in total, which led to them pulling back a little from the area.

By the time spring of 1943 rolled around, the Germans were ramping up their efforts in the Black Sea. The Gulf of Finland was protected by mines, and the Soviets were unable to break through the anti-submarine net barrage across the gulf. Over sixty thousand naval mines were spread out in the area. The Soviets were prevented from raiding German shipping or from getting anywhere close to the German U-boats. Their repeated attempts came at a high cost since they lost six submarines.

However, the Soviets did sink one of the Finnish minelayers and caused damage to gunboats through an air raid. In the fall of 1943, one of the Soviet Union's torpedo planes sank a Finnish escort vessel.

By 1944, the Soviets were starting to crush the Axis powers in land battles. The Siege of Leningrad had been lifted, and things were looking up for the Allied powers.

Air raids on Helsinki by the Soviets led to the sinking of two Finnish patrol boats; however, the Soviets were unsuccessful in their attempt to attack the south coast of the Gulf of Finland. In the end, that didn't matter. In September, the Soviet Union and Finland signed the Moscow Armistice, agreeing to peace.

Prior to the armistice, the Soviet offensives against Finland resulted in several German vessels becoming damaged. After the successful invasion of Normandy, the majority of Germany's surface fleet was sent to the Baltic Sea to help the floundering navy there. A series of battles ensued between the two countries, with the Soviets advancing further into Nazi-occupied territories and the Germans evacuating people. Both sides continued with their bombings and torpedoing, resulting in boats and vessels sustaining significant damage.

By this time, the German forces were also dealing with a desperate shortage of supplies, including fuel. In order to save whatever resources they had left, the Germans began to reduce the number of escort ships, leaving the convoys open to the Soviets' mercy.

After liberating Leningrad, the Soviet Union's weakened and crumbling surface fleet stayed put because of the mines the Germans had laid out in the area. Its submarines, however, continued to attack and sank several German liners that were being used to transport refugees, resulting in heavy losses. The war ended soon after that, bringing an end to the Baltic Sea campaigns.

Pacific Theater

When people discuss WWII, Europe tends to get more attention, but Japan played a very critical role in the war. Japan, which was part of the Axis, was in conflict with much of Asia and later the United States and the Allies.

After the attack on Pearl Harbor, the United States went into the war with guns blazing. Defeating Germany was certainly a priority for the US but so was crushing Japan.

Japan's sphere of influence and control extended over a large portion of central Pacific and Southeast Asia, including Burma, present-day Malaysia, New Guinea, and Wake Island.

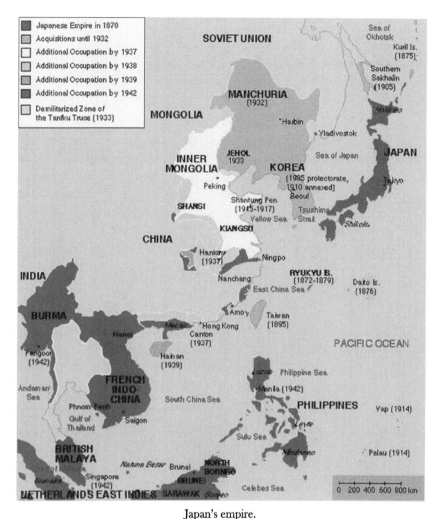

Japan's empire.

The US was determined to end Japan's control. The Americans took charge of the Allied forces battling in the Pacific theater and began to organize counteroffensives against Japan, leading to a series of battles.

One of the major conflicts to take place in the Pacific theater was the Battle of Iwo Jima. It was fought between Japan and the US and is one of the deadliest battles ever fought by the US Marine Corps.

In 1942, the Joint Chief of Staff (JCOS) was established and put in charge of directing the war effort. The JCOS was made up of officers from the US Air Force, Navy, and Army, with General Douglas MacArthur and Admiral Chester Nimitz commanding one-half of the Pacific theater.

The two leaderships meant a divided opinion on how the US should advance into the Japanese homeland. MacArthur believed the best way forward was to head toward Tokyo and regain the Philippines on the way, while Nimitz wanted to focus on regaining smaller islands throughout the Pacific. After much discussion, it was decided in 1944 that a combination of both strategies would be used against Japan.

In October 1944, MacArthur took his troops to the Philippines, while Nimitz took control of the Mariana Islands, leading to the significant destruction of Japan's air force and navy.

One of the JCOS officers, General Henry Arnold, felt the Bonin Islands—over two dozen small volcanic islands scattered throughout the central Pacific Ocean—could be the key to attacking Tokyo via air raids. Iwo Jima was ideally placed, as it was located between Tokyo and the Mariana Islands.

Battle of Iwo Jima – February 19ᵗʰ to March 26ᵗʰ, 1945

Arnold had initially planned to take the island of Formosa (present-day Taiwan), but his admirals felt Iwo Jima and Okinawa might be a better bet instead. Once the plan was approved by JCOS, Nimitz began to plan the invasion, which would become known as Operation Detachment.

Iwo Jima was a tiny, volcanic island covered in sand and ash. It contained hundreds of small caves and two airfields named Motoyama 1 and 2. Lieutenant General Kuribayashi Tadamichi was put in charge of defending Iwo Jima. Japan was determined that, win or lose, it would make the US troops suffer.

Tadamichi first built a network of tunnels on the island and then set up blockhouses and gun sites aboveground for protection. His soldiers were stationed either in the caves or the tunnels. The plan was to get the American soldiers deep inland and then attack through a barrage of artillery and infantry fire. Tadamichi also ordered the troops to forego the traditional banzai charge—the Japanese battle cry—and instead use their hideouts to kill as many

American soldiers as possible.

When the US finally began its invasion, the small island had over twenty-one thousand Japanese soldiers ready to attack and fend off the invaders.

On the American side, Operation Detachment was made up of naval forces and Marines. They had eleven warships and approximately seventy thousand troops. American intelligence believed the island was being defended by thirteen thousand Japanese troops and were confident that the invasion could be successfully won in four days.

General Joel Alan Schmidt, who was commanding the Marines, had put in a request to bomb Iwo Jima for ten days in a row in preparation for the invasion. He got permission for three due to the narrow timeframe. Nimitz was aiming for a quick win before turning his attention to Okinawa.

The bombing did not go as planned. The weather did not cooperate, and the bombings hardly made a dent on the well-protected island. When the Marines began to land on the island on the morning of February 19th, 1945, they were expecting a quick and efficient landing. But the shore was surrounded by volcanic ash, making the landing more difficult than anticipated. Bulldozers were sent by the US Navy to clear the ash, and they began to make some progress.

Pressing his advantage, Tadamichi ordered his troops to start firing on the confused, disoriented soldiers. A few days after the landing, Tadamichi launched kamikaze attacks on navy vessels. These attacks were a type of suicide attack via bombing with the goal of destroying enemy warships; this same type of attack was used at Pearl Harbor. A Japanese fighter pilot would take their kamikaze aircraft, which was basically a plane that had been converted into a missile, and crash into a ship. More often than not, the ship and the aircraft would explode, leading to complete destruction or severe damage.

A kamikaze attack on the USS Essex during operation in the Pacific theater, 1944.
https://commons.wikimedia.org/wiki/File:USS_Essex_(CV-9)_is_hit_by_a_Kamikaze_off_the_Philippines_on_25_November_1944.jpg

Tadamichi's kamikaze attacks severely damaged some of the American ships, but the US Marines pressed on, undeterred. By February 23rd, the 28th Regiment managed to secure Mount Suribachi, firmly announcing their win by raising an American flag on the summit.

The raising of the American flag on Mount Suribachi.
https://en.wikipedia.org/wiki/File:Raising_the_Flag_on_Iwo_Jima,_larger_-_edit1.jpg

This image has become one of the most enduring and famous images from WWII.

In the meantime, the other regiments continued to advance forward, but their progress was hampered by the extremely strong Japanese defense. American troops were fired upon relentlessly. The US suffered heavy casualties, but little by little, they managed to gain control of some key areas, including Hills 362A and 362B.

By March 10th, the Amphitheater and Turkey Knob were under US control. Less than a week later, on March 16th, the US announced that the last of the Japanese defenses had crumbled and that the invasion of Iwo Jima had been a success.

However, this would not be entirely true until March 26th. On that day, several hundred Japanese troops killed one hundred sleeping Allied troops and then committed suicide. After this, the invasion was considered over, but it came at a very steep cost. Japan lost approximately 18,500 soldiers. Close to 7,000 US Marines died, with another 19,200 wounded.

Nearly every single Japanese soldier was killed or committed suicide, a testament to their unyielding loyalty to their country. The realization that the Japanese would rather die than surrender would go on to influence Harry Truman's decision to bomb Hiroshima and Nagasaki.

The cost for the Americans was high, but the victory benefited them. Iwo Jima's airfields were used for the rest of the war.

Battle of Okinawa – April 1st, 1945 to June 22nd, 1945

As planned by Nimitz, within days of winning the Battle of Iwo Jima, the focus turned to Okinawa. Pre-invasion bombings were started by the US Navy on March 24th, 1945. They continued until March 31st, and on April 1st, 1945, over sixty thousand American troops and Marines stormed the beaches of Okinawa, officially beginning the battle.

This would be the last planned island battle. Okinawa was one of the larger islands. If the Allies could successfully gain control of it, they would have an airbase from where they could launch air strikes on Japan. The island would also provide a base for the Allied fleets and help them blockade important routes for Japan.

The codename for the battle of Okinawa was Operation Iceberg.

The initial landings by the American forces went smoothly, and they met with no resistance from the Japanese troops. However, this would soon change. Much like at Iwo Jima, the Japanese troops put up a fierce and determined defense.

Also like Iwo Jima, Okinawa was not a quick and easy victory. The battle took place over a period of almost three months. Some of the deadliest kamikaze attacks were seen during this battle, destroying or crippling thirty-four US ships.

Okinawa was also the first time when the Japanese began to use *baka*, a suicide weapon like the kamikaze planes. The glider was loaded with explosives and powered by rockets. A Japanese pilot was tasked with guiding the glider to its target and hitting it. A series of offensives and counteroffensives throughout the months of April, May, and June saw the US troops slowly gain ground.

Back home in the US, in the midst of the battle, President Franklin Delano Roosevelt died. Harry Truman became president.

Finally, by June 22nd, the American forces managed to overwhelm and defeat the Japanese, bringing the Battle of Okinawa to a close. Yet again, the US suffered heavy losses. It is estimated that twelve thousand soldiers died, with an additional thirty-six thousand wounded.

Reminiscent of Iwo Jima, many of the Japanese troops chose to kill themselves instead of surrendering.

Japan's Surrender

Once the Battle of Okinawa ended, the Allied powers began to plan the invasion of Japan. Germany had already surrendered, bringing the war in Europe to an end, and the Allies were hoping the same would happen with Japan.

However, the Potsdam Declaration (the Proclamation Defining Terms of Japanese Surrender) was not accepted as planned.

In the declaration, the Allies demanded Japan's unconditional surrender and the complete disarmament of the country's military. It also outlined the intention of trying the Japanese for war crimes and the intent to establish a democratic government in the country. If Japan agreed to the points, it would be allowed to maintain any and all industries that were not related to the war. Furthermore, it would be given access to raw materials and, over time, be allowed to trade internationally again.

However, if they refused to surrender or agree to the terms, the Allies would carry out an aerial and naval attack.

Shortly before the Potsdam Conference was set to begin, Truman received word that the Manhattan Project scientists had successfully carried out a test of the first atomic bomb. He passed the information along to Stalin and outlined his plan to use it should Japan refuse to surrender.

As we know, Japan rejected the Potsdam Declaration. Japan's war minister Korechika Anami said the terms were dishonorable and refused to accept them, thus sealing the fates of Nagasaki and Hiroshima.

Soon after, Truman made the decision to drop the atomic bombs as a way of bringing the war to a swift and final end. Although the decision is heavily criticized to this day by many, it is quite likely that the events of the battles of Iwo Jima and Okinawa heavily influenced Truman's decision.

He firmly believed that by bombing the two cities and forcing Japan to surrender, he had prevented the deaths of thousands of American troops. If previous battles were anything to go by, Japanese troops would choose death as long as it meant taking Allied lives with them.

Truman perhaps felt that he had one shot at crippling Japan completely, and he took it. If he hadn't, would Japan have continued with their kamikaze and baka attacks? Impossible to say for sure, but it is quite likely. However, others have said that Japan was on its last legs, which means the war likely would have concluded without the use of such extreme force.

Whether it was a good call or not, the bombings led to Japan's unconditional surrender and its acceptance of the Potsdam Declaration.

Chapter 6: The War on Land

Life in the Trenches

It's no secret that war is very often glorified. In books, movies, art, and even music, fighting for an ideological cause is seen as the ultimate glory. There are images and stories of camaraderie, of troops marching through lush, green fields, shoulder to shoulder, fighting for a just cause.

However, the reality is very different. Land warfare was absolutely horrendous. It was physically, mentally, and psychologically draining and damaging.

British soldiers in the trenches.
https://ww2db.com/image.php?image_id=5769

World War II was a devastating war, shocking in its bloody savagery. It was by far the most destructive conflict ever witnessed by the world.

The Germans perfected the science of the blitzkrieg. It was a fast-paced, efficient way of invading, destroying, and occupying. Each country the Germans invaded was taken completely by surprise and bombed into submission. This highly effective method accounted for Germany's series of successful invasions at the start of the war. But as Great Britain and the Allies organized themselves, the German forces had a harder time finding victory.

As the Axis and Allies began to battle each other, what followed was one of history's deadliest periods. Bombs were dropped left and right, destroying entire cities. Whatever the bombs might have missed were ravaged by the massive tanks that rolled through the streets. At this point in history, technology was quite advanced, and each side had an arsenal of sophisticated weaponry at their disposal.

The troops fought with a wide array of weapons, such as the following:

- Guns, including rifles, shotguns, submachine guns, and pistols;
- Grenades and mines;
- Machine guns;
- Missiles;
- Poison gas;
- Tanks, including tank destroyers and flame tanks;
- Artillery, such as anti-tank guns, self-propelled guns, rocket launchers, and heavy mortars;
- Atomic bombs;
- Simple things like knives and blades.

A good portion of the battle was fought on foot, with soldiers either on horses or marching on the ground. If an enemy shot at a soldier, mortally wounding them, chances were high that they would die right there on the spot. Those who were lucky were sent back home for a proper burial. Hundreds of thousands of soldiers would never return home again.

Life of a Soldier

The life of a soldier at the front was hardly the romantic experience depicted in books and movies. It was also rather different than military training. Life on the front was unpredictable, traumatic, and potentially deadly.

People who registered for military service were sent to basic training to develop skills and receive training in military life, the chain of command, and weaponry. Depending on what the soldier wanted to do, specialized training might follow basic training. For instance, some people were trained for combat, while others were taught how to operate radios and transmit codes.

Since a large portion of WWII was fought on land, the soldiers who fought on the ground had a tougher experience. Once they were thoroughly trained, they were taken to a holding camp to await further instructions and for their heavy equipment to arrive. The camps were the calm before the storm. There was food, companionship, and a bunk to sleep in at night. And if a soldier was lucky enough to arrive during the warm months, they would find camp life was infinitely more pleasant.

When they finally had to move on, each soldier was given a pack to carry everything they would need to survive: food, clothes, personal items, boots, and helmets, just to name a few things. A separate bag with ammunition and weapons was also carried. In total, each soldier was carrying roughly eighty additional pounds with him at all times. The soldiers also carried a rifle and other items that were distributed amongst them.

The squads of soldiers then marched to their destination, led by a junior officer and sergeants. As they marched, they were acutely aware that enemy forces could be lurking nearby, ready to take them out.

Most of these soldiers had very little idea of what was actually happening with the war. Were they losing? Winning? Nobody knew for sure. Some of the updates that would eventually reach their ears were weeks old.

Depending on where they were headed and the weather, these marches could be horrendous. Soldiers had to slog through mud, rain, ice, scorching heat, or knee-deep snow. There was no respite from the weather, and for those going over mountainous terrain or through dense woods, the march was even more miserable.

Soldiers often ended up with painful blisters on their feet or got trench foot, which happens when your feet are wet for a long period of time. The men had little opportunity to bathe or shave, often going for months without an opportunity to properly clean themselves or wear fresh clothes. Some showers were taken using a bag that was hung several feet off the ground. There would be just enough water in the bag to allow the soldier to soap up and rinse off.

When the soldiers finally reached their destination, they had to set up a camp for the night. Camp consisted of foxholes that had to be dug up individually using an ax or a pick. This was back-breaking work, especially if the ground was frozen and rock-hard. Craters could sometimes be found as a result of artillery; the men would use these craters as camps.

In the winter, soldiers slept in sleeping bags, but most soldiers did not like using them since it made them less mobile. There was always the fear they would be attacked at night.

Even the camps were never truly safe. If they were close to an enemy camp, soldiers were forbidden from smoking or lighting a fire. Some were assigned to patrol at night, while others slept or at least tried to sleep. Soldiers had to get up at dawn and be ready for an attack at any moment from the enemy camp.

The battles themselves were bloody, dangerous, and violent. Most infantrymen carried an M1 Garand semi-automatic rifle, a tough, reliable weapon. This rifle had an eight-round clip that could be fired just by pressing on the trigger for each shot and could even be converted into a grenade launcher!

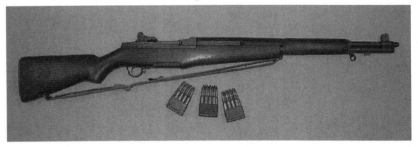

M1 Garand semi-automatic rifle.
Curiosandrelics, CC BY-SA 3.0 <https://creativecommons.org/licenses/by-sa/3.0>, via Wikimedia Commons; https://commons.wikimedia.org/wiki/File:M1-Garand-Rifle.jpg

Wounded soldiers were treated on the field by a medic, if the squad even had one. Soldiers with severe wounds were sent to a surgical post or a hospital.

Through the course of these sometimes very long battles, soldiers barely had time to think or process anything that was going on except for the enemy before them. They did what they had to do; if they were lucky, they were able to get some rest and maybe a bite to eat before battling the enemy again.

On and on it continued, night and day, until the enemy was vanquished. And then the squad would march to their next stop. Along the way, they would witness horrifying things. They would see the dead bodies of their friends and allies, villages razed to the ground, and innocent civilians killed or wounded. Day in and day out, they lived this horror until the war finally ended.

As we can see, life on the front was not easy or filled with glory. The description above was a basic rundown of a soldier's journey; the actual details were much worse. It is lucky for the world that men were willing to live through this and fight for a just cause because it was not an easy feat.

Key Land Battles during WWII

World War II was fought mainly on land through a series of battles scattered throughout Europe and other parts of the world. While every battle contributed to the war effort, some battles were more decisive than others.

Here is a short list of the most important land battles.

- Operation Barbarossa (June 22nd-December 5th, 1941): This was the German invasion of the Soviet Union. It resulted in the Soviets entering the war on the side of the Allies. After a series of mishaps and heavy losses, the Soviets would end up playing a key role in defeating Germany and the Axis.

- Siege of Leningrad (September 8th, 1941-January 27th, 1944): The city would be under siege by the Germans for nearly nine hundred days. The lifting of the siege was seen as a huge victory for the Soviets and a turning point in the war.

- Battle of Stalingrad (August 23rd, 1942-February 2nd, 1943): Germany's invasion of Stalingrad was met with fierce resistance by the Red Army. The German Army was soundly defeated.

- Battle of Normandy (June 6th-August 30th, 1944): This battle is often seen as the beginning of the end. With Normandy, the Allied troops were able to start pushing the Germans out of France, liberating the country.

- Battle of the Ardennes (December 16th, 1944-January 25th, 1945): Germany's last great offensive and attempt to destroy the Allies initially began with a lot of promise. Germany even believed it could reverse its losing streak, but in the end, the Americans' persistence paid off. The German offensive was pushed back and wrecked.

- Battle of Berlin (April 16th–May 2nd, 1945): This battle spelled the end for Hitler and the Nazis. The Red Army fought fearlessly and captured Berlin while waiting for American reinforcements to arrive. Hitler committed suicide during this battle when he finally came to the realization that Germany had lost.

Additional details and a more in-depth look at these battles can be found in other sections and chapters of this book.

Propaganda and Conscription

Propaganda played a huge and important role in World War II, especially in Nazi Germany.

Various types of propaganda were used to sway civilians to a certain way of thinking. While propaganda helped to increase support for the war and gain troops, conscription was one of the primary ways in which each country was able to enlarge its armies.

Germany

Nazi propaganda would become so strong and effective that people were more than willing to join the Nazi cause, but before they arrived at this stage, Hitler got troops by reintroducing conscription. The announcement for conscription was made on March 16th, 1935.

Hitler stated his plans for Germany's rearmament program and the need to increase the German Army to over half a million troops. The German military would also be renamed Wehrmacht, and the Wehrmacht High Command would be responsible for overseeing the air force, the army, and the navy.

When world leaders began to question Hitler's moves, he assured them he was doing this for defensive purposes and that all Germany wanted was peace. Of course, this was not true. Within a year of reintroducing conscription, the buffer zone between France and Germany was swarming with German soldiers.

The skies above the Rhineland—the buffer zone—were covered with German fighter planes. Hitler's generals felt nervous and worried that France or Great Britain might object since doing this was in direct violation of the Treaty of Versailles. Hitler correctly surmised that they would do nothing.

Over the next three years, Hitler waited, biding his time. He built his armies through conscription. Between 1935 and 1939, 1.3 million men were drafted, and an additional 2.4 million joined the military voluntarily, including women. Over half a million women were volunteer uniformed auxiliaries in the Wehrmacht. Additional volunteers served in aerial defense, nursing, and other units.

When Hitler felt he was ready, he struck.

The United States

In the United States, conscription is typically referred to as "the draft" and has been used a total of six times throughout history for major conflicts, such as the Civil War and WWI.

In 1940, after Germany's successful invasion of France, the general consensus among Americans was that young men should be drafted and begin training just in case. Even though the government wasn't interested in declaring war, there was still worry that the US might be in danger.

The Selective Training and Service Act was signed by Franklin D. Roosevelt, requiring men between the ages of twenty-one and thirty-five to register. The plan was to cap the number of conscripts to 900,000 men, and they would only have to serve for one year unless anything changed. The initial one-year date would be amended once the war was underway.

Voluntary enlistment was closed through Executive Order 9279 one year after Pearl Harbor. Instead, the military chose troops from the Selective Service System.

The draft was active from 1940 to 1946 and was highly successful, with forty-nine million men registering for duty throughout the course of the war. More than ten million men would go on to active military service.

WWII poster in the US encouraging people to enlist.
*https://commons.wikimedia.org/wiki/File;J. M. Flagg, I Want You for U.S. Army po
ster_(1917).jpg*

Great Britain

Conscription was imposed in Great Britain immediately after the country declared war on Germany. Within hours of the declaration, Parliament passed the National Service (Armed Forces) Act, requiring men between eighteen to forty-one years old to sign up for the military.

There were, of course, some exceptions. For instance, men who were physically unable to fight were exempt. Men who had essential jobs were also exempt. The Act led to a significant increase in the number of British troops.

Two years after the first National Service Act was passed, Parliament passed another one, this one aimed at women between twenty and thirty years of age. The practice of conscription in Great Britain ended in 1963 and is no longer used.

Chapter 7: The War in the Sky

Aircraft played a huge role in WWII. In many ways, it was the first aerial war. Aircraft worked with and supported the naval and land forces and served a wide variety of purposes beyond dropping bombs on cities.

In this chapter, we will look at the role of aircraft in the war and how it was used by both sides. We will look also take a brief look at the different air force groups.

Luftwaffe

The Luftwaffe was Germany's aerial branch and was established before the start of WWII. Germany's previous air force had been dismantled, as per the conditions of the Treaty of Versailles.

When Hitler came into power, he reestablished the air force. The Luftwaffe fell under the purview of the Wehrmacht High Command.

By 1939, the Luftwaffe was extremely advanced. It was the latest, greatest thing in terms of technology, and when Poland was invaded, it quickly became evident just how superior the Luftwaffe was.

The invasions of Norway and France were successful because of the Luftwaffe's contribution; in fact, the Luftwaffe helped get Germany over seventy thousand air victories during the war. The Luftwaffe bombed both military and non-military targets, resulting in the deaths of thousands of innocent civilians. The hardest hit was the Soviet Union.

However, as the war continued, there was a visible weakening of the Luftwaffe, and it began to lose its superiority. Its effectiveness also began to decline steadily. After a particularly spectacular loss during Operation Bodenplatte (an operation that targeted the Low Countries) on January 1st, 1945, the Luftwaffe was no longer considered to be useful or effective.

One of the Luftwaffe's major flaws was the lack of a solid air defense system. The war in Germany began before the Luftwaffe's defenses were complete. This meant it had to develop defenses on the go while fighting a war. There was also a problematic lack of communication between the various flying branches, which, in turn, resulted in poor coordination.

Just over a year after the invasion of Poland, the Luftwaffe was dealing with heavy losses. They badly needed new aircraft but were bogged down by production issues, partially as a result of poor planning and partially due to not having enough resources. Germany was unable to develop the technology further, again due to supply issues and the lack of access to raw materials such as aluminum or oil. This greatly hampered the war effort.

The Luftwaffe played a rather sinister role in the concentration camps, namely Auschwitz and Dachau, where prisoners were used as subjects for experiments for the Luftwaffe. For example, in one of the experiments, prisoners were used to figure out at what altitude someone could be ejected safely from their seats.

When the war finally ended, several Luftwaffe commanders were put on trial for the crimes they had committed during the war.

Similar to Japan's kamikaze, a special task force within the Luftwaffe called the Sonderkommando carried out attacks on air where aircraft were purposely used to attack Allied bombers mid-air, causing them to explode. More often than not, the pilots on these missions died.

Japanese Imperial Air Force

Japan's air force was named the Imperial Japanese Army Air Service (IJAAS). While Japanese aviation played a role in WWI, the Japanese government only began to take the development of military aviation seriously after the war ended. They quickly realized how advantageous it would be to develop new technologies, so they got to work.

An aircraft factory was built in 1916. At first, Japan was using the services of people like Dr. Richard Vogt, an engineer from Germany, to create designs for them.

Imperial Japanese Air Force Mitsubishi Ki-21-II bombers.
https://commons.wikimedia.org/wiki/File:Mitsubishi_Ki_21-2s.jpg

By the late 1920s, they were producing their own designs, and several years after that, they had created an extensive collection of aircraft.

The Imperial Air Force was recognized as a distinct yet equal branch to the Imperial Army's other branches of the military: the cavalry, the infantry, and the artillery.

By the time WWII was well underway, in 1941, Japan's Imperial Air Force was made up of 1,500 aircraft, with the country continuously developing new technology. The aircraft they used for combat were incredibly advanced machines. They utilized fighter planes, bombers, transports, trainers, and reconnaissance planes, to name a few.

One of the deadliest aspects of the Japanese air force was the kamikaze pilots. These pilots were essentially given a suicide mission and used to destroy important posts. They were used more extensively by Japan toward the end of the war.

Even though Japan started strong, Japan's air force was unable to maintain momentum. They didn't have enough aircraft. Poor planning and limited cooperation between the army, navy, and air forces also contributed to Japan's failures as the war progressed.

Like Germany, Japan was having production difficulties. They couldn't replace the aircraft fast enough to make up for their heavy losses. They also did not have enough pilots to man the aircraft. And as existing pilots began to be killed or wounded in battle, their situation worsened.

Difficulties finding resources like fuel and mechanics didn't help matters either.

After the war was lost and Japan was defeated, the Imperial Air Force, navy, and army were disbanded.

Soviet Air Forces

The Soviet Union was very strong and capable on many fronts; however, their air force was not one of them. In fact, the Soviets had one of the weakest aerial forces, which is ironic given that in 1938, the Soviet Union's air force was the largest one in the world. However, the planes were poorly designed, not the most technologically advanced, and not prepared for a war in any way.

Soviet engineers had been more focused on creating bomber planes, which were loud, showy, and could fly really far, instead of developing planes that would be good for tactical warfare.

Along with the bomber and attack planes, the Soviet Air Forces also had fighter planes, transport planes, trainers, and reconnaissance and patrol aircraft. But none of these aircraft were particularly advanced. Stalin himself admitted in the early 1930s that the Soviet military was lagging decades behind in terms of modernization.

The Yak 9 aircraft.

As a result of this poor planning and poor organization, the Soviet Union was woefully unprepared for Germany's invasion in 1941. A week after the invasion, roughly four thousand Soviet aircraft had been decimated by the Luftwaffe.

The Soviets also experienced a significant lack of pilots and other support crews to man the aircraft. A program was created during the war that allowed women with prior flying experience or training to engage in air combat.

When the Lend-Lease Act was launched in March 1941, the Soviets were able to receive US-built aircraft. They received nearly fifteen thousand aircraft under the program. These far more sophisticated and powerful aircraft went a long way toward helping the Soviet Army during the war.

The Soviet Union also began to increase its production of aircraft. As a result, between 1941 and 1945, it produced over 157,000 machines, the majority of which were built for combat.

After the war ended and the Cold War began, the Soviet Union's focus turned to creating and developing the newest, most advanced technologies for its military, with an emphasis on its aircraft.

United States Army Air Forces (AAF)

The AAF was established on June 20th, 1941, and fell under the umbrella of the United States Army. The AAF was the country's aerial warfare service, and it was disbanded after the end of the war.

In 1938, Germany's Luftwaffe began to play a more prominent role by supporting ground forces in German-occupied Czechoslovakia and Sudetenland. President Franklin D. Roosevelt realized that Europe may have been dragged into another war and that the US might have to get involved. In order to win the war, the US would need a strong air force.

A year later, Roosevelt received $300 million USD to establish an air corps. When Hitler began his invasions in Europe, the air corps began to rapidly expand, as new bases were established in the US and overseas.

The air force had an extensive collection of various aircraft for different missions and purposes. The most common ones used for combat included bomber planes; fighter planes; observation, transport, and trainer planes; and utility, glider, and rescue planes.

The AAF was extremely organized, and over the course of the war, it only got stronger and more powerful. Within a period of three years (1942 to 1945), the US produced nearly 275,000 aircraft! This number was higher than the total number of aircraft produced by Japan, Germany, and Great Britain.

From the moment the US joined the war until the end, the AAF played a critical role in helping win battles and victories. They dropped bombs, conducted air raids, engaged in air-to-air combat, brought supplies for ground troops, defended the airs, and provided support to naval and ground support.

During D-Day, the AAF played an important role by clearing the path for troops to land and invade Normandy. To reduce combat fatigue, the AAF made sure to replace and rotate crews frequently to give their pilots and air personnel a break.

The AAF's organization, communication, experienced crew, and ability to produce hundreds of aircraft made it the most powerful and superior air force on the battlefield. With the AAF's help, the Allies ended up with a far more destructive air force. In 1947, the United States would create a permanent air force.

The Royal Air Force (RAF)

Great Britain's air force is called the Royal Air Force or RAF for short. It was established in 1918, and by the end of WWI, the RAF had become the world's largest air force. During WWII, the RAF played a hugely important role, especially during the Battle of Britain.

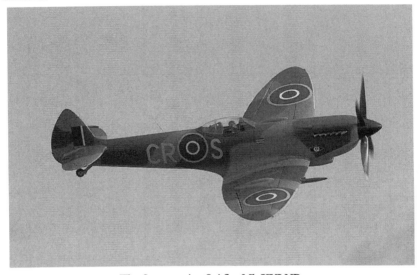

The Supermarine Spitfire Mk XVI NR.
Chowells/Noise reduction and shadows lifted by Diliff., CC BY-SA 2.5
<https://creativecommons.org/licenses/by-sa/2.5>, via Wikimedia Commons; https://commons.wikimedia.org/wiki/File:Supermarine_Spitfire_Mk_XVI_NR.jpg

Before the start of and during WWII, the RAF was considerably expanded. Like most of the countries embroiled in the war, the RAF's aircraft included fighters and bomber planes, torpedo and dive bombers, level bombers, patrol and reconnaissance planes, trainers, and transport planes.

During the war, one of the RAF's primary focuses was an offensive bombing campaign against Germany. The RAF wanted to make sure Germany was weak and unable to fight as efficiently. The RAF's contributions to the war helped the Allies win numerous victories and ultimately end the war.

The contribution from the RAF also included female fighter pilots who joined the war effort. In January 1940, there were only eight women who were part of the effort, but within a few very short years, over 165 women pilots were flying fighter planes and spitfires.

The Battle of Britain

The RAF's single greatest victory during the war is likely the Battle of Britain, which it won singlehandedly.

After a series of stunning German victories, including the fall of France, Hitler turned his eye on Great Britain, invading it in July 1940. He expected a quick victory.

However, the RAF managed to successfully defend Great Britain from the Luftwaffe's relentless bombings and air raids. No matter what the Germans did, the RAF's superior aircraft and strategies could not be broken through. Over 1,700 Luftwaffe planes were shot down by the RAF. The RAF lost about 1,250 aircraft.

When Germany began to lose aircraft at an alarming pace, Hitler was forced to give up and turn his attention elsewhere. The battle ended on October 31st. This would be the first serious loss for Germany, which had only tasted success up until that point. The Luftwaffe was never quite able to recover from these losses. If the RAF had failed, it is almost certain that Germany would have invaded and occupied Great Britain as it did with France.

Chapter 8: The War in the Media

Propaganda

Regardless of which side of the war one was on, the propaganda used to conscript people were similar. Each side had strong ideological beliefs, and each portrayed the other side as the enemy.

Nazi Propaganda

One of the most powerful and important tools in Adolf Hitler's meteoric rise to power was propaganda. He and the Nazi Party used it extremely effectively, legitimating the party and increasing party membership. The skillful use of propaganda is what helped Hitler get elected, and it's what he used to eventually become a dictator.

In order to connect to the masses, Hitler's focus was on relaying clear and simple messages that appealed to the wider public while exploiting their fears. Hitler's timing was impeccable, as Germany's economy had tanked. People around the world were living through the Great Depression, but Germany was severely hit because of the terms implemented by the Treaty of Versailles.

For example, one of Hitler's messages that targeted the working-class people was "Bread and Work." This message tapped into people's fears and instability surrounding the lack of employment, wages, and food shortages.

Another message, "Mother and Child," showed what the Nazi idea of a woman was.

One of Hitler's most trusted advisors was Joseph Goebbels. He joined the party early on, doing so in 1924. Goebbels would become the force behind the Nazis' highly successful propaganda machine. He was so successful that he became the Minister of Propaganda in 1933.

Goebbels used a combination of various types of media, such as art, posters, film, music, radio, and newspapers. He worked hard to reach the maximum number of people. He also carefully began to craft Hitler's image, turning him almost into a mythical leader who was strong and powerful. A leader who would be Germany's savior, who would help the country get back on its feet.

Hitler promised jobs and economic recovery and assured the people that Germany would rise once again with his guiding hand at the helm.

As you can imagine, the "Hitler myth" was highly successful and very effective.

The methods of propaganda that led to Hitler's rise to power were later used to portray the Jewish people as the enemy, an enemy that would be the downfall of Germany.

Hitler recognized the key role propaganda played in his rise. Once he became the chancellor of Germany, he established the Ministry of Public Enlightenment and Propaganda. This in itself was a brilliant move since governments typically only organized committees to spread propaganda while at war. By establishing the ministry during a time of peace, Hitler further legitimatized what he was doing.

Goebbels, who was put in charge of the ministry, envisioned Germany as an enormous empire with absolute control over the people's education and beliefs, as well as the media. He used the anger most Germans felt about their defeat in World War I and emphasized national pride.

In Goebbels's own words, "The essence of propaganda consists in winning people over to an idea so sincerely, so vitally, that in the end they succumb to it utterly and can never again escape from it."[8]

One of the propaganda ministry's first moves was to gain control of the guild that allowed journalists and editors to get jobs. On October 4th, 1933, after gaining control of the Reich Association of the German Press, a new law requiring all journalists and editors to be pure of race was passed without protest. The Editors Law would be the start of a long campaign that banished Jewish people from nearly every aspect of German society.

Under the ministry's governance, the press had to follow mandates and laws passed by the ministry. The press could not print or put out anything that might make Hitler's regime look weak to the German people or the world. The news was controlled even further when daily guidelines and directives on what should be written and how they should be written were issued from Berlin and sent to the offices of local papers.

What happened if anyone defied these directives? They were sent to a concentration camp. Before long, everyone was doing exactly what they were instructed to do. Opposition newspapers were forcefully shut down, while any media or publishing businesses owned by Jewish people were taken away from them and given to "racially pure" Germans. Within months, the idea of a free press had evaporated. The Nazis now controlled everything from the radio to the theater, and they used all these mediums to advance their ideologies and beliefs.

During the war itself, propaganda was used extensively by the Nazis to depict the German Army as a brave, powerful, and conquering force fighting for German nationality. In sharp contrast, Soviet troops were portrayed as heartless, inhumane machines who felt no fear. The Allied powers were misguided cowards who didn't know any better.

Over time, people were brainwashed to believe all these things were true. And more horrifying still, most believed that Jews were evil and did not deserve to live. Nazi propaganda encouraged and

---

[8] "World War II Propaganda."
https://www.pbs.org/wgbh/americanexperience/features/goebbels-propaganda/.

ignited hatred in the people's hearts toward Jews and others who were not of the Aryan race.

So, when hundreds of thousands of Jews, Romani, Soviet prisoners of war, and other Nazi victims were shipped off to concentration camps, most people were either indifferent or felt relieved. Very few people had the courage to fight back against what the Nazis were feeding them.

Propaganda's "task is not to make an objective study of the truth, in so far as it favors the enemy, and then set it before the masses with academic fairness; its task is to serve our own right, always and unflinchingly."[9] This was written by Hitler in his book *Mein Kampf,* and it perfectly captures what the Nazis did and why they did it. They twisted the media and used propaganda to serve Hitler's cause.

British Propaganda

When WWII broke out, Great Britain once more reestablished the Ministry of Information that had been set up for WWI. The purpose of the ministry was to create propaganda that would rally the population together and provide support to the troops and the war effort.

Like Germany, Great Britain also used a mix of modern and traditional media, including films and leaflets. While much of the propaganda was filled with hostility for the Axis powers, especially Germany, the general themes of the advertisements or posters were more positive or motivational than those put out by Goebbels. Emphasis was placed on supporting the Allies, fighting for freedom, and being brave. Each civilian was supposed to do their own part to help the war effort.

People were encouraged to be frugal, grow vegetables, and volunteer for work that could be done within the country. Women were pushed to join the Land Army or the ATS (Auxiliary Territorial Service) or work in munitions factories. In short, everyone was made to feel they had a role to play during the war, whether at the front or at home, and that winning the war depended on everyone pulling together.

---

[9] "Hitler on Propaganda." http://fcit.usf.edu/holocaust/resource/document/docpropa.htm

A British propaganda poster encouraging women to join the war effort.
https://commons.wikimedia.org/wiki/File:Kriegsplakate_6_db.jpg

A lot of the propaganda was devoted to making people feel good about the war effort. Every German defeat and every victory by the British forces were joyfully announced to boost the country's morale and assure the people the Allies were headed down the right path. No matter what was happening, British propaganda tried to focus on the positive. When the tide started to turn for the Allies, British propaganda and radio commentaries became even more inspirational.

Much of the government's information about the war was relayed through propaganda, such as encouraging children to be sent away from the city and how to stay safe during a blackout or air raid.

And, of course, there was the propaganda related to why the British were fighting the war. The issue was depicted simply: it was a fight between light versus darkness, good versus evil.

Hitler was an evil that needed to be rooted out, and the Allies were the ones responsible for doing so, not only to help themselves but also to save the world. As the war went on, the tone shifted. Images and accounts of the war became more sinister to increase the dislike and hatred for the Germans and the Axis powers.

British propaganda about Hitler.
https://commons.wikimedia.org/wiki/File:INF3-238_Anti-rumour_and_careless_talk_Mr._Hitler_wants_to_know.jpg

Sentiment toward the Japanese was lukewarm. While their actions on the Pacific were seen as deplorable, the main target for hatred continued to be the Germans. However, when recruiting African troops, British propaganda placed greater emphasis on anti-Japanese sentiment since that was the more imminent threat to them. The Italians also did not face the same kind of anger as the Germans.

British propaganda also created specific campaigns to bolster public opinion about the other Allies. For example, after the Battle of Stalingrad, the British put out leaflets and posters about the

Soviet Union's great victory, painting the Soviets in a very favorable light.

Much propaganda was aimed at the United States with one goal in mind: to have them join the war. The British were careful not to present it as propaganda; instead, they were delivered as news reports and information. While Franklin D. Roosevelt was keen to join the war effort, the American public wanted nothing to do with it. Both FDR and the British government hoped that news coverage of the battles and the situation in Europe would sway public opinion.

In short, the British used propaganda in a skillful way to bolster morale, gain international support, and provide hope, all while making sure that the people knew exactly who their enemy was.

American Propaganda

As mentioned earlier, President Franklin D. Roosevelt was keen to join the war, but having fought in the First World War, most of the US had no desire to get involved in what they viewed as yet another European problem.

While the British had begun to use propaganda to change American minds, the American government was reluctant to use any type of propaganda, even after they officially joined the war in 1941. This mindset eventually shifted due to increasing pressure from a number of industries that wanted clearer directives, including businesses and the media. When the government began to use propaganda, they wanted to be clear the materials would be used to provide information to the public.

Propaganda was used effectively to garner public sympathy toward the Allied forces and instill a desire within the public to support them. All types of media were used to ignite hatred for Germany and the other Axis powers.

The media of choice for the US seemed to be posters, with the country producing the most posters than any other country engaged in the war. Nearly 200,000 unique posters were designed and printed, mostly with encouraging, supportive messages. For instance, the US made posters of Rosie the Riveter, who was supposed to represent the women joining the workforce.

The woman in this poster was never identified as Rosie the Riveter during the war, although many Americans today mistakenly call her by the name. The poster did not become the famous symbol it is today until the 1960s.

https://en.wikipedia.org/wiki/File:We_Can_Do_It!_NARA_535413_-_Restoration_2.jpg

Advertisements for a number of different causes were released by the country, including selling war bonds, encouraging production in factories, and urging everyone to contribute what they could to the war effort. These advertisements were a key factor in maintaining public morale.

The running theme for most of America's propaganda was patriotism. The Allies were portrayed as the "right" side, while the Axis powers were made to look like weak, cowardly creatures who could not be taken seriously. Hitler was often ridiculed and depicted as a foolish man who was doomed to fail. The Nazi Party was portrayed as the ultimate evil, worse than anything anyone could imagine.

Like Great Britain, the point of the war was simplified to good versus evil. President Roosevelt especially wanted people to understand what a catastrophe it would be if Europe and Asia were ruled by dictators.

In 1942, the Office of War Information was established. The agency would go on to be involved with propaganda in Hollywood movies and other forms of media.

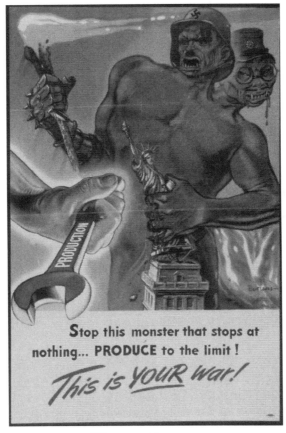

US propaganda poster.

Another organization that was put together to produce and publish propaganda was the Writers' War Board. The board was closely linked to President Roosevelt's administration and established a link between writers and the government. Oftentimes, the writers were far more blistering and took a bolder approach than the government.

Comic book writers also got involved in the war effort to sway people to the "right" side. Superheroes were now battling real-life villains instead of fictional ones.

Advertising played a big role in war propaganda. Companies and big businesses used the war as a way to promote their own brand and what they were doing. Advertisements either supported the war or depicted a company's contribution to the war effort. The companies that could find a way to link their products to the war did so. For example, Coca-Cola advertised that its products were consumed by factory workers and troops. Ads like this supported the war and were good for business. The soldiers at the front also liked getting magazines that were filled with colorful ads. It was a win-win.

Effectiveness of Media

In general, propaganda was spread mainly through modern and traditional media, such as radio programs, newspapers, magazines, films, and posters. In an era where not everyone was exposed to media or had access to media, word of mouth played an important role.

The media was extremely effective at passing on the ideologies and beliefs of the governments and leaders in charge. This was especially true for the Nazi Party. The Nazis had absolute control over every form of media and had complete power over what the population did or did not see. The German population had little access to anything beyond what the Nazi-controlled state told them. Years of being brainwashed by Nazi propaganda is one of the reasons why nobody seemed particularly horrified by the idea of concentration camps or the idea of a supreme Aryan race.

For the Allies, propaganda was effective because it clearly depicted an "evil" that had to be fought by the "good" guys. It helped garner sympathy and support from the population and increased the number of volunteers. Men felt compelled to defend innocent people and rid the world of an evil presence. Women were inspired to step up and take action as well.

Of course, almost every bit of propaganda had some element of untruth to it. Nazi propaganda, for instance, was almost entirely based on lies and fabrications. Allied propaganda was more truthful and factual; however, to keep up morale at home, they worked hard to put a positive spin on what was happening on the front. Most people who were removed from the war had no idea of the actual horrors being endured by those on the battlefield. In the

US, the war was often spun in a heroic, glorified way.

Civilians in Europe lived through nightly raids and bombings, so they knew better. Letters sent from soldiers at the front also painted a different picture. For example, one soldier at the front described in a letter back home:

"Our first evidence of actual battle is anything but poetic. Behind a wall-like hedgerow is a series of abandoned foxholes, each surrounded by a litter of used K-ration cartons, tin cans, empty cartridge casings, dried human feces. This has been the front line. It is eloquent of a new reality, the feces perhaps most eloquent. There'd been no time to relieve yourself leisurely, cover your deposit afterward, and no such niceties as toilet paper. Like an animal afraid for your life you jumped out of your hole, excreted, jumped back in. The dead or wounded had of course been removed to the rear long before we passed. The able-bodied had gone forward as we were going. Again the courage and blood of others paved the way."[10]

Adversely, soldiers were reluctant to lay bare the true horrors of the war to their loved ones and often didn't mention anything negative at all. They tried to write brave, happy, positive letters. What follows is an example of such a letter from Private Harry Schiraldi:

"Dear Ma, Just a few lines tonight to let you know that I'm fine and hope everybody at home is in the best of health. I just finished playing baseball and took a nice shower and now I feel very nice. Hope every thing is going alright at home and don't forget if you ever need money you could cash my war bonds anything you want to. This afternoon I went to church and I received Holy Communion again today. Getting holy, ain't I?"[11]

Henry died the following day on D-Day when an enemy machine gun fired on him on the beaches of Normandy.

Propaganda, media, and letters aside, the true horrors of the

---

[10] "Letters from the Front." https://www.pbs.org/wgbh/americanexperience/features/dday-letters-front/.

[11] Sharmi, Swati. "A U.S. Soldier's Last Letter Home before He Died on D-Day." https://www.washingtonpost.com/news/worldviews/wp/2014/06/05/a-u-s-soldiers-last-letter-home-before-he-died-on-d-day/

war were only really revealed once it ended. The terrible truths were laid bare among the rubble, the dead, and the concentration camps.

Each side did what they had to in order to garner support for their cause, and they did it very effectively.

Section Three: Ideology and Involvement

At first glance, World War II was about defeating Adolf Hitler and the Nazi Party. But when one digs a little deeper, one can see how the major powers were motivated and led by their core ideological beliefs.

It was not just an ideological war. As discussed in Part One, there were many other factors that led to and contributed to the war. However, numerous ideologies were at play that did have a significant and important influence on the war effort, notably fascism, Nazism, communism, nationalism, and democracy.

Over the next few chapters, we will examine the extent these ideologies influenced the course of the war.

Chapter 9: Nazism, Hitler, and the Death Camps

What is Nazism?

National Socialism, otherwise known as Nazism, was a totalitarian movement with Adolf Hitler at the helm. It shared a lot of commonalities with Italy's fascism. Both movements appealed to the masses, were led by a dictator who wielded absolute control, and focused on intense nationalism. However, Nazism was more extreme. In many ways, Nazism was the younger, more radical, and more violent brother of fascism.

The roots of Nazism go back much further than Hitler and can partially be linked all the way back to the 1680s. However, for the purpose of this book, we will look at Nazism during Hitler's time.

The Nazi Party has its origins in the German Workers' Party, which was established in 1919. It was a political organization that was made up of anti-Semites who were angry about the humiliation Germany had been subjected to under the Treaty of Versailles. They believed Germany had been treated unfairly by the international world and that the treaty was unacceptable. They focused on promoting German pride while also spreading anti-Semitic beliefs.

Hitler joined this party in 1919. When he became its leader in 1921, the name of the party was changed to Nationalist Social German Worker's Party or, as it would become known throughout the world, the Nazi Party.

Nazis rejected the notions of democracy or liberalism. They did not believe in the concept of human or equal rights or the rule of law. They viewed women as inferior to men, believing their sole purpose in life was to procreate. Nazis also believed the state should rule the people and demanded absolute obedience from them. Above all, they believed that pure Germans or Aryans were not only superior but that they should also control the world. The Nazis' worldview was that the world needed to be purged of racially impure, weak, fragile, and damaged people until only the Aryan race existed.

According to the Nazis, pure Aryans had a Nordic background. They were tall and had pale white skin and blue eyes. Their heads were long and shapely, and they had slim, narrow noses, blond hair, and a defined chin.

One of the Nazi Party's top priorities was to further the Aryan race. They encouraged people who fit the criteria of "strong and pure" to breed and have children together. For example, young people who were planning to get married and have children were eligible for interest-free loans from the Nazi Party. However, they had to prove they came from the Aryan race. Nazis also required the bride to have worked at a job for six months, which she would then quit to get married. In this way, the Nazis were assured of a job vacancy that could be filled by a man.

Couples who received the loan were forgiven one-quarter of the loan for every child they had. It was an incentive for each "perfect" couple to have at least four "perfect" children. They also believed a woman's role was at home as a wife and mother, and this program helped keep them there. This encouragement of procreating to bring more "superior" beings into the world was called "positive eugenics."

"Negative eugenics" was the opposite. It was designed to prevent flawed, disabled, and undesirable people from having children. For instance, in July 1933, the Nazis passed a law giving the government permission to sterilize people who suffered from genetic or hereditary diseases like schizophrenia, deafness, and blindness, just to name a few.

For the Nazis, the next logical step in their obsession with racial cleansing and desire to create a "master race" was eliminating anyone who did not fit the criteria. It, therefore, wasn't a stretch to house non-Aryans in concentration camps and have them exterminated.

Adolf Hitler

The most talked about Nazi is, without a doubt, Adolf Hitler.

He was born on April 20th, 1889, in a small town in Austria. As a little boy, Hitler loved the arts and wanted to become an artist. He applied to the Vienna Academy of the Arts but didn't get in. When he was eighteen, his mother died, and he moved to Vienna, hoping to pursue a career in the arts.

Within a year, Hitler had gone through the substantial money he had inherited from his parents and was living in poverty and sleeping in homeless shelters. His family encouraged him to enter the civil service, but he refused.

Over the next few years, he managed to scrape together enough money to live on by painting the scenery of Vienna. During his time there, he developed relationships with Jewish people, both personally and professionally. In fact, he earned a portion of his living by selling to Jews in Vienna.

While in Vienna, Hitler was strongly influenced by politician Georg Ritter von Schönerer's racist nationalism and the views of the mayor of Vienna, Karl Lueger. Lueger openly promoted anti-Semitic views and reinforced views that Jews were the ultimate threat and Germany's enemy.

At the time, Austria had a universal three-year conscription. Hitler did not want to fight for the Habsburgs. Since he was at risk of getting arrested for shirking his duty, he moved to Munich, Germany, instead. His life continued in much the same way in Munich; he earned a basic living by painting.

And then the First World War broke out. Suddenly, Hitler found a purpose in life. He enlisted voluntarily and joined the Bavarian Regiment. Luck clung to him like a shadow throughout the war, as he managed to escape life-threatening situations time and time again. Hitler didn't have a military bearing and was a loner, but he was an eager soldier. He never took leave and never complained about the conditions.

In 1916, during the Battle of the Somme, Hitler's leg was injured. After a brief recovery at the hospital, he was assigned to other duties in Munich. While he was there, he saw and heard Germans expressing anti-war sentiments and a general sense of indifference. This upset him greatly, and he placed the blame squarely on the Jews, believing they were hampering the war effort.

Hitler asked to return to the thick of the action. He performed extremely well and even received five medals; however, he never progressed past corporal. Ironically, his commanding officers felt he did not have the personality or skills to command respect from the troops or be a leader.

When it started to become clear that Germany was losing the war, Hitler became depressed and spent a lot of time thinking. When the war finally ended, he wasn't on the battlefield but was instead recovering from a gas attack in a hospital. He was devasted by the news of the Kaiser's fall, and seeds of hatred began to grow in his heart for the people who had let down Germany. Again, inexplicably, he blamed the Jews.

Once more, Hitler felt adrift. And then the Nazi Party came along. When the party was founded, Hitler joined as a party member, and within two years, he climbed the ranks to become the party's leader.

In 1923, Hitler, feeling inspired by Mussolini's march on Rome, decided he had had enough of the Weimar Republic. He tried to stage a coup with the Nazi Party's backing to displace the government, but he failed. He was arrested two days later and sentenced to five years in prison. However, he only served nine months. While in prison, he wrote *Mein Kampf.*

Adolf Hitler.
Bundesarchiv, Bild 183-H1216-0500-002 / CC-BY-SA, CC BY-SA 3.0 DE
<https://creativecommons.org/licenses/by-sa/3.0/de/deed.en>, via Wikimedia Commons;
https://commons.wikimedia.org/wiki/File:Hitler_portrait_crop.jpg

In this autobiographical work, Hitler outlined his views and beliefs on many things, including his deep hatred for communists and Jews. He talked about how he wanted to get rid of parliamentary systems and establish a new world order where the weak and sickly would be exterminated in order to make room in the world for strong, capable people.

The volumes were written mainly for his party, but as his power grew, people began to be interested in what he had to say, and sales began to increase. He made over a million Reichsmarks from his books back then. That would be equivalent to over six million euros today!

As time passed, Hitler's popularity grew. He was well-spoken, utterly mesmerizing, and had a way of appealing to the masses. He used the country's desperate situation to his advantage. He spoke at length about how democracy was to blame for unemployment and the depression. Hitler promised the people prosperity and to get rid of Jewish bankers and financiers who were bringing them down. He spoke with confidence about a new world order under which Germany would no longer be weak or crippled but would rise strong and proud, filled with people of the Aryan race.

The people were hooked. They flocked to the Nazi Party in droves. By 1932 (less than a decade after Hitler's failed coup), the Nazi Party had become the Reichstag's biggest political party.

In 1933, Hitler was appointed chancellor of Germany by President Paul von Hindenburg. He got to work immediately. Almost overnight, civil liberties began to be suppressed. Democratic institutions began to crumble, and anyone who opposed his changes was murdered or taken away.

After Hindenburg's death in 1934, Hitler seamlessly slid into absolute power. He named himself Führer and became the army's commander in chief. The expansion of the army, including a new air force, began quickly, while troops were gathered through the reintroduction of conscription.

Laws and decrees began to be passed against Jewish people, segregating and isolating them from German society and slowly stripping them of their civil rights. These laws would lay the groundwork for what would follow.

The steps Hitler took and the money he spent on the military brought prosperity to the country. He also held up his promise to widen Germany's natural boundaries. The first thing he did was annex Austria. He then forced Czechoslovakia to hand over the Sudetenland.

Since the international world did nothing, Hitler became bolder. The people began to go along with his policies and beliefs since everything he had done so far had been to their advantage. They were convinced he would guide them down the right path.

A year after that, Hitler invaded Poland and started WWII.

The invasion was just the beginning; there would be so much more to come. So many horrors and terrible truths would only be revealed much later.

Nazi Concentration Camps

Concentration camps are commonly associated with the Holocaust; however, the first camp was built by the Nazi Party as soon as Hitler became chancellor in 1933, years before the war began.

Throughout the course of the war, the Nazis would go on to set up over forty-four thousand concentration camps, incarceration camps, and ghettos.

Dachau, the first camp, was set up right outside Munich and used to house political prisoners, including communists and socialists. It would become the model to follow for future camps.

In 1938, the first set of Jewish males was sent to Dachau. After Kristallnacht (the "Night of Long Knives"), the Nazis began to round up more Jewish men. Over thirty thousand men were held in concentration camps.

The term concentration camp has become synonymous with gas chambers and death, but not all the camps were used for the same purpose. Some camps were used for forced labor, some to house prisoners of war, and some were transit camps where Jewish people were held until they could be deported. More often than not, deportation meant being sent to a killing center.

The Nazis built five killing centers in total. While people died in the other camps too, the killing centers were designed specifically for mass extermination. Hitler and the Nazis were obsessed with the idea of racial superiority and wanted to wipe out the Jews. These camps were the "final solution" to the Jewish problem.

Concentration camps were guarded by the SS (the Schutzstaffel). The SS was a paramilitary organization that evolved from a small guard unit to a police force tasked with security and enforcing the Nazi Party's policies.

Heinrich Himmler inspecting a prisoner.

https://commons.wikimedia.org/wiki/File:Himmler_besichtigt_die_Gefangenenlager_in_Russland._Heinrich_Himmler_inspects_a_prisoner_of_war_camp_in_Russia,_circa..._-_NARA_-_540164.jpg

Deportation

Soon after Kristallnacht and the mass imprisonment of Austrian Jews, Jewish people became the Nazis' main target. The Nazis didn't even try to make up an excuse for arresting them. Being a Jew was crime enough. Nazis began to round up Jewish people and deport them. Most prisoners were told to pack a suitcase and fed lies about where they would be sent. They were always invariably led to believe they would simply be taken outside of Germany and released.

This was, of course, false.

Sometimes, families were deported together. Other times, people were called up randomly. In either case, the prisoner was put on a train headed for a camp.

The journey could take anywhere from a few days to several weeks. The prisoners were crammed together in a boxcar with no room to sit, move, or even kneel. There were no bathroom breaks and no pauses for sleep or rest. They were given very little food to share between them. Pain, hunger, and inhumane conditions led to many deaths during the transport.

The conditions inside these compartments were awful beyond belief, but the worst was still to come.

Camp Life in Auschwitz-Birkenau

While there were many different concentration camps, we will look at the most infamous camp of all, Auschwitz, which was established in 1940. The camp originally served as army barracks for the Polish army and was adapted to serve the Nazis' purpose.

The Nazis added more buildings and second stories to the existing buildings. Every building was meant to house roughly seven hundred prisoners, but the actual number was much higher, well over one thousand.

When the train finally reached the camp, most prisoners felt an immense sense of relief. They had reached the end of their horrifying journey and would now be released. But the minute they stepped out, they were greeted by a massive sign curled around the iron gate that read, *"Arbeit Macht Frei"* ("Work makes one free").

The prisoners were sorted into two groups: one for men and another for women and children. They would then be lined up for inspection. The SS would decide who would live and who would die. Those who looked too weak or sick were sent to the gas chamber while the rest were moved forward for identification.

Each prisoner's suitcase and personal effects would be taken away. The people were assigned a number, which was tattooed on their arms. The registration process also included the assigning of barracks and work.

Once this was complete, the prisoners had to undress so their heads could be shaved. This was followed by a public shower under the ever-watchful eye of the SS. After the shower, they were given blue and white striped pajamas.

Bald, tattooed, and dressed the same, the prisoners were stripped of their individual identity and dignity.

Most prisoners were woken up at four in the morning. They were given a half hour to eat, get dressed, go to the bathroom, and clean their barracks. This was followed by morning roll call, which could sometimes take hours. This was especially harsh during the winter months when prisoners had to stand shivering in the snow and sleet.

After roll call, everyone went to their assigned work. The lucky ones were assigned jobs in the administration building or sorting through clothing and personal belongings, while others were assigned to break rocks or dispose of dead bodies.

Meals were provided but in such small quantities that everyone was malnourished. After working all day, the prisoners were subjected to hours-long roll call again before being given some "free time." Most of the people were so exhausted and weak that they simply went to sleep.

The beds were either wooden planks or mattresses stuffed with straw and laid out on the floor. Most beds were shared by eighteen to twenty people.

Brick bunks at Auschwitz; four prisoners would sleep in one of these partitions.
Bookofblue, CC BY-SA 3.0 <https://creativecommons.org/licenses/by-sa/3.0>, via Wikimedia Commons;
https://commons.wikimedia.org/wiki/File:Auschwitz_1_concentration_camp_bunks_6006_4162.jpg

Disease and illnesses were rampant in the extremely unsanitary conditions of the camp, which were infested with vermin, rats, and lice.

This daily routine was the best the prisoners could hope for. As horrible and inhumane as these conditions were, it was far preferable to the atrocities that befell many prisoners. Throughout the day, the prisoners were watched carefully by the SS and were at the mercy of their whims and desires. For the bored SS guards, torturing the prisoners was something of a sport for them. They would mercilessly beat anyone they felt was out of line or "not behaving." It was not uncommon for them to simply shoot someone dead on the spot just for fun.

Women were raped and violated, with some camps even setting up brothels. During the Holocaust, approximately five hundred brothels were operated in the camps. The women who became pregnant were subjected to abortions. Many died from the procedure.

Gas Chambers

Early in the war, prisoners were typically shot dead by the SS in mass killings. As time went on, the SS realized they needed a more efficient way of getting rid of so many people. Thus, the gas chamber was designed.

Four gas chambers and crematoria were built in Birkenau in 1942. By June 1943, they were up and running. The crematoria could burn approximately 4,416 prisoners a day. If they ran every day, it worked out to 1.6 million people a year. For the Nazis, this was a far more effective solution than individually shooting each person.

During the first selection, the old, weak, disabled, pregnant women, babies, and children were almost immediately sent off to the gas chambers upon arrival. Those who were young, healthy, and looked strong enough to work were allowed to live, at least for the moment.

The Nazis were careful not to cause panic in the people since it would make the process less efficient for them. So, the people who were led to the chambers were made to believe they would be taking showers. The prisoners handed over their belongings, undressed, and entered the massive "shower." Once it was packed, the doors closed, and gas (Zyklon B) was piped into the chamber.

This photograph was taken at Auschwitz and shows a group of Jews headed toward the gas chambers.

https://commons.wikimedia.org/wiki/File:Birkenau_a_group_of_Jews_walking_towards_t he_gas_chambers_and_crematoria.jpg

It only took minutes for the prisoners to die. Other prisoners from the camp were then tasked with stripping any leftover valuables from the corpses, like gold teeth, and putting the bodies in the crematoria ovens. Sometimes, the bodies were dumped in a huge hole that was used as a mass grave.

There is no precise number of how many people died during the Holocaust. It is believed around six million Jews died, along with millions of other "undesirables." It is thought that one in six Jews died at Auschwitz.

Medical Experiments

Nazi concentration camps were also used to conduct medical experiments on humans with total disregard for human life.

There were three specific goals:

- To conduct research on how to best keep German troops alive on the battlefield or how to heal wounded troops;

- To test out new medications, surgical procedures, or make new medical discoveries;

- To confirm that the Aryan race was indeed superior.

Over seven thousand such experiments have been documented; however, the real number is likely much higher.

The cruelest Nazi physician was Josef Mengele, who was at Auschwitz. Known as the Angel of Death, he was particularly vicious and enjoyed torturing his victims in the name of medicine. He especially liked using twins as test subjects. One was used as a test subject, while the other was the control. The test subject was put through unimaginable horrors, such as being injected with diseases, receiving blood transfusions, or having their limbs amputated. When the test subject inevitably died, Mengele cut open the bodies to study the internal organs. The control twin was then also killed so they could be studied.

Mengele was also obsessed with eye color and collected eyeballs to study them. He hoped to find the key to ensuring that all Aryan women would carry blond-haired and blue-eyed children. Mengele believed that if this could be done, the world could easily be populated by the Aryan race.

He conducted hundreds of other torturous experiments. It is estimated that about three thousand twins were tortured at his command. Less than two hundred of them made it out of the camp.

When the war ended, Mengele managed to escape to South America. He died in 1979 without ever being prosecuted for his crimes.

The Brutality of the Camps

Concentration camps were made to sound like labor camps. The prisoners were led to believe that if they worked hard enough, they would one day be set free. The truth was most would never leave.

The actual horrors of the camps will never be known fully. When the Nazis realized they were losing the war, a desperate attempt was made to destroy the camps to hide what they had done. Camps were burned and razed to the ground. Some prisoners were killed while the rest were made to march to another camp. Many prisoners died during the Death March. The prisoners were just days away from liberation.

What we know of the camps is based on survivor stories, the remnants of the camps, and what the Allied troops witnessed and discovered.

Chapter 10: Fascism and Mussolini

What Is Fascism?

Fascism is a political ideology that developed after Vladimir Lenin's Bolshevik communists led a revolution in Russia and successfully seized power. The ideology spread in a number of countries between the 1920s and 1945. Fascism spread all over the world, including the Middle East, Europe, South America, Asia, and even the United States!

World War I was seen by fascists as a great social upheaval that opened the door to a new era, one in which liberalism was no longer relevant. Some viewed fascism as a radical movement that brought about positive change, similar to the French Revolution, while others viewed it as a violent, oppressive, authoritarian movement. Given that both Hitler and Mussolini were fascists and given the events of WWII, fascism today is viewed in the latter light and is seen as one of the causes of WWII.

Some of the key beliefs associated with fascism include:

- Strong emphasis on nationalism;
- Racial hierarchy and protecting the rights of nationals;
- The military's supremacy;
- Opposition to liberalism, democracy, and Marxism.

- Opposition to equality and individual rights;
- Rigid gender roles and the firm belief that women are lesser than men.

Fascism and Nazism share some common beliefs and core values; however, fascism wasn't nearly as extreme as Nazism. While fascists believed in a racial hierarchy, they did not possess the same hatred for Jews as the Nazis. Historically, Italians had always been tolerant and humane. So, in 1938, when the fascist government in Italy began to announce policies that were clearly anti-Semitic, most people were surprised. It is generally believed that Hitler's influence and beliefs swayed Mussolini.

In order for a fascist government to enforce beliefs and ensure obedience from its population, it needs to wield absolute control, which is why most fascist governments end up with a dictator who controls everything. In Italy, the man who led the fascist movement was Benito Mussolini. While fascism existed in other parts of the world, it is most closely linked to Mussolini because he was the first one to create a political party based on the fascist movement and stand for election.

Benito Mussolini

Born on July 29th, 1883, in Italy, Mussolini was likely destined to be a revolutionary from birth as his radical father named him after a revolutionary leader in Mexico, Benito Juárez. His family was very poor, and his childhood was hardly an ideal one. He grew up to be an aggressive and disobedient child who once attacked a classmate with a penknife. Mussolini was also a very intelligent child, and although he didn't excel in school, he received a teaching diploma and became a teacher.

After some time, he left his job and moved to Switzerland, where, like Hitler, he drifted aimlessly. But he read a lot of books on philosophy, ideologies, and theories. He began to gain a reputation as a good speaker and political journalist.

Mussolini was arrested numerous times for his views, and by the time he went back to Italy in 1904, he had already been mentioned several times in the Roman newspapers. For a while after that, he repeated the cycle of drifting, writing, and being imprisoned. During a lull in 1909, he fell in love and got married, although he was arrested soon after.

By this time, Mussolini was becoming fairly well known as "Comrade Mussolini." After his release, he continued writing in socialist papers before creating his own, *La Lotta di Classe* ("The Class Struggle"). The paper was incredibly successful and led to his appointment as the editor of *Avanti!* ("Forward!"), a socialist newspaper.

With the outbreak of World War I, Mussolini believed the government should support the Triple Alliance. His views on the war clashed with those of the Socialist Party, which was supportive of joining the Allies. As a result, he cut ties with the party. He eventually joined the Royal Italian Army and served in the war as a corporal. He stopped serving after being wounded and went to Milan, where he became the editor of a right-wing paper, *Il Popolo d'Italia* ("The People of Italy").

His new political viewpoints were outlined in this paper, which would essentially become the rallying cry of fascism. He wrote, "From today onward we are all Italians and nothing but Italians. Now that steel has met steel, one single cry comes from our hearts – Viva l'Italia!"[12]

Mussolini had been advocating the need for a dictatorship in Italy and began to drop hints in speeches that he might be the perfect man for the job. He slowly created a party based on his new political philosophy. Two hundred people followed him early on; this group was mainly composed of disenchanted and restless people looking for direction and people who wanted to create a new force. They were ex-soldiers, revolutionaries, anarchists, and socialists. The force was aptly named *Fasci Italiani di Combattimento* ("fighting bands").

Fascism in Italy was born.

It didn't take long for the strong, confident Mussolini to mesmerize the crowds. He was also visually appealing and quite striking against the backdrop of his supporters, who wore black shirts as a uniform. It didn't matter that Mussolini was sometimes cruel or that his opinions were not always based on fact. The

---

[12] Davis, Kenneth. *Strongman: The Rise of Five Dictators and the Fall of Democracy.* Macmillan Publishers, 2020.

people were hooked.

Inspired by Mussolini, fascist squads began to crop up all over Italy, attacking local governments and terrorizing socialists and the people. These acts were encouraged by Mussolini.

By 1921, the lawless fascists' control was spreading throughout the country. Mussolini planned his next step. Blackshirts (members of Mussolini's fascist squads), armed and ready for violence, marched to Rome. They wanted Mussolini to be appointed prime minister. King Victor Emmanuel III bowed to pressure, and Mussolini became the new prime minister. His party began a campaign of steadily undoing Italy's democracy.

Mussolini, in the meantime, began to merge his party with the military and established anti-union laws to protect wealthy industrialists. He promised them protection from socialism.

However, people from Mussolini's party felt they should move quicker. In 1924, Giacomo Matteotti, the leader of the Unitary Socialist Party, was assassinated. The time to take decisive action had come.

On January 3rd, 1925, Mussolini gave an address to Parliament, saying he was responsible for everything that had happened, indirectly implying he had Giacomo killed. No action was taken against him. Assured of his absolute control, Mussolini openly became the dictator of Italy, naming himself *Il Duce*.

Under his rule, Italy was a police state, and everyone was expected to obey him. While there is no doubt that big businesses benefited from Mussolini's rule, the truth is he did very little to help the regular people. They saw a continued decline in their standard of living, especially once the Great Depression hit.

Internationally, Italy wasn't as big an empire as Great Britain, the Soviet Union, or even Germany. Italy had a few colonies in Africa, which they promptly lost during WWII.

After Lenin's death, Mussolini and Stalin were on friendly terms. They had diplomatic relations but likely wouldn't have hesitated to turn on one another if the need arose.

As discussed previously, although Hitler would go on to greatly influence Mussolini and bring Italy into the war, Mussolini's first impression of Hitler was not positive. The two men eventually developed some degree of loyalty and friendship toward each other.

At first, Mussolini had no intention of joining the war, but he changed his mind in 1940, feeling that he had to stand by Germany. Italy's participation in the war was doomed almost from the start. In 1943, when the Allies invaded Italy, the people were ready to surrender and switch sides.

A certain amount of bitterness and anger had been brewing against Mussolini for some time, as they blamed him for putting them through an unnecessary war. By the time Italy surrendered, they were already plotting his downfall. Mussolini was partially shocked by how things had turned out but sensed that his time was up, readily agreeing to resign.

Within hours of his resignation, he was arrested and imprisoned.

As the war neared its end, Italian communists made the decision to have Mussolini executed. He tried to cross into Austria but was discovered and stopped. On April 28th, 1945, he was killed along with his mistress. Their bodies were hung upside down in Milan for the public to see. The swelling crowds celebrated the end of his dictatorship and the end of the war.

If we look at the evolution and eventual downfall of fascism, it is clear that it was an abject failure. Mussolini had nearly fifteen years to "fix" Italy and bring prosperity and happiness to his people, but he did not or could not.

Was Fascism a Failure?

Ideologies like fascism and Nazism promise great things to the people, preying on their weaknesses and desires. But in the end, the only people these ideologies serve are the dictators who thrive on total control and their entourage. They snatch power with the promise to help and empower others, but in the end, they do nothing for them.

One might have expected fascism to die out completely after the end of the war. While the original fascist regimes have more or less died out, fascist ideologies and ideas have not. They have simply morphed into a milder form. Countries like France, Denmark, Greece, and the United States have fascist parties, but politicians are (understandably) hesitant to openly describe themselves as such.

Chapter 11: Stalin's Red Wave

After the Russian Revolution in October 1917, the Bolsheviks' leader, Vladimir Lenin, came to power. The Russian Soviet Federative Socialist Republic was formed by the Bolsheviks, triggering the Russian Civil War (1918–1920) between the Bolsheviks (the Reds) and the anti-Bolshevik forces (the Whites).

During the Russian Civil War, the Whites were supported by major international powers like Great Britain and the US, but the Reds had a lot of support within the country and managed to win the war in 1920. Sporadic uprisings occurred until 1924. After the revolution, Russia became a communist country and was renamed the Soviet Union.

Communism is a political ideology that fiercely opposes ideas like liberalism and democracy. Communists do not believe in a class system or in private property. Under communist rule, everyone is supposed to be treated equally. No one should have more wealth than another, the basic necessities of life are provided to all, and everything is owned as a collective.

In short, everyone works in harmony to reap the same benefits and rewards. A capitalist, profit-based economy is replaced by communal ownership and control. In theory, an equal world sounds like a great idea, a dream come true for the struggling masses, but in practice, it doesn't quite work like that.

For communism to work, the people have to be governed by a totalitarian system. There can be no democracy. Because one person's actions may not benefit another, rights become restricted. There is the threat that exposure to other ways of thinking will make people want a different life, so the government imposes censorship. This way, the people only know what they want them to know. Finally, a country's economy thrives when people are gainfully employed, earning a living that they are then spending on material things. Material things are produced in factories, which provide employment.

Capitalism, while flawed, is a full circle that keeps a country running and boosts the economy. Communism is viewed as completely undesirable by developed, capitalist countries.

When Lenin died in 1924, there was a brief struggle for power. Joseph Stalin ultimately became the leader of the party.

Joseph Stalin

Stalin was born on December 18th, 1878, in Georgia (not Russia) to a very poor family. His full name at birth was Iosif Vissarionovich Stalin. He later simplified it to Joseph Stalin.

Joseph Stalin.
https://commons.wikimedia.org/wiki/File;JStalin_Secretary_general_CCCP_1942.jpg

Stalin did not have a happy home life, as he was savagely beaten by his father. He learned Russian at school and was never quite able to get rid of his Georgian accent.

His mother wanted him to become a priest, but this would not be the path he followed.

As a young boy, he secretly read the works of Karl Marx, and at twenty-two, he became politically active. In 1903, Stalin joined the Bolsheviks and became an ardent supporter of Lenin. Slowly, he moved up the hierarchy of the party, proving his value, especially during the Russian Civil War.

Stalin held two ministerial positions in the Bolshevik government, which helped him gather a following. By the time Lenin died, the two were no longer getting along. Lenin was supportive of the quasi-capitalist New Economic Policy, with which Stalin did not agree.

Luckily for Stalin, Lenin died in 1924 before any lasting damage could be done to Stalin's reputation. He became the new leader of the country.

Under Stalin, the Soviet Union became a totalitarian state mired in class-based violence. The country did industrialize rapidly but at a high cost. Many beautiful historical relics in Russia were destroyed and replaced with statues of Stalin.

He ruled using fear and violence but developed a cult-like following, which was central to the idea of Stalinism. After the Great Terror, the people were so scared of him that they did not even dream of straying.

Stalin didn't make many friends in the international world either. He had a strained, distrusting relationship with the United States and tenuous diplomatic relations with countries like Great Britain. Russia and Germany always had a tense relationship. Fearful of a German attack, Stalin agreed to a non-aggression pact with Germany in 1939. He promised to turn a blind eye to Poland's invasion and even helped Hitler. In exchange, Hitler would stay out of the Soviet Union. Of course, Hitler broke the pact when it suited him to do so.

Stalin was a deeply paranoid man; he trusted no one, and it seems nobody trusted him. After the Germans invaded the Soviet Union, he was forced to work with the Allies in order to defeat their common enemy. But throughout all the discussions, no side fully trusted the other. The Potsdam Conference, where the leaders of Great Britain, the US, and the Soviet Union met, was filled with tension and suspicions. Almost as soon as the war officially ended, the threadbare relationship between the Soviet Union and the US fell apart completely.

And once the greater threat of Hitler was finally resolved through mutual cooperation, the Soviet Union and communism became the new threat, with the world entering the Cold War era.

Stalin's Great Purge

The Great Purge or the Great Terror is exactly what the name implies. Stalin led a campaign in which anyone he considered to be a threat to himself or his rule was purged.

He first got rid of members from his own party whom he felt were starting to turn away or were questioning his authority. Political opponents were his next target, and then the purge began to include regular civilians, peasants, minorities, intellectuals, scientists, and the list goes on. Basically, anyone was a target.

In 1934, a Bolshevik leader by the name of Sergei Kirov was assassinated at the headquarters of the Communist Party. The purge was launched after this and resulted in over a million people being sent to the Gulag camps. More than 750,000 people were killed.

Stalin's purge caused fear and terror to spread through the country, especially when he began killing without discrimination. He even had thirty thousand generals, officials, and troops from the Red Army executed! He was convinced they were planning to overthrow him.

It is estimated that roughly one-third of the Soviet Union's Communist Party was purged. However, the actual number is likely much higher, maybe even double, as many people simply disappeared. The Soviet Union was also known for hiding statistics.

The Gulag

And what about those who were lucky enough to escape death? Were they truly better off? Many prisoners in the Gulag have said they would rather have been executed than sent to the labor camps.

The Gulag was the government agency in charge of the Soviet labor camps. Political prisoners and criminals were sent to them. It was used as a way to politically repress the people.

While the Gulag labor camps were not used on the same scale or for the same purpose as the Nazi camps, the two forms of camps are comparable in how they were used and the treatment of prisoners. This is especially true of the forced labor camps. In both Nazi and Gulag camps, prisoners were starved, beaten, and worked to the bone, having to do grueling work for fourteen or fifteen hours a day. In the Gulag, the prisoners were given minimal tools and tasked with jobs like cutting trees or digging into the frozen ground. Some people felt so desperate they maimed themselves to become handicapped.

Nazi camps saw similar types of work. In both camps, prisoners lived in overcrowded shacks in inhumane conditions. Prisoners were often abused, shot, or killed by guards.

But the similarities end here. The Nazi camps' main purpose was to kill and exterminate a population. That was not the Gulag's purpose, even though most prisoners did end up dying.

The SS, incited by hatred and racism, made it their personal mission to kill as many people as they could. This was not the case for the guards in the Gulag. The Gulag did not have gas chambers or a crematorium. When a prisoner's prison term was completed, they were allowed to leave. Some were even granted early release for work well done. This did not happen in Nazi camps.

The Gulag housed the highest number of inmates during Stalin's rule. In the 1920s, the Gulag had roughly 100,000 prisoners. By 1936, there were five million! This number only continued to increase drastically until Stalin's death in 1953. A few days after Stalin's death, the Gulag set millions of prisoners free, most of whom were completely innocent.

Over time, the camps were converted into prisons. In 1987, when Mikhail Gorbachev came to power, he got rid of them completely. His grandfather had once been imprisoned in the Gulag.

The psychological, emotional, and physical trauma and horror endured by the survivors of the Gulag will never be understood properly by the world and continues to haunt and impact generations of Russians today.

Chapter 12: The Role of America

Historically, America's foreign policy was isolationism and non-interventionism. Its government had no desire to get involved with other powers, expand its empire on a large scale, or fight battles. Its focus was almost entirely on its own affairs. Of course, this is no longer the case, and this shift began partially with World War I.

When the Great War broke out on July 28th, 1914, it was very much a European war and problem. But it didn't take long for it to become a global war, with more than thirty nations picking a side. Most countries sided with the Allies, which was made up of powerful countries like France, Great Britain, Russia, Italy, and Japan. The United States, while privately siding with the Allies, remained neutral.

But as the war dragged on, it became impossible for the US to maintain its neutral stance. The war hit particularly close to home when a German U-boat torpedoed the *Lusitania* in 1915. The US ship had been carrying civilians.

Americans were outraged, and even Cabinet members were in favor of war, but President Woodrow Wilson continued to be cautious. He threatened war, and Germany promised it wouldn't sink passenger ships again without proper warning.

But in 1917, a telegram from Germany was intercepted saying Germany would be returning to submarine warfare and sinking ships with no restrictions. The Zimmerman telegram was the final straw for the US. On April 6th, 1917, the United States declared war.

Historically, it is believed that the US helped to turn the tide of the war, leading the Allies to a win and officially ending the war on November 11th, 1918. Its endless supplies of troops, artillery, equipment, and skilled commanders were a much-needed boost to the war-weary Allied troops who had been fighting for years. The Americans came like a vengeful force, defeated the enemy, and retreated back to isolationism.

And then WWII happened.

Interestingly enough, the events of WWII unfolded in a similar manner to WWI. At first, the US did nothing. It sided with the Allies but remained neutral until the war hit too close to home.

Pearl Harbor

The United States had already been experiencing some conflicts and tensions with Japan as the Asian country looked to expand its empire. Japan wanted to ensure the US would not interfere with its interests and wanted to cripple the US before it could make a move.

The direct result of this was the attack on Pearl Harbor on December 7th, 1941, when the Imperial Japanese Navy Air Service launched a surprise strike on the American bases located at Pearl Harbor, Hawaii.

An image of the USS Shaw exploding.
https://commons.wikimedia.org/wiki/File:USS_SHAW_exploding_Pearl_Harbor_Nara_80-G-16871_2.jpg

During the attack, 2,403 US personnel lost their lives, as well as 68 innocent civilians. Nineteen ships, including eight battleships, were also destroyed.

Without a doubt, Japan won this attack, but it would pay for the move dearly toward the end of the war.

In retaliation to the attack, the United States did the one thing Japan had hoped to avoid: the US government declared war and officially joined WWII.

Nagasaki and Hiroshima

By the end of the summer of 1945, it had already been a few months since Germany's defeat at the hands of the Allies. However, the war in the Pacific continued to rage with no definitive end in sight. President Harry Truman received warnings that if Allied troops tried to invade Japan to bring the war to an end, the number of casualties would be horrifying. Still, it was clear the war needed to end quickly and decisively.

After the start of WWII, fearful of what Germany might do, the US started developing atomic weapons. By July 1945, the first atomic bomb was tested in a US desert. By then, Germany was no longer a threat. But with this technology on hand, President Truman decided the best way to cripple Japan was to use the new weapon.

Before attacking, the Allies presented Japan with the Potsdam Declaration, which did not specifically mention the atomic bombing but did warn of severe consequences if it did not surrender. Although the US dropped leaflets about air raids before, they chose not to do so with the atomic bomb. It was better to leave the people in the dark and use this major shock-and-awe tactic to force a surrender.

The declaration was rejected. The American bomber *Enola Gay* was armed with one five-ton bomb, which was dropped on Hiroshima on August 6th, 1945.

The blast decimated the city. Over 92 percent of the city's buildings and structures were either completely destroyed or severely damaged. Between 80,000 to 180,000 people died at the time of the blast and in the weeks after from radiation poisoning, injuries, and wounds.

Truman told Japan that more would follow if it did not surrender. The Soviet Union even jumped in at this point, declaring war on the Asian nation.

There was no indication that Japan would surrender, so Truman decided to follow through on his threat. On August 9th, three days after the first bomb, a second bomb was dropped on the Japanese city of Nagasaki, but there was less damage because of Nagasaki's hilly landscape. Some key parts of the city had been shielded from the blast. The second bombing led to between 50,000 and 100,000 deaths.

Nagasaki before and after the bombing.

Several days after Nagasaki, Japan surrendered, and the war was over. Japan would formally sign its surrender on September 2nd, 1945,

Although many historians now believe that Japan was close to surrendering before the bombings, at that time, there was no indication that this was the case. After Germany's surrender, Truman believed the swiftest way of ending the war on all fronts was to knock Japan out.

His plan was not approved by all; Secretary of War Henry Stimson, General Dwight Eisenhower, and some American scientists objected to the dropping of the bombs. But Truman believed that if the war wasn't brought to an immediate end, thousands of American lives would be at risk.

The bombs were dropped without the approval of Congress, but Truman had the power to do it without their permission, so their approval was inconsequential.

While the bombs definitely had their desired effect, with Japan surrendering and WWII coming to a complete end, over seventy years later, many still debate whether it was really necessary to take such a drastic step. Unfortunately, whether Japan would have surrendered without the bombs is a question we will never have an answer to.

What we do know is that the bombing of Hiroshima and Nagasaki had long-reaching effects. Generations of people suffered as a result of the bombs. Survivors of the bombs and their offspring were susceptible to a range of illnesses, such as leukemia, blindness, and delayed development. It took Japan years to recover from the devastation. The bombings served as a warning of what could happen if there was another global war.

One could argue that the devastation and tragedy of Hiroshima and Nagasaki kept both the Soviet Union and the United States in check during the Cold War. Both countries witnessed firsthand what could happen if things got out of control.

The Marshall Plan

After the war ended, both the United States and the Soviet Union emerged as superpowers; however, it was soon clear the two countries were headed down very different paths and had very different goals. Stalin wanted the Soviet Union to expand into Eastern Europe and promote communism, while the US wanted democracy and capitalism and to stop the spread of communist nations.

Recognizing that the best way of stopping communism was to ensure that countries could stand on their own feet and improve economically, President Harry Truman signed the Economic Assistance Act, which allowed for the creation of an aid program in Europe. The Marshall Plan, as it would come to be known, would be one of the more brilliant moves by the US after the war.

The basic premise of the Marshall Plan was that the United States would provide financial help to Western European countries. In exchange, they would need to find a way of working together and develop a plan that would allow economic integration between them. The goal was to stimulate economic growth and trade. The US felt confident it would prevent communism from spreading globally.

In total, the US sent over thirteen billion dollars in aid to sixteen countries. The money helped with investments, went toward the modernization of industries, helped reduce debt, and, perhaps most importantly to the US, ensured Western Europe was led by democratic, capitalist governments. The gross domestic product (GDP) in each of these countries grew alongside their economies.

The Marshall Plan set the tone for America's foreign policy and firmly established the country as a global leader and superpower. Many countries were grateful to the US, and there was also a sense of being indebted to the nation, which further cemented its role as a superpower.

Another outcome of the Marshall Plan was that it led to the beginning of the Cold War. Stalin wanted nothing to do with the plan. Under his direction, all of the Eastern European countries under his rule were forced to reject it.

With the start of the Cold War, tensions were once again high. The US maintained a strategy of "containment." Containment basically meant playing the long game. It meant being patient but firm, vigilant but conciliatory, and helping out countries that were resisting external influences.

The Cold War would last for four decades. During this time, both sides built nuclear weapons, knowing that one attack would signal the end of both countries. Although there were a few international incidents that almost came to a head, events thankfully never escalated that far.

Between 1989 and 1994, the Berlin Wall came down. It was clear that the writing was on the wall, and the Soviet Union and the Cold War officially came to an end on December 26th, 1991.

To this day, the United States is still considered to be one of the world's superpowers, yielding considerable global influence.

Key Figures from Wartime

Much of the United States' reaction and approach to the war and the post-war world was shaped by several key figures. We will take a brief look at four people who played a key role in the war.

Dwight D. Eisenhower

Eisenhower is best known today for being the thirty-fourth president of the United States. He also played an important role in World War II.

Eisenhower was born in 1890 and had a nice, loving family life. His family had moved to the US from Germany in 1741, which is ironic given the role he would eventually play in defeating Germany. He served during WWI as a commander of a tank crew training unit and displayed great skills, although he was upset that he never got to go to the front.

When the US joined the war, Eisenhower was assigned to work in Washington in the War Plans Division before becoming the commander of the American troops stationed in the United Kingdom. He led the successful invasion of Allied troops in North Africa, and in May 1943, he forced an Axis surrender in Tunisia.

Given this glowing track record, it's no surprise that after Pearl Harbor, Eisenhower was tasked with creating war plans to defeat Germany and Japan. In 1942, he was appointed as the Supreme Commander Allied Expeditionary Force of the North African Theater Operations. A year later, he was appointed Supreme Allied Commander of Europe. This organization would go on to plan D-Day (or Operation Overlord) and eventually liberate France and Western Europe from German occupation.

As you now know, D-Day was a successful campaign. Through it all, Eisenhower demonstrated fantastic diplomatic and leadership skills and was greatly respected by his troops, his colleagues, and global leaders.

In December 1944, Eisenhower became the general of the US Army. It was a big honor and a significant promotion.

During the Battle of the Bulge, Eisenhower's strategic skills helped the Allies counter the German offensive and send them back. When the war finally ended, Eisenhower asked the liberating

Allied forces to thoroughly document and photograph everything they could from the Nazi concentration camps. He had a feeling that people would attempt to cover up or deny the horrifying events of the Holocaust. Of course, he was right. And much of the evidence we see today of the Holocaust is in large part thanks to his foresight.

After the war, Eisenhower was urged by many people to throw his hat in the presidential ring. He declined to do so and instead accepted the position of president at Columbia University.

In 1950, he took an extended leave from the university to take on the position of supreme commander of NATO. He was given command of the organization's European forces. Two years later, Eisenhower retired from active service and finally decided to run for president. He won and is generally seen as a popular president today.

Franklin Delano Roosevelt

Franklin D. Roosevelt, commonly referred to as FDR, is the only US president in history who was elected to office four times. He guided the country through both the Great Depression and WWII.

Franklin Delano Roosevelt.
Photograph: Leon A. Perskiedigitization: FDR Presidential Library & Museum, CC BY 2.0 <https://creativecommons.org/licenses/by/2.0>, via Wikimedia Commons; https://commons.wikimedia.org/wiki/File:FDR_1944_Color_Portrait.jpg

Roosevelt studied at Harvard and became a lawyer. His childhood was one of privilege, far removed from the realities of most Americans. Roosevelt's wife, Eleanor, who was also his fifth-cousin once-removed, and his fifth cousin President Theodore (Teddy) Roosevelt, greatly influenced him and opened his eyes to the plight of the American population.

He eventually entered politics and won a seat on the New York State Senate at the age of twenty-nine. As he became immersed in politics, he lost his air of superiority and was a great champion of progressive reforms. His health also played a significant role in shaping the man he would become.

When he was thirty-nine, he contracted polio, and for several years after, his focus was on recovery. He briefly removed himself from politics. In 1924, three years after being diagnosed with polio, he participated in the 1924 Democratic convention, his first political event in years. FDR felt uncertain about rejoining politics, but with his wife's help and support, he soon moved up the political ladder. Although it was challenging dealing with his disability, it made him a better politician. He was more relatable and sympathetic.

In 1932, he was elected president. He guided the nation through the Great Depression, earning him reelection. When WWII broke out, Roosevelt was careful to remain neutral, but privately, he felt strongly that the US should join the war. After the neutrality ended, Roosevelt did an excellent job of leading the nation at war.

Internationally, he worked hard to build a solid partnership and alliance with Great Britain, the Soviet Union, and other Allies. He helped supply over $50 billion of supplies to the Allied forces.

He also talked extensively about why America was fighting the war and gave the country and its troops a sense of purpose. FDR talked to the people he was leading in the fireside chats, which were radio programs that had started back in 1933. One of his most famous speeches, the Four Freedoms speech, stated the war was being fought for the freedom of speech, freedom from fear, freedom of religion, and freedom from want.

One of Roosevelt's most shameful and less than stellar contributions to the war was the signing of Executive Order 9066, which led to the displacement of thousands of Japanese Americans.

While Roosevelt led the nation through the war, he was unfortunately unable to see the final outcome, although he was pretty confident of how it would end. Struggling with poor health, he died on April 12th, 1945, less than a month before Germany's official surrender. He is often remembered as one of the greatest American presidents.

Harry Truman

When FDR died, his vice president, Harry Truman, became president.

Born on May 8th, 1884, Truman was the oldest child in a family of three. His father was a farmer, so he grew up on the farm. After finishing high school, Truman briefly became a banker before joining the National Guard.

When his father died, he went back to manage the farm, but as soon as WWI broke out, he volunteered for active duty. Truman fought in the trenches of France. After the war ended, he returned home and entered politics. His career continued to advance, and eventually, he became vice president and then president.

His two significant contributions to the war were overseeing its end and the Marshall Plan.

Truman also attended the Potsdam Conference and finalized the strategies to end the war. But after Germany's surrender, he needed to finish the war with Japan. Under Truman's orders, atomic bombs were dropped on Nagasaki and Hiroshima, leading to Japan's surrender. It was perhaps one of the most difficult decisions he ever had to make. Right or wrong, we cannot know. We know thousands of people died, but would thousands more have died if the war with Japan had continued? It remains a polarizing conversation today, and rightfully so.

When the Charter of the United Nations was signed in June 1945, Truman was there to witness it. Perhaps his biggest and most lasting contribution to WWII was the Marshall Plan, which was discussed above in greater detail. And, of course, Truman's biggest crisis after the end of WWII was the beginning of the Cold War. Truman won reelection in 1948, beating Republican Thomas Dewey; the election is still seen as one of the greatest upsets in US history. It was the last election before term limits were placed on presidents.

James Doolittle

WWII was peppered with extraordinary men and women who courageously fought for freedom and democracy, but there are some who deserve special praise. US Army General and aviator James Doolittle was one such person.

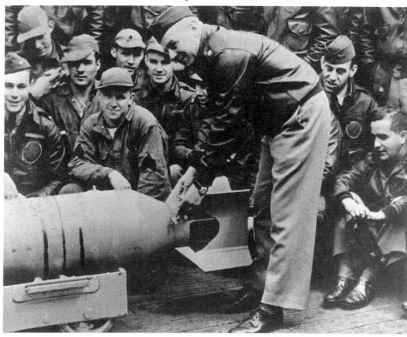

James Doolittle placing a medal on a bomb. This ceremony took place shortly before the April raids on Japan.

When WWI broke out, he was eighteen years old. He enlisted in the army and learned how to be an aviator and flight instructor. After the war ended, he continued his career in the US Army Air Corps, returning to active duty during WWII.

Several months after the attack on Pearl Harbor, he was tasked with leading air raids in Japan. It was a daring attack that required nerve and courage. The raid was carried out overnight on April

18th, 1942. Sixteen B-25 bombers dropped bombs over numerous Japanese cities like Yokohama and Tokyo. After the mission, the planes were unable to return to the USS *Hornet*, which was where they had taken off, because they ran out of fuel. They ended up crash-landing in Soviet and Chinese territories.

While the raid didn't cause significant destruction, it went a long way to boosting the morale of the American population. It also left Japan feeling spooked enough that it moved critical resources away from the South Pacific to Japan.

Conclusion

There can be no doubt about America's role in WWII. The country played a critical role and helped tip the balance in favor of the Allies. However, other countries played a significant role as well, such as Australia, Canada, India, Malaysia, and Kenya, among many others.

The Allies worked together to secure a victory; the win was not due to one country alone. However, we can deduce that America's support, diplomacy, and seemingly infinite resources, combined with cooperation between the major players, helped bring the war to an end.

Section Four: Key Moments

In this final part of the book, we will revisit a few key moments and battles from the war. But first, let's look at a basic timeline of the war from start to finish.

- January 30th, 1933 - Hitler is appointed chancellor of Germany.
- September 1st, 1939 - Hitler invades Poland. Great Britain and France declare war on Germany.
- September 1939 to May 1940 - Phony War
- May 26th to June 4th, 1940 - Operation Dynamo (Dunkirk)
- June 14th, 1940 - Paris falls
- June 22nd, 1941 - Operation Barbarossa
- July 10th to October 31st, 1940 - Battle of Britain
- December 7th, 1941 - Japan attacks Pearl Harbor. The next day, Great Britain and the US declare war on Japan.
- April 18th, 1942 - Doolittle raids on Japan
- June 1942 - Battle of Midway
- October 23rd, 1942 - Battle of El Alamein
- August 23rd, 1942 to February 2nd, 1943 - Battle of Stalingrad
- July 1943 - Allies invade Sicily.
- September 3rd, 1943 - Italy surrenders.
- November 1943 - Tehran Conference
- January 1944 - Siege of Leningrad lifted
- June 6th, 1944 - D-Day
- August 25th, 1944 - Paris is liberated.
- December 16th, 1944 - Battle of the Bulge
- March 1945 - Allies cross the Rhine.
- April 1945 - Russians reach Berlin.
- April 28th, 1945 - Mussolini is executed.
- April 30th, 1945 - Hitler commits suicide.
- May 7th, 1945 - Germany surrenders.

- May 8th, 1945 – VE Day
- August 6th to August 9th, 1945 – Atomic bombs are dropped on Japan.
- August 14th, 1945 – Japan surrenders. World War II ends.

Chapter 13: Barbarossa - Causes and Consequences

In some ways, Operation Barbarossa was like a pebble thrown into still water. The ripple effects of the campaign were far-reaching and eventually played a role in Hitler's downfall and Germany's ultimate defeat.

Hitler and Stalin had signed a non-aggression pact in 1939, so Stalin sat back as Hitler invaded Poland, believing himself to be safe from a German invasion. Therefore, it was quite the shock when Hitler reneged on the pact and launched an invasion of the Soviet Union, which was something he had been planning for some time.

Approximately three million troops (150 divisions) were assigned to invade the Soviet Union. The force was made up on 19 Panzer divisions, 7,000 artillery, 3,000 tanks, and 2,500 aircraft. It remains the largest invasion in recorded history.

Hitler divided his forces into three groups, with each group being given a specific task. Army Group North was tasked with taking Leningrad. Army Group South's objective was to invade Ukraine, while Army Group Center's main target was Moscow.

Hitler felt confident this would all be achieved in a matter of ten weeks. Their invasion began strong. In fact, on the first day, approximately 1,800 Soviet aircraft were destroyed.

While the Soviet Union had an enormous air force, none of their aircraft were very effective. They were unable to put up a serious fight against the far more powerful Luftwaffe. Within a month, the Germans were less than 350 kilometers away from Moscow. The efforts to capture Moscow continued until December 2nd, with the German troops a stone's throw away from the object of their desire.

But the harsh winter crippled the German troops, which were ill-prepared for the cold. By January of 1942, Germany was forced to concede that it would not be able to capture Moscow.

While Operation Barbarossa ultimately failed, the German troops *were* able to successfully blockade Leningrad, and it would remain under siege for nearly nine hundred days.

Operation Barbarossa wasn't a surprise to anyone who knew Hitler. The pact he had signed with Stalin was simply a way to give him some breathing room. His end goal had always included an invasion of the Soviet Union. Hitler's dream was to expand Germany to the east and gain a proper space (*Lebensraum*) for the German people. He intended to rid the Soviet Union of all its Jewish people, get rid of communism, and set up his own Nazi government. In his larger plans, Hitler's ultimate goal was to exterminate the Slavic people as well. To that end, millions of Soviet prisoners of war were killed by the Nazis. The only reason his larger plans did not come to fruition was because the Nazis were defeated.

Things did not go exactly as planned with Operation Barbarossa. The Soviets ended up being more resilient and powerful than Hitler had anticipated, and while the Soviet aircraft were not good, they had superior tanks. The weather also worked in their favor.

The Red Army did suffer some heavy losses, and the German troops did gain a lot of territory, but they were not able to eviscerate the Soviet forces or get them to surrender. Hitler's dream of taking over the Soviet Union failed.

And now he had made an enemy. The consequences of the operation would be quite high.

Enraged by Hitler's double-cross, Stalin allied himself with Great Britain and eventually the United States. Together, the three powers planned and strategized Hitler's defeat. When the time came, the Soviets crushed Germany.

As discussed in a previous chapter, the war could not have been won without the Soviet Union or the Red Army. Had Operation Barbarossa never been launched, Stalin would likely have joined the Axis powers, and the final outcome of the war could have been a very different one!

But Hitler did, and he failed. With Moscow a hopeless cause, Hitler instructed his troops to march farther into the Soviet Union to capture Stalingrad.

Chapter 14: Stalingrad - Causes and Consequences

The Battle of Stalingrad was fought halfway through WWII. After the failed Operation Barbarossa, another offensive was launched in June 1942 to destroy the rest of the Soviet Army and take control of Stalingrad.

The city was named after Stalin. It was an important city, as the Volga River ran right through it and was used as a shipping route that connected different parts of the country to each other. As an industrial center, Stalingrad produced many goods and products, including artillery. In short, it was an ideal city in a great location. And the fact that it had Stalin's name on it was a bonus that Hitler fully intended to exploit in his propaganda.

Hitler instructed his troops to kill all the men as soon as the city was captured and send the women away. Stalin ordered every Russian who was capable of doing so to arm themselves and defend Stalingrad.

The battle began on August 23rd, 1942. At first, the Soviet forces managed to hold back the Germans, but the Luftwaffe's relentless air strikes began to pay off. By the fall, the Volga River was rendered useless, the Luftwaffe was controlling the skies, the city was left in shambles, and tens of thousands of civilians and troops had been killed, wounded, or captured by the Germans and shipped off to camps.

The situation was getting increasingly desperate, but Stalin would not let his forces retreat or surrender. Reinforcements began arriving from other parts of the country, and other generals organized additional forces to launch a counterattack named Operation Uranus.

Soviet soldiers running through the trenches in Stalingrad.
https://commons.wikimedia.org/wiki/File:62._armata_a_Stalingrado.jpg

Through careful strategizing, the Soviet forces managed to wall in the enemy. The blockade meant the trapped troops had limited supplies. They began to starve and weaken. Things quickly deteriorated as winter approached. In the meantime, Soviet troops began working hard to break the lines of the Axis forces.

It was clear to Hitler the battle had failed, but he would not surrender. His troops continued to starve and die. By February 1943, the Soviets had taken Stalingrad back.

Roughly 100,000 German soldiers were sent to Soviet prison camps. A few groups tried to resist and continue the battle, but even they gave up in less than a month.

The victory for the Soviets and the crushing defeat for the Germans was a foreshadowing of how the war would ultimately end. Historians often point to this battle as the turning point for the war since Germany was finally on a downward spiral.

Chapter 15: VE Day

May 8th, 1945, was an important day. It was the day the Allies had been working toward since the invasion of Poland. It was Victory in Europe Day!

After six violent, bloody, awful years, the war was finally over in Europe. Hitler and the Nazis had been defeated, and the Allies had won. However, the war wasn't officially over; Japan still had to be defeated. But on May 8th, 1945, the people weren't thinking about Japan. They just wanted to celebrate their newfound freedom and their major victory.

People celebrated in the United States, Great Britain and its colonies, and the formerly occupied European countries.

At the beginning of 1945, the Yalta Conference took place. The Allied leaders sat down to strategize what they hoped would be the final offensive that led to the Nazis' defeat.

The Battle of the Bulge had been Hitler's last-ditch effort to regain some ground, but the Allies crushed him. In the meantime, Hitler's troops also had to deal with the Soviet forces on the Eastern Front. The Red Army was gunning for Germany's capital, and by the spring of 1945, they had attained their objective. On April 16th, 1945, the Soviets began their invasion of Berlin.

The German troops were exhausted and had shrunk dramatically. Even as the Soviet troops began to take over Berlin, Hitler, sitting in his underground bunker, refused to surrender, calling instead on every civilian, children included, to defend the capital. On April 20th, Hitler's fifty-sixth birthday, he came up to give out medals.

Soviet shelling began on the same day. Within days, less than 100,000 German troops were fully encircled by 1.5 million Red Army soldiers. The Germans knew there was nothing they could do anymore.

Hitler must have known the same thing because a week later, on April 30th, he married his long-time mistress Eva Braun and committed suicide. Their bodies were brought out of the bunker and burned to prevent any further indignities and insults. The Nazis were perhaps worried that Hitler's body would be strung up like Mussolini's and spit upon or abused. Shortly after, the Soviets secured the ruined and devastated Reichstag.

Red Army soldiers raise the Soviet flag in Berlin after its capture.
Mil.ru, CC BY 4.0 <https://creativecommons.org/licenses/by/4.0>, via Wikimedia Commons; https://commons.wikimedia.org/wiki/File:Raising_a_flag_over_the_Reichstag_2.jpg

Germany's official surrender came on May 2nd, 1945; however, there were a handful of troops that continued to fight until May 8th.

In the weeks and months after, Berlin was in total chaos, with the Soviet troops reorganizing the city according to their desires and imposing their rules. Some Soviet troops treated the civilians horribly, raping women and inflicting other atrocities on the people. Other troops, however, gave out food and basic necessities to the people.

Meanwhile, the Allied troops were on their way to Berlin. American troops arrived on July 4th, 1945, and British troops entered the city two days later, on July 6th.

Given the situation, Germany had no choice *but* to surrender. It was a humiliating and despairing moment for the people. After initiating the war, after spending six years of fighting, after depleting all of their resources and losing millions of German lives, the end result was German troops on their knees begging the Soviets for mercy.

After the defeat and humiliation of WWI, this defeat must have been utterly demoralizing. In the short term, there were severe consequences to Germany's surrender. As part of the peace treaty, Germany was occupied by the four Allied forces. The country that had gone to war hoping to become a global power was now being run by foreign powers. Germany also had to pay steep reparations, which further crippled its economy.

However, in the long run, this was the best thing that could have happened for West Germany. After nearly fifty years of occupation by France, the US, and the UK, West Germany emerged as a powerful, developed nation. East Germany, unfortunately, was not quite so lucky. Falling under Soviet rule, East Germany's suffering continued until the end of the Cold War.

For the Allies and the world in general, Germany's surrender was critical to ensuring that democracy and freedom prevailed. Without timely Allied intervention, without the Marshall Plan, and without the defeat of Japan, would most of the world be enjoying the type of life that we do today? Or would fascism and communism have spread throughout the world, becoming the dominant ideology?

One thing is for sure, without Germany's defeat, the world would have looked very different today.

Fun Facts – Hitler's Death

It's hard to imagine that there could be any such thing as a fun fact when talking about WWII, but given the heavy subject matter, it might be interesting to look at a few random facts and myths.

One of the most common myths or conspiracy theories is that Hitler did not actually commit suicide. Seventy-seven years after Hitler's death, historians and conspiracy theorists alike still hotly debate whether he actually *did* die. Books, movies, and documentaries have been written and produced regarding this matter. Amateur sleuths and historians have spent years sifting through evidence and looking for proof to validate this claim.

It is believed that Hitler managed to escape his bunker and make his way to South America (like many other high-profile Nazi officers), where he lived out the rest of his life in quiet retirement. Some of the confusion stems from the fact that nobody credible saw Hitler's dead body. There is also some debate on whether he died by a self-inflicted gunshot wound or by ingesting poison. The lack of physical, visual, and concrete proof has given rise to wild theories.

Of course, there is no way to know for sure; however, there is no reason not to believe that Hitler died. One would think that, at some point, somewhere, someone would have caught a glimpse of him. Finally, given what we know of Hitler, was he really the type to simply disappear quietly and not seek the spotlight for decades on end?

Whatever the truth is, Hitler's death is one of the most persistent theories that still exist and will likely continue to exist.

Other Fun Facts

- VE Day, the abbreviation for Victory in Europe Day, was coined as early as September 1944, nearly eight months before Germany's surrender, because the Allies felt confident that they would win the war.

- In the movies, surrendering to an enemy is often portrayed by waving a white flag. Reality is not quite that simple. Finalizing the documents for surrender took over twenty hours to complete and was done days in advance of Germany's surrender. When victory was certain, cables were sent by **SHAEF** (Supreme Headquarters Allied Expeditionary Force) to world leaders telling them that Germany would likely be surrendering soon, and the documents began to be drafted. Comments, opinions, and changes from all parties took twenty hours to complete, and the document was finished at 2:30 a.m. on May 7th.

- On May 7th, 1945, a surrender ceremony was held in Reims when General Alfred Jodl signed the unconditional surrender of Germany. Stalin was not happy about this and made a fuss about the wording of the document and objected to where it was signed. He refused to accept a surrender that had been signed in France and insisted on a second surrender ceremony. This caused confusion for all parties, and some believed that Germany was still at war with the Soviet Union. A second ceremony was quickly organized on May 9th in Soviet-occupied Berlin. This means that in Russia, the celebration of VE Day is on May 9th, not May 8th.

- VE Day happened to fall on President Truman's sixty-first birthday. When Germany surrendered, it had been less than a month since he took office. It would be his first birthday as president. What a great birthday present!

- Hiroo Onoda was an intelligence officer from the Imperial Japanese Army who fought in WWII. He missed the memo that the war was over and was hiding out in the Philippines with three other soldiers. They carried out guerilla activities months after the war ended. In October, they saw a flyer saying the war was over, but they didn't believe it and refused to surrender. Over the next few years, many efforts were made to convince the group the war was over, but they refused to believe it. By 1972, Onoda was on his own; the other men had either died or left. He finally surrendered in 1974 (twenty-nine years after the end of the war!) when his former commander found him and officially relieved him from active duty. Now that's loyalty!

Chapter 16: Comparing Two Evils

World War I and World War II are often compared to each other. Both wars were triggered by Germany and fought by mostly the same countries. Both resulted in German defeats. And both were extremely bloody, violent wars that would have a lasting impact on the world.

However, there are many differences between them. How were the wars similar? How were they different? Was one war worse than the other?

Trench Warfare versus Air Warfare

World War I is closely associated with trench warfare, as most of the battles took place in the trenches.

With trench warfare, there is minimal mobility, with both sides digging deep, zig-zagging trenches. During WWI, the soldiers lived in the trenches for weeks since they offered some protection against bullets, artillery, machine guns, and poisonous gas (giving the soldiers time to put on gas masks).

Trench warfare was brutal, and nighttime attacks became the norm. If the initial attack led to a breach in the trenches, the enemy would then go around the trench to attack from the back while others attacked from the front, essentially trapping the soldiers in the trench.

Sitting in trenches for weeks while dealing with shelling and bombardments led to many soldiers developing PTSD. Physically, they were prone to becoming very sick from things like cholera, typhoid fever, and trench foot. Trenches were not sanitary, so diseases spread very quickly.

During WWII, the use of trench warfare was minimal; instead, there was a rise in air warfare. Aircraft had been used during WWI but were mainly used for reconnaissance. Due to the lack of mobility, it was important for planes to fly behind enemy lines to gather intelligence and draw maps. Later on in the war, planes began to be used to take out the enemy and conduct bombing campaigns. By the time World War I ended, it was clear to everyone that aircraft were the future of warfare.

Unfortunately, the next war came much quicker than anticipated. And when WWII started, air warfare really took off. Air superiority would become a deciding factor on who would win or lose.

Aircraft supported the ground forces and the navy for both the Axis and the Allies. Much of Hitler's early success was due to the Luftwaffe. Great Britain was saved from Nazi occupation due to its strong RAF.

For the Allies, air warfare was a huge support during battles. When the Americans joined the war, their technology and aircraft were far superior to anyone else's. Their planes played a key role in the Normandy landings and eventually helped the Allies win the war.

Machine Guns, Gas, and Close Combat versus Artillery and Modern Technology

Some of the most enduring images from WWI are soldiers trekking through the trenches wearing gas masks that make them look like aliens. WWI saw the arrival of new weapons, such as quick-firing artillery, or the development of old weapons that made them deadlier, such as machine guns, grenades, rifles, and mortars.

Armed with this slew of weapons, the war in the trenches was fought viciously with only one goal in mind: kill the enemy. Once the enemy managed to get into their rival's trenches, the combat turned physical, with soldiers fighting each other with whatever they could get their hands on, including shovels, knives, and clubs.

And then, to complicate things further, the Germans introduced the use of poison gas. The gas would be carried in metal canisters and then released to float toward the enemy. The gasses used early in the war did not inflict much damage, but by 1917, the Germans were using mustard gas. Mustard gas attacks the skin and leads to blindness. It is lethal, and the gas masks offered very little protection against it. Sadly, the victims who survived would go on to suffer from the effects of the gas for the rest of their lives.

During WWII, the Nazis accidentally developed a gas called sarin. They had enough to kill millions of people, and high-ranking Nazi officials wanted Hitler to give the go-ahead to unleash the gas. But for whatever reason, Hitler didn't want to. We'll never know his reason for not doing so, but many historians believe he didn't want to because he himself had been a victim of a mustard gas attack during WWI.

Instead of gas, WWII was fought with artillery units and modern technology. The main weapon of choice for the infantry was the M1 Garand, a semi-automatic rifle that was easy to use, light to carry, and very deadly. Machine guns, grenades, flamethrowers, and submachine guns were also used.

Like WWI, tanks were also used. However, WWII introduced new technologies, such as radar systems, computers, penicillin, and the atomic bomb. The atomic bomb led to Japan's surrender, bringing the war to an end.

Death Tolls

Both wars resulted in massive casualties, but the death toll in World War II was significantly higher.

During WWI, an estimated forty-six million people were affected directly by the war.

- 10 million military troops died.

- 7 million civilians died.

- 21 million people were wounded or injured.

- 8 million people went missing or were imprisoned.

In contrast, the estimated death tolls for WWII vary between fifty and eighty million people.

- 20 million military troops died.

- 38 to 45 million civilians died (from injuries, mass bombings, or other war-related diseases).
- 11 million deaths as a result of Nazi extermination programs.
- 3.6 million deaths in Soviet Gulag.

These are just estimates; the true numbers will never be known.

WWII wiped out over 3 percent of the world's population. It is the deadliest military conflict in recorded history (likely in all of history) and far surpasses WWI's death toll.

Conclusion

It is said we must learn from the past, that we must learn from history.

What did World War II teach us? Millions of lives were lost and destroyed during the war. Millions more became displaced refugees, losing their homes and identities. Countries and cities were ravaged, becoming ruins.

When we look around at the world we live in today and reflect back on the events and tragedies of this war that happened not even a century ago, was it worth it? Or was it all for nothing? What did the world gain?

There is perhaps no single answer to that question because what the world gained depends on your viewpoint and likely where you live in the world.

Regardless of what one personally thinks, the cost of the war was great. The sacrifices made were enormous. The genocide that was perpetrated is a black mark in history, and sadly enough, sentiments that brought about the rise of Hitler are still being touted today.

Based on numbers alone, WWII is definitely the bloodiest war in recorded history. It reshaped the world and changed the old way of doing things, ushering in a new era of foreign policy, diplomatic relations, and the rise of capitalist democracies.

Prior to WWII, many countries, like the United States, practiced isolationism. The war changed the global landscape, making isolationism impossible. Countries had to work together and maintain ties in a way they never had to do before. Many of these ties still exist today through global or regional organizations like NATO.

Without a doubt, World War II changed the face of the world. It is hard to imagine what would have happened if Hitler had succeeded. Thankfully, we will never know, but it is important to remember what happened during this war. People often say history repeats itself, but this is one event that should never be repeated.

Here's another book by Enthralling History that you might like

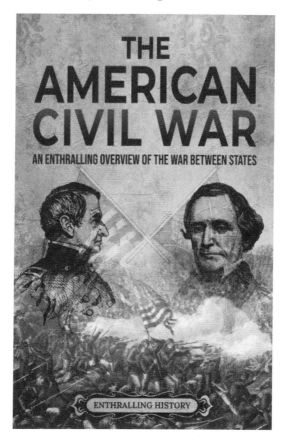

Free limited time bonus

Stop for a moment. We have a free bonus set up for you. The problem is this: we forget 90% of everything that we read after 7 days. Crazy fact, right? Here's the solution: we've created a printable, 1-page pdf summary for this book that you're reading now. All you have to do to get your free pdf summary is to go to the following website:

https://livetolearn.lpages.co/enthrallinghistory/

Once you do, it will be intuitive. Enjoy, and thank you!

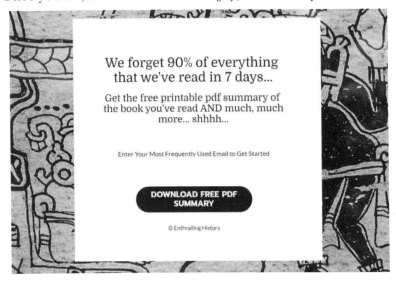

We forget 90% of everything that we've read in 7 days...

Get the free printable pdf summary of the book you've read AND much, much more... shhhh...

Enter Your Most Frequently Used Email to Get Started

DOWNLOAD FREE PDF SUMMARY

© Enthralling History

Sources

- Mann, Tara. *World War I*, edited by Jacob Steinberg, Rosen Publishing Group, 2016. *ProQuest eBook Central*, https://ebookcentral.proquest.com/lib/jacob/detail.action?docID=4573489.

- Rajczak, Nelson, Kristen. *World War I*, Cavendish Square Publishing LLC, 2021. *ProQuest eBook Central*, https://ebookcentral.proquest.com/lib/jacob/detail.action?docID=6710737.

- Gagne, Tammy. *World War I Technology*, ABDO Publishing Company, 2017. *ProQuest eBook Central*, https://ebookcentral.proquest.com/lib/jacob/detail.action?docID=5263040.

- 50MINUTES. *World War I: Part Two: 1915-1917: Stalemate*, Lemaitre Publishing, 2017. *ProQuest eBook Central*, https://ebookcentral.proquest.com/lib/jacob/detail.action?docID=4815644.

- Williamson, Samuel R. "The Origins of World War I." *The Journal of Interdisciplinary History*, vol. 18, no. 4, 1988, pp. 795–818. *JSTOR*, https://doi.org/10.2307/204825

- Van Evera, Stephen. "The Cult of the Offensive and the Origins of the First World War." *International Security*, vol. 9, no. 1, 1984, pp. 58-107. *JSTOR*, https://doi.org/10.2307/2538636

- Kaiser, David E. "Germany and the Origins of the First World War." *The Journal of Modern History*, vol. 55, no. 3, 1983, pp. 442-74. *JSTOR*, http://www.jstor.org/stable/1878597

- Gompert, David C., et al. "Woodrow Wilson's Decision to Enter World War I, 1917." *Blinders, Blunders, and Wars: What America and China Can Learn*, RAND Corporation, 2014, pp. 71-80. *JSTOR*, http://www.jstor.org/stable/10.7249/j.ctt1287m9t.13

- Crook, Paul, and David Paul Crook. *Darwinism, War and History: The Debate over the Biology of War from the "Origin of Species" to the First World War.* Cambridge University Press, 1994.

- Hart, BH Liddell. *A History of the First World War.* Pan Macmillan, 2014.

- Horne, John. "The Global Legacies of World War I." *Current History*, vol. 113, no. 766, 2014, pp. 299-304. *JSTOR*, http://www.jstor.org/stable/45388568

- Chamberlin, William Henry. "The First Russian Revolution." *The Russian Review*, vol. 26, no. 1, 1967, pp. 4-12. *JSTOR*, https://doi.org/10.2307/126860

- Wade, Rex A. *The Russian Revolution, 1917.* Vol. 53. Cambridge University Press, 2017.

- Yeh, Puong Fei. "The Role of the Zimmermann Telegram in Spurring America's Entry into the First World War." *American Intelligence Journal* 32.1 (2015): 61-64.

- Schindler, John. "Steamrollered in Galicia: The Austro-Hungarian Army and the Brusilov Offensive, 1916." *War in History*, vol. 10, no. 1, 2003, pp. 27-59. *JSTOR*, http://www.jstor.org/stable/26061940

- John A. C. Conybeare, and Todd Sandler. "The Triple Entente and the Triple Alliance 1880-1914: A Collective Goods Approach." *The American Political Science Review*, vol. 84, no. 4, 1990, pp. 1197-206. *JSTOR*, https://doi.org/10.2307/1963259

- Morgan, Elizabeth, and Robert Green. *World War I and the Rise of Global Conflict*, Greenhaven Publishing LLC, 2016. *ProQuest eBook Central*, https://ebookcentral.proquest.com/lib/jacob/detail.action?docID=5538452

- Baldwin, Faith, and Stig Förster. *The Treaty of Versailles: A Reassessment after 75 Years.* Cambridge University Press, 1998.

- Lu, Catherine. "Justice and Moral Regeneration: Lessons from the Treaty of Versailles." *International Studies Review*, vol. 4, no. 3, 2002, pp. 3–25. *JSTOR*, http://www.jstor.org/stable/3186461

- Burkham, Thomas W. "League of Nations and Japan." Encyclopedia 1914-1918. 10 June 2021. https://encyclopedia.1914-1918-online.net/article/league_of_nations_and_japan#:~:text=The%20Assembly%2C%20by%20a%20vote,from%20the%20League%20of%20Nations.

- Swift, John. "Mukden Incident." Britannica. https://www.britannica.com/event/Mukden-Incident

- "Leaders and Controversies." The National Archives. https://www.nationalarchives.gov.uk/education/leaders-and-controversies/g3/cs1/#:~:text=A%20year%20earlier%20Mussolini%20had,Mussolini%20demanded%20an%20apology.

- A&E Television Networks. "German General Erwin Rommel Arrives in Africa." History. 10 February 2020. https://www.history.com/this-day-in-history/rommel-in-africa

- National Army Museum. "Second World War - Battle of El-Alamein." NAM. https://www.nam.ac.uk/explore/battle-alamein

- Jeff Wallenfeldt. "Atlantic Charter." Britannica. 7 August 2022. https://www.britannica.com/event/Atlantic-Charter

- Office of the Historian. "The Atlantic Conference and Charter, 1941." https://history.state.gov/milestones/1937-1945/atlantic-conf

- Jennifer Llewellyn, Jim Southey, Steve Thompson. "Hitler and Mussolini." Alpha History. 26 August 2015. https://alphahistory.com/nazigermany/hitler-and-mussolini/

- Tharoor, Ishaan. "Don't forget how the Soviet Union saved the world from Hitler." Washington Post. 8 May 2015. https://www.washingtonpost.com/news/worldviews/wp/2015/05/08/dont-forget-how-the-soviet-union-saved-the-world-from-hitler/

- History Stories. "How D-Day Changed the Course of WWII." https://www.history.com/news/d-day-important-world-war-ii-victory

- Italy Since 1945. "The First Decades after World War II." Britannica. https://www.britannica.com/place/Italy/Italy-since-1945

- Occupation and Reconstruction of Japan, 1945–52. https://history.state.gov/milestones/1945-1952/japan-reconstruction#:~:text=After%20the%20defeat%20of%20Japan,%2C%20economic%2C%20and%20social%20reforms

- Wikipedia. "German Casualties in World War II." https://en.wikipedia.org/wiki/German_casualties_in_World_War_II

- BBC. "How Britain lost an empire – war and government." BBC Bitesize. https://www.bbc.co.uk/bitesize/guides/zyh9ycw/revision/4#:~:text=World%20War%20Two%20had%20been,the%20rebuilding%20of%20the%20country.

- Kids Britannica. "British Decolonization in Africa." https://kids.britannica.com/students/article/British-Decolonization-in-Africa/310389

- Goodwin, Doris. "The Way We Won: America's Economic Breakthrough during World War II." The American Prospect. 19 December 2001. https://prospect.org/health/way-won-america-s-economic-breakthrough-world-war-ii/

- The Man Behind Hitler. "World War II Propaganda." PBS. https://www.pbs.org/wgbh/americanexperience/features/goebbels-propaganda/

- D Day – Eyewitness Accounts of WWII. https://www.normandy1944.info/home/battles

- Holzwarth, Larry. "A Day in the Life of an Infantry-Man in World War II." American History. 14 July 2018. https://historycollection.com/a-day-in-the-life-of-an-infantry-man-in-world-war-ii/10/

- Whitman, John. "Japan's Fatally Flawed Air Forces in World War II." HistoryNet. 28 July 2006. https://www.historynet.com/japans-fatally-flawed-air-forces-in-world-war-ii-2/

- Imperial War Museum. "RAF Bomber Command during the Second World War." https://www.iwm.org.uk/history/raf-bomber-command-during-the-second-world-war#:~:text=The%20Royal%20Air%20Force's%20(RAF,strategy%20for%20winning%20the%20war.

- The History Place. "The Rise of Adolf Hitler." https://www.historyplace.com/worldwar2/riseofhitler/warone.htm

- United States Holocaust Memorial Museum. "Prisoner bunk bed from Auschwitz concentration camp." https://collections.ushmm.org/search/catalog/irn94891 Auschwitz-Birkenau. https://www.auschwitz.org/en/history/life-in-the-camp/

- Holocaust Encyclopedia. "At the Killing Centers." https://encyclopedia.ushmm.org/content/en/article/at-the-killing-centers

- A&E Television Networks. "Gulag." History. 17 August 2022. https://www.history.com/topics/russia/gulag#:~:text=Conditions%20at%20the%20Gulag%20were,still%20permeates%20Russian%20society%20today.

- Campaign for Nuclear Disarmament. "Hiroshima and Nagasaki." https://cnduk.org/resources/hiroshima-and-nagasaki/#:~:text=Almost%2063%25%20of%20the%20buildings,of%20a%20population%20of%20350%2C000.

- World War II. "Timeline of World War II." https://wwiifoundation.org/timeline-of-wwii/

- The National WWII Museum. "Worldwide Deaths in World War II." https://www.nationalww2museum.org/students-teachers/student-resources/research-starters/research-starters-worldwide-deaths-world-war

- Canadian War Museum. "Canada and the First World War." https://www.warmuseum.ca/firstworldwar/history/battles-and-fighting/weapons-on-land/poison-gas/

- The National WWII Museum. "The Cost of Victory." https://www.nationalww2museum.org/war/articles/cost-victory

- Wikipedia. "World War II." https://en.wikipedia.org/wiki/World_War_II